P9-DWJ-558

POSTER CHILD

POSTER CHILD

A Memoir

Emily Rapp

BLOOMSBURY

Some of the names, locations, and details of events in this book have been changed to protect the privacy of persons involved.

Published by Bloomsbury USA, New York
Distributed to the trade by Holtzbrinck Publishers

All papers used by Bloomsbury USA are natural, recyclable products made from wood grown in well-managed forests. The manufacturing processes conform to the environmental regulations of the country of origin.

Library of Congress Cataloging-in-Publication Data

Rapp, Emily.
Poster child : a memoir / Emily Rapp.
p. cm.
ISBN-13: 978-1-59691-256-4
ISBN-10: 1-59691-256-1
1. Rapp, Emily. 2. Femur—Abnormalities—Patients—Biography. I. Title.

QM117.R37 2007
362.197'580092—dc22
[B]

2006012555

First U.S. Edition 2007

1 3 5 7 9 10 8 6 4 2

Typeset by Westchester Book Group
Printed in the United States of America by Quebecor World Fairfield

For my parents, Mary and Roger Rapp
and for Glen and Ann Rebka

First, are you our sort of person?
Do you wear
A glass eye, false teeth or a crutch,
A brace or a hook,
Rubber breasts or a rubber crotch,

Stitches to show something's missing? . . .

—Sylvia Plath, "The Applicant"

Prologue

HIDDEN TRUTHS

After the van dropped me off in the middle of ChunCheon, I turned the map around in my sweating hands, trying to figure out where I was in relation to where I needed to be. The map was written in Korean, and my limited knowledge of the language meant I could decipher only a few letters and words. To my left, pedestrians and bicyclists were vying for space on a street lined with noodle huts. Walking in the direction of people and activity seemed a better plan than standing on a street corner fumbling with an incomprehensible map.

Traffic was bumper-to-bumper. Cranes swung in the air over buildings-in-progress. Digital billboards advertised cars, bourbon, cigarettes, and cruise holidays. A Chinese opera blared out of a record store. A chaos of smells—car exhaust, rotting vegetables, melting tar, and frying garlic—moved through the sweltering mid-afternoon air. I turned off the main road onto a smaller street when my left leg buckled beneath me; I fell backward into a puddle of motor oil in front of a small roadside stand.

Sitting in the hot street, I tried to inspect the damage: Had my prosthesis lost a screw or some other part that had caused it to malfunction? Perhaps I had simply lost my balance and fallen, as I often had as a child. Using my fingertips to grope through the cosmetic socks that covered the leg, I found the hydraulic system at the back of my knee, searching for loose parts, searching for the source of the trouble. The knee was hot to the touch from the friction of walking and the heat of the city. My prosthetist had warned me that it was possible for the seals and fluid in the hydraulic unit to fail under such conditions. I knew from many prosthetic fittings that an artificial leg without a single part was like a car with a flat tire. The whole machine was useless.

I was afraid to stand up and walk for fear that the leg would fall completely apart and all the technology, all the tiny, carefully aligned parts that held me together, would be ruined or lost on a strange street with a name I couldn't pronounce. Two schoolgirls, arm in arm, stopped a few feet from where I had fallen and stared down at me, whispering to each other behind their hands. A bicyclist swerved around me just in time, yelling at me as he sped away.

I was failing my first survival test as a Fulbright scholar. Although I had been out in the city numerous times, I had a terrible sense of direction, and I had been dreading this activity for days. After all twenty of us had piled into the van, Mr. Adams, the program administrator and the man in charge, had dropped us off one by one, instructing us to find our way back from our individual "drop points" (as he called them) to the dormitory at the university, where we were receiving a six-week crash course in Korean and conversational English lesson planning. "Use your Korean if you get lost!" Mr. Adams encouraged. In another three weeks, each of us would be teaching in public schools throughout South Korea.

I had come to Korea for several reasons. During my junior year abroad in Ireland, I had enjoyed the challenge of living in a new place and making a life for myself in a country where so much was exciting and different: food, holidays, songs, electrical outlets, habits, fashion, and expressions. The Fulbright scholarship appealed to me because it offered another chance for me to reinvent myself and seek adventure. It was also prestigious; this was of absolute importance to me, because I was constantly seeking proof that I should believe in myself. I was affirmed when, through my achievements, I received attention for being smart and fearless.

With all those issues in play, I had given scarcely any thought to the country in which I would live and work. Foolishly, I thought place was of little consequence, as long as it was new, different, and far from home. I chose Asia because I'd never been there; I chose Korea because it was described, in some of the materials I happened to read, as "the Ireland of Southeast Asia." I investigated the country and my responsibilities as a Fulbright English teacher no further than that. I applied and got the scholarship. Six months later, I was on a plane bound for Seoul.

I thought of the other scholars, and a fear that I might finish last finally motivated me to move. I told myself that I could not fail: I would survive the survival test! I pushed myself into an upright position.

After I slowly stood up, I found myself face-to-face with the vendor of the stand where I'd fallen. Rivers of wrinkles ran from the man's forehead all the way down his neck and arms. He wore a loose blue shirt and a green plastic visor that read, "Get It On!" Behind him were his goods piled up for sale.

Although I clearly needed help, I was nervous about asking for it. Mr. Adams had told me when I arrived in the country three weeks ago that people with disabilities were often institutionalized in Korea. "I've never seen one in public," he'd said at our first group meal. "It might be difficult to find a host family that will accept you." If people with disabilities were so disliked and mistreated, this man might refuse to help me. What would I do then?

I felt ridiculous and desperate. My hands and my backside were covered in oil, my body was covered in sweat, and I kept bending down to feel the four-bar hydraulic knee. I tried to remember the way my prosthetist looked at the leg when I visited his office for regular tune-ups; I tried to recall where all the different parts belonged. The truth was, I knew little about the leg's mechanics. I simply handed it over and waited for it to be fixed. I didn't want to be bothered with the way it was constructed or how it worked. The only thing I knew how to do was tighten the hydraulics with a small wrench in order to change the speed at which my leg swung through as I walked. Why hadn't I paid more attention to what my prosthetist did? Was it a screw, the foot, the fit, the socket, the weather?

People were watching, staring. I tried to pretend that their looks were rolling off me like water—a little visualization I used to withstand people's stares when I wore shorts or short skirts during the summer. In Korea, I wore long dresses or loose pants. Except for the artificial foot, which was covered in two layers of thick orthotic support hose two shades darker than my pale skin, and a slight limp, the most obvious physical sign of my disability—the artificial leg itself—was always hidden beneath my clothes.

I hobbled over to the stand, slowly dragging my left leg behind me. The prosthesis had been in a state of disarray for weeks. During the day, I could practically smell the latex spray that covered the leg burning off. The heel of my Flex-Foot, an expensive foot made of carbon fiber, was poking out slightly through the back of the cosmetic shell like a bone jutting out of my heel. I felt ratty and badly put together.

My heart was beating at an alarming speed. The vendor fanned his face and blew smoke into mine. I offered a smile. I did not know the Korean word for "Allen wrench": the ideal tool to fix the problem, if the hydraulics were, in fact, the problem. "Uh, screwy thing?" I said, pointing at the back of my leg and twisting my finger. I felt helplessly idiotic and as if I might laugh or cry at any moment.

This state-of-the-art leg had always been absolutely reliable; the fall was an unfortunate accident. Being in a country I knew so little about quickly created worst-case scenarios in my mind. What if I couldn't make myself understood or the leg couldn't be fixed? Would I have to *hop* somewhere for help? And where would that be? Although, as promised, we had not been driven that far from the dormitory, without the use of the leg, even several blocks would seem like a mile. I was starting to make myself sick with worry, but I tried to look exceptionally friendly. "Help?" I asked, beaming.

The man responded with a deep, textured, smoker's laugh. I understood then, without words, that he was laughing less at me than at my situation. He motioned for me to follow him, and he led me to a stool behind his stand. There was an impressive collection of items for sale: lacy pink bras, cans of beans, Hershey bars, Manwich, outdated *Playboy* magazines, Obsession cologne, dusty jars of Skippy peanut butter, Buddha statues, and tape recorders. Hanging from hooks on the walls were colorful *imikabang,* or "immigration bags," which could expand or contract.

He returned with a tiny screwdriver held aloft in one hand. Perfect. I rolled down the cosmetic sock, and using the screwdriver and my fingers, I tightened the hydraulics enough, I thought, to hold the leg together. The vendor watched me as I worked underneath the cover of my long skirt. I returned the tool and rolled up the sock. When I stood up to take a tentative step, his hands hovered just beside my shoulders as if he would catch me if I fell. The leg felt steady, at least for now. Disaster had been averted.

We bowed to each other—*Kahmsamnida Anhyonghi kyeseo,* Thank you and good-bye, I fumbled in Korean, hoping I'd chosen the appropriate farewell. I walked out under the deep pink sky and jungle of neon.

Eventually I made it back to the dorm. I walked until I found a main road, and then, using landmarks I remembered from previous nights out in the city with the other scholars, I found my way. Moving as quickly as I could, I panicked the whole time, afraid that I would finish last. I was afraid to look weak, the way I had been revealed and made vulnerable in the street. I was afraid that if I arrived at the dorm last, people would think it was because of my disability, and they would either pity me or look down on me. Both thoughts were equally intolerable and made me almost physically ill. I was afraid to put my full weight on the leg; this created an uneven gait and made the lip of the socket dig painfully into my left hip. I tolerated this pain, because it was normal and expected: part of living with a prosthesis. I had grown up wearing a progression of wooden legs that grew taller as I did, until in college I was fitted with a state-of-the-art prosthesis that was the model I will wear, with various modifications, for the rest of my life.

I felt sweat pooling at the bottom of the silicone socket, making it slip and chafe against the small ankle bone on my stump (the residual limb), creating sores that would later itch and bleed. Still I walked on. I knew the torn skin would heal after a few days, and I could not lose. If I arrived last, I thought, I would be nothing but a cripple.

By the time I reached the dorm, I was hobbling and in a great deal of pain, but making it back was the only thing that mattered to me. I was thrilled to be one of the first to arrive at the meeting point. I felt a rush of relief mixed with a kind of intoxicating pride.

I went upstairs and scrubbed my hands clean in the sink at the end of the hall. I walked to my room, put my ruined clothes in a plastic bag, and removed my leg. It was hot and stinking between my hands as I held it upside down and peered into the hydraulic unit. With the Allen wrench I had thrown into my suitcase at the last minute, I tightened the hydraulics, bending the leg back and forth until the knee moved as stiffly as possible; now I would be able to tell when and if it loosened. I also cleaned out sand, dirt, oil, and dust that had collected behind the knee joint. Finally, worried that the leg smelled badly, I gave it a light mist with my favorite French perfume.

I had been unaware of what was going on with the leg. Because South Korea had been such an adjustment in so many other ways, I had neglected my prosthesis. Adapting to a new language, weather, and all the other aspects of a different culture was important, but now I realized I needed to keep an eye on the leg, too. I scolded myself for not thinking of this earlier. Angrily, I thought, *Why should I have to deal with this shit?* The rest of the Fulbrighters seemed magnificently composed and carefree; for me, wearing shorts in public was a big deal, and I did it very rarely. I took a deep breath. In my head, I listed all my accomplishments—this made me feel better. Bitterness and anger would never help. I had learned to manage my disability by putting on a determined smile and believing that with the right adaptive strategies—the right clothes, the right attitude, and a sense of humor—I could adjust to any situation. I revisited those coping mechanisms and told myself that everything was fine: I was here, wasn't I? For now, that would need to be amazing enough.

After I applied antibiotic ointment to the wounds I had acquired while walking home, and had cleaned out the sweaty silicone socket with a towel, I reassembled myself. With years of practice, I reattached the leg in less than a minute. I rolled the silicone back over the stump, put on the polyester-and-spandex Soft Sock, slipped the stump into the leg, tucked the socket's string through the hole on the side of the leg near my right inner thigh, pulled it tight, fastened the Velcro side of the string to the corresponding strip on the artificial thigh, and then twisted my stump inside the leg a bit to be sure everything was secure. I folded the sock over the leg's edge and pulled up the flesh-colored hose; they gripped the top of my artificial leg like the thigh-high stockings sold in lingerie stores. I carefully smoothed out the fabric near the ankle so it wouldn't bunch up and look like loose, flabby skin. I grabbed a long cotton dress from the closet and pulled it over my head. I put my sandals back on. Fully reassembled, I left the room and joined the others who were headed down the stairs to dinner. I strolled away into the world of my evening, laughing.

Chapter One

MISS AMERICA

Everyone has predictions about her future when a baby girl is born, and my parents were no different.

A few hours after my birth on July 12, 1974, after I had been cleaned of blood and swaddled in a pink blanket, two nurses brought me in to see Mom and Dad. My mother, a nurse herself, found it odd that two nurses accompanied me instead of one, which was the standard arrangement, but she was preoccupied with my red hair, my hands, my small ears.

"Look at her long fingers," she said. Throughout the arduous seventeen-hour labor and delivery, my father had been present as Mom's Lamaze breathing coach; he was the first to tell her that I had her dad's red hair, a feature she'd hoped I would inherit.

"A pianist," Dad said, lifting my new hand with his own. "An orchestra conductor." As with most newborns, my legs were still tucked up into my chest, having not yet broken entirely free of the fetal position.

On this midsummer morning, warm light spilled into the room of the maternity ward at St. Francis Hospital in Grand Island, Nebraska. I was healthy, and everything looked fine. Before Dad left to pick up my grandmother at the airport and bring her to the hospital to meet me, he called the leader of his congregation's prayer chain to update the parishioners, who had been praying since Mom's water broke: "It's a girl with dainty hands; she has red hair just like Mary wanted. Weighed in at seven pounds even. Her name is Emily."

Later that afternoon while Dad was gone, the doctor returned to

Mom's room, carrying me in his arms. The room was hot now; the air conditioner struggled to counteract the humidity and bright sunshine that pressed against the hospital walls.

Dr. Baxter set me on the bed and opened up my blanket. "We have a problem here," he said. He stretched my legs out and away from my chest. I wailed. One leg was visibly shorter than the other.

"What is it?" Mom asked, taking hold of my legs. "One leg is shorter? What does it mean?"

"It's a birth defect," Dr. Baxter said. "I don't know much about it, but I'm doing research." The defect remained unnamed, unnamable.

"But you said she was fine."

"We just noticed it," he said.

"Will she walk?"

"I don't know."

"What does it mean?" Mom asked.

She had been healthy and fit throughout her pregnancy: She gained weight, ate well, and had very little morning sickness; at thirty, she was a normal childbearing age. There had been no warning signs that there might be trouble. Mom and Dad had assumed that I was in the clear. Now, it appeared, I was not. Mom touched my legs and looked at the doctor.

"We'll just have to wait and see," he said.

Mom realized why two nurses had brought me in that first time: They had already known about this mysterious problem. Apparently, it was a situation that required backup. She felt strangely light, released of the heaviness of my body inside her, freed from the burden of physical pain. But now she was filled with the panic of fear, a different lightness.

When Dad returned from his airport run, he had no idea what awaited him. My grandmother had traveled from Illinois to Nebraska assuming that I was normal, healthy, and beautiful. This last bit, especially, was crucial and especially important for a girl. Girls were born to be pretty and desired. She had told everyone about me: "Gorgeous baby girl, the prettiest anyone has ever seen."

When Mom finally told Dad and Grandma the truth about me, that they were still trying to determine what the next few days would bring, not to mention the future, Grandma burst into tears. "It's my fault," she said. Everyone in the small farming community of Flanagan—population 900—knew about her fast boyfriend from the neighboring town of Streator who went to war; about her long, mysterious vacation to Chicago; about her return to town with a baby boy—my father—nine months later.

"Oh God, it's my fault," she repeated. She was hysterical. She took the blame for me, for what I was: deformed. There is that tricky line in Exodus she'd memorized as a child, the verse that promises that the sins of the fathers (and mothers) will be visited upon their sons and, in this case, their daughters. Here I was, a condemnation of her life, when all of her life she had been searching for the status and respectability that being a grandmother might restore. My older brother's birth two years before must have felt like a dream come true, a success. Now here I was, the revisitation of an earlier, irrevocable mistake. *It's my fault.* A statement with a whole lifetime in it: a christening of shame.

As Grandma cried, Dad stayed silent. Mom looked at him. The room was full of unasked and unanswered questions: *Will she live with us forever? Will she die young? Will she walk, run, skip, play, read, and write? What will she be? When she speaks, what will she tell us, what will she say?* And also the other questions that would never be answered: *Why us? Why her?* The air conditioner rattled in the window.

Still waiting for the official diagnosis, Mom was taken to a private room for my first feeding; the nurse thought there might be trouble. Mom couldn't imagine how a short leg would affect my ability to breast-feed, but she was too tired and overwhelmed to argue.

"I don't understand how this could happen to you," the nurse said as Mom opened her gown to feed me. The nurse addressed Dad, who was wearing his white clerical collar tucked inside his black cotton clergy shirt. "You two must live closer to God than anyone else." Blame again: To whom or what does it belong?

The nurse gave Mom a look she would get used to. Later, I would also come to know it well: a look of pity, sadness, with kindness and a bit of unexplainable triumph mixed in. A strangely open yet mysterious look—penetrating and diffuse. "We just don't know what God is going to do," said the nurse, fluffing the pillows as Mom shifted away from her. "We just don't know His plan. Isn't that right, Reverend?"

Dad stared at the nurse, fuming, until she looked away.

"I wanted to smack that nurse for her messed-up theology," Mom once told me. "She might have been trying to be helpful. Anyway, I said nothing. You ate and we did fine."

The next day, a woman my mother had never met before walked into her hospital room and said, "I hear you have a baby with a birth defect."

Mom watched this stranger move crisply about the room, rolling up the window blinds and filling the water glass by the bed. The woman told the story of her son, who was born with a brain disorder; she explained his functional and cognitive problems and her struggles as a parent. Mom realized that news of my deformity had been spread around the maternity ward; she knew this extreme breach of patient confidentiality was unethical and unprofessional. Too angry to speak, she refused to answer the woman's questions or respond to her expressions of concern. She had been *sent in* like a messenger of disaster. "If I'd had the energy," Mom said, "I would have sued that hospital's ass."

I was finally diagnosed with proximal focal femoral deficiency (PFFD), a congenital bone-and-tissue disorder that caused my left femur to develop abnormally in the womb and left it irrevocably damaged. The left leg would always be shorter, deficient. There would be asymmetry in the growth pattern of the limbs; the body would continue to grow unevenly, maintaining its strange, incorrect shape as if it had intended to look that way all along. There might be hip, joint, kidney, and back problems. The problem now had a name: What was the solution?

After Dr. Baxter explained the diagnosis to the best of his ability, Dad leaned against the wall in the hospital room and repeated, "Oh boy, oh boy," until Mom asked him to stop. They were both, unsurprisingly, still in shock. After a long and difficult labor, all had been declared normal, then abnormal. Now there was a name for the problem—the defect—but there were still no answers. The prayer chain at the church was activated again, but for a different reason; Mom's best friend arrived to offer what support she could; my older brother, Andy, was whisked away to a neighbor's house to stay for several days.

I would have needs, different from those of other babies, that my parents might not be able to meet, problems they might not be able to solve, and these would be more serious than colic or refusing a bottle. My needs might carry me into an institution. That word: institution. It is gray and heavy. I was newly diagnosed with a birth defect that seemed to have already set the stage for my life before the curtain had even gone up. The play had just begun, and the audience was already disappointed and stressed, mulling about in their seats, complaining about the actors, the set, the plot.

Over the next few days, more doctors came to visit, together with rotating groups of sleep-deprived medical interns who perked up at the thought of examining a problem-case baby with a congenital defect in the first crucial days after birth. The room was busy and crowded. I think back on that time—of Mom and Dad, me, the doctors and interns, the X-ray machines, Andy in a strange bed at a neighbor's house—as though everything were in a snow globe. Snow falls lightly around the bed, onto the tile floor, onto the fabric of Mom's pastel-colored nightgown; it dampens the bedsheets in irregular patterns that connect and spread. The X-rays gleam in the corner. On the flat surface are the lit shadows of two long leg bones, one not quite long enough, a bit twisted, a bit tentative, searching for its remainder; the left foot points out toward the X-ray's edge as if it is trying to leap away from the body, although at second glance it looks snuggled up close to the chest as if it never wants to leave. One limb looks strong, ready to walk, kick, and fight. The other, smaller one seems brighter, a warning. Turn the globe upside down and the snow keeps falling. The bones glow.

While Dad was preaching at his church that Sunday, Mom padded down the hallway in her pink bathrobe to look at me through the glass windows of the newborns' room. She felt other mothers looking at her, searching her eyes, and she stared back at them. She had longed for a redheaded girl; I had arrived, but in slightly different form from what had been expected or wished for. The nurses had attached a small sign to my crib that read "Miss America" in blue, carefully printed letters. Mom tapped on the glass; she blew me a kiss.

I believe that deep in my memory I hold this image of my mother behind the glass, sending me a kiss and looking at me as if I were the most precious and beautiful baby in the world. Although these circumstances of my birth are factual, it's difficult for me to imagine the scenes: being talked about in the maternity ward; being different, feared but pitied, classified as deformed. But this look, this look of love—this gift—I can easily imagine, because I would know it for the rest of my life.

Mom's eyes found my body in that room of new bodies. She looked into my eyes and told me: *You are perfect, you are enough, you are beautiful, you are mine.*

Instead of predictions about my future, there were decisions to be made, a much darker prospect and not nearly as enthralling. I was a baby that required decisions. I was a baby that people had to come to terms with.

Mom and Dad took me to Dr. O'Hara, who was setting up his first pediatric practice in Grand Island. He said that although he could not test mental capacity or determine intelligence level until I was older, he thought I looked clever. Mom liked him.

Very little about my birth defect appeared in medical journals, and Mom became consumed with making sure that I had the best and latest medical treatment. At the local library, she checked out every book she could find that might help her understand children with special needs; most of these texts were outdated and unhelpful.

More than any other doctor, Mom remembers Dr. O'Hara as "her savior." He answered the lingering questions about her role in my birth defect, offering reassurance that she was not to blame. I was conceived in Carol Stream, Illinois, a suburban area that had expanded into former farmland. When Mom had asked the doctors if there might be fertilizer or other toxic chemicals in the water of the area, they told her it was perfectly safe to drink it. As a nurse, she trusted medical advice and opinions, although another girl in the area had also been born with PFFD. "Nobody brought bottled water in then, and we didn't have filters," she told me. "When I asked the doctors, they always said the water was fine."

"It's not your fault," Dr. O'Hara promised her. "This defect is just one of those things: a fluke of nature, an accident." What about mental complications? At this time, there were still some suspicions that physical disabilities brought with them mental deficiencies as well. "No," he said. "Her eyes look bright. Don't worry." He also treated my frequent ear infections. Each time Mom brought me in, he reassured her that I would be fine, that I was okay.

Dr. O'Hara referred me to Dr. Brown, an orthopedic specialist who recommended the amputation of my left foot. After this procedure and other operations to modify my body, he believed I could be fitted with an artificial limb and have hope for a normal life. Before making a final decision, Mom and Dad collected other opinions from several doctors. Some recommended not amputating the leg, but instead trying the Van Ness procedure, which involves rotating the lower leg and foot 180 degrees so that the ankle joint functions as the knee joint; others suggested waiting until I was older to have the leg amputated. Mom didn't fully understand the first alternative ("How would that look?" she wondered), and she thought postponing amputation was risky because it meant losing a foot after I had already formed clear and precise memories of the body's shape and contours. She thought it best that I grow up with the knowledge of a body that was already altered.

Dr. Brown prescribed Buck's traction from two to nine months of age. This called for wrapping my left leg in an Ace bandage and weighting it so that it would be flexed, abducted, and externally rotated. This was done every night and at nap time. The leg was kept as straight as possible so that it would not begin to turn and twist like the gnarled roots of an old tree. The traction was designed to prevent contractions in the weaker muscles and keep the left leg from springing up into my chest while I was asleep. By keeping tension on the muscle, it made sure the head of the femur bone (the thigh bone) was placed solidly in the hip joint. I would often wiggle out of my stretching machine, my body already resisting the efforts to make it straight.

In May 1975, when I was ten months old, I got my first brace, which was made by a small company in Grand Island. "They weren't exactly used to making kids' stuff, but they did a good job," Mom recalls. She said that I reminded her of Chester from *Gunsmoke,* who walked with a straight leg and couldn't bend his knee. "You were cuter, though," she said.

The brace was made of straight metal rods, a flexible but durable plastic sleeve that hugged my thigh, and a thick cloth bandage around the knee. It was attached by a long canvas strap that wrapped around my waist twice and buckled in the front. Wearing a stiff orthopedic shoe, the left foot was strapped inside a foot cage and suspended a few inches above a moon-shaped rubber bolster that, with its slight sponginess, mimicked the natural energy return in a flesh-and-blood foot and eased forward motion.

Mom wanted me to walk by myself at a time consistent with normal developmental standards, but she wasn't sure how I would maneuver the brace. She tried to imagine having one, thinking she might be able to teach me if she learned how to do it herself. She sat on the floor and attempted to keep her left leg straight as she stood up. "I couldn't do it," she told me. "I just kept falling on my butt."

So Mom tried something else: She put my favorite doll in my stroller, rolled the stroller into the dining room, and then locked the wheel brakes. She sat me next to it and went into the kitchen, where she wouldn't be as tempted to help me stand up but could check my progress periodically by poking her head around the corner. I loved that doll—a little teddy bear with a soft cloth book in the middle of its tummy—and I went for it, just as Mom had expected I would. "You puttered around for a little while, tried to lift yourself, and fell. You grunted a little; it took effort. I watched you then from the kitchen, keeping my hands busy with dinner so I wouldn't run over to help you. Finally, you gripped the edge of the stroller with your hands, pushed yourself up with your right leg, and used the knob of the brace to lift up the final few inches." After that, she told me, "you were steady on your feet and walked as well as any kid. You got used to the brace and learned how to move. You took your first steps at thirteen months and were walking alone at fifteen months." Mom was very proud each time I accomplished a particular physical skill at the correct developmental time, and she dutifully recorded these triumphs in my baby book.

As soon as I became mobile, the questions began. Whenever she was asked, "What happened to your baby?" Mom replied, "Oh, she is okay. She just has one leg shorter than the other, and the brace helps her walk." She became comfortable with this standard response. It didn't bother her when children asked her what was wrong with me; she felt that their curiosity was innocent and natural. She got annoyed only when adults asked or, worse, expressed condolences ("I'm so sorry; it must be so hard") or dispensed useless advice like "There are medical advances every single day" or "God works in mysterious ways; at least she looks happy." And according to my mother, I was.

Around this time, a picture of me and Andy appeared in the local paper. We are on the merry-go-round in the town park on a warm autumn afternoon. Andy balances on one foot, one hand gripping a metal pole; his brown hair is lifted off his forehead by the light wind our slow spins create. I stand with my brace and my right foot locked together on the platform, both arms wrapped tightly around one of the poles. Andy is looking straight at the camera, and I am looking at him; we are laughing. I loved the merry-go-round, especially when Andy pushed me around so fast that the ground and the trees began to blur to colors instead of objects. I loved that feeling of floating, of being released from my body, spinning through the air, unable to see how I moved, just knowing that I was moving.

In March 1976, when I was one and a half years old, Dr. Brown performed my first surgery at Lutheran Hospital in Grand Island. I had an osteotomy, a surgical incision into the bone to control a deformity. The controlled fracture corrects the angulation of the femur bone so that its head will fit firmly into the hip socket and provide good motion of the joints. My femur wasn't as straight as it needed to be—the months of Buck's traction had apparently done little—and this operation would allow my body weight to be carried by both legs more easily. Later, at orthopedic appointments, I poked at the thigh bones of skeletons, watching the rounded knobs of the two perfect femurs move in the hip sockets and listening to the bones rattle.

The operation took place during the season of Lent, when followers of Jesus are asked to prepare themselves through self-reflection and repentance for the death and resurrection of Christ. For this reason, Mom remembers feeling particularly dark and somber. This first surgery was not performed in a children's hospital, and there was trouble inserting the IV into my small veins. The nurse tried to enter the vein again and again; it was painful and frightening. Finally, Dr. Brown, with the help of Mom and Dad, held me down as the appropriate vein was accessed with the needle. My parents would be sure that the rest of my operations took place in a children's hospital, where the nurses and doctors would have experience poking tinier veins. After this incident, I was an uncooperative patient: I pulled out the hard-won IV twice after the operation. If I saw a needle coming in my direction, I pitched a screaming fit. Pills given to calm and sedate had the reverse effect, making me more agitated and belligerent.

During the surgery, a full (hip spica) body cast was fitted over me from midchest to knee. My right leg, from knee to foot, was the only part of the lower body not covered with stiff white plaster. My thighs were held apart by a metal bar; my bottom half looked like a wishbone ready to be pulled apart. Some friends rigged up a walker by removing the regular seat from a small table with wheels and suspending a bicycle seat in the middle of it. I could sit upright and play with my toys on the table and eat standing up. I was also propped up on pillows on the floor or in my crib.

My parents often put me in their bed and slept one on either side of me, because Mom thought it was important that I be turned during the night. They woke up at two-hour intervals and carefully, slowly, turned me onto my back, then my stomach, then my back again, all through the night. The cast was on for eight weeks; after that, I was back in the brace.

In February 1978, our family moved to Laramie, Wyoming, where Dad had accepted a job as the pastor of Trinity Lutheran Church.

Laramie, called "the gem city of the Plains," is set in a valley between two mountain ranges in southeastern Wyoming, about one hour west of Cheyenne and three hours from the Colorado border. The land was not as green as it had been in Nebraska, but the air was fresh and arid; the streets were lined with cottonwood and aspen trees. The foothills in the distance were spotted with evergreens and scrubby sagebrush. At night, you could almost always see the stars.

Mom worked long hours as a nurse in the local hospital. I felt her warm presence, late at night, at the edge of my bed. She put her hand on my forehead and kissed me. I heard the soft click as she turned off my kitty-cat-shaped radio, the music gone now to static when all of the Wyoming stations finally went off the air. I often fell asleep in church, and Dad scooped me up in his arms as he left the sanctuary at the end of the service. I woke up staring at the faces of parishioners who had turned in their pews to watch the two of us. I felt Dad's steady steps—his practiced, processional prance—and inhaled the scent of his heavy clerical robes: pine trees, musky sweat, and dust. The deep notes of the organ vibrated through the air.

Surrounding our new house were rows of yellow shrubs that Andy and I called "bee bushes" because there were always fat bumblebees hanging from the bright yellow flowers. We took empty jelly jars, trapped a bee on a branch inside the jar, and then ripped off the branch and screwed the lid on tightly, with the bewildered bee still inside. We punched holes in the top with a screwdriver and watched to see how long the bees lived; they flung their fat, disoriented bodies against the glass, buzzing wildly. After they died, we dumped their shriveled corpses in the backyard.

Daddy longleg spiders were also easy victims, as they were relatively easy to capture. I picked them up and pulled off one of their legs—as easy to do as unwinding a long hair from a hairbrush. It seemed to cause the spider no pain at all, but when it tried to move, its coinlike body fell over to one side; it could not walk when it was so lopsided. Finally, at Andy's insistence—"Kill it, just kill it!"—I crushed it with the palm of my hand, pressing the flat body into the driveway and leaving a gooey smudge on the concrete.

Andy and I also had a rotating collection of salamanders that we pulled out of "Stink Lake" in LaBonte Park. In the springtime we took them from the water, and during the summer we found them under logs and piles of damp leaves. After we had removed them from their natural habitats, we waited for them to die in the old fish tank we used as their temporary home, denying them food and water. Their moist skin began to dry up and they began to look shorter and shorter, even with their long tails. It didn't take long: A salamander averaged several days; the sturdiest one lasted a week. We called them "Chip" and "Bob," short names to match their short lives. We often had one or two captives in various states of near demise. When they were about to croak, they went from green to brown to a sickly gray color that matched the rocks where we'd found them or lifted them from the dirty water.

I found a shameful but exhilarating joy in this cruelty to helpless creatures. I experienced a guilty, unsettling power when I took control of these small lives. I knew I was going to have "the big operation"—as my parents called it—and I was going to have it soon. I knew that my left foot would be taken away. Instead of walking with a brace, I would use a fake leg made of wood. I would be able to run and skip and even ride a bike. I didn't mind the brace so much, and although I didn't like needles or the smells of hospitals, and I hated being immobile in a hospital bed, I did enjoy the attention I received from Mom and Dad, from people in my church, from neighbors, nurses, and classmates. The one good thing about going under the knife was getting to be the center of attention, getting to be the star.

As Andy and I conducted our experiments, I watched how the small creatures I tortured dealt with deformity when it was thrust upon them. What I learned was that they didn't survive very long, yet there was something powerful about their struggle that was horrible but fascinating to watch. Andy always wanted to end the suffering by squashing the bug before it died. "Stop!" he pleaded.

"No," I often replied to his requests for mercy. "Wait."

Part of me wanted to see how long these creatures could last. I wanted to be a witness to their resourcefulness, as if their limits were in some way a gauge of my own. Part of me expected a miracle, as if the daddy longleg spiders could grow back their thin, eyelashlike legs or the salamanders would swim away when we dumped their lifeless bodies into the polluted lake. The expectation of the miracle always seemed much more important than whether or not it actually occurred. "God be with you," we said to one another at church. "The Lord be with you. Peace be with you." Certainly if there was going to be a miracle, God—who was with me always, every moment of every day—would make sure that it happened to me. The smaller, more helpless creatures of the world were on their own.

Chapter Two

THE BRICK HOUSE

In April 1978, still wearing the metal brace, I met Dr. Elliot at Denver Children's Hospital. He had successfully treated several other patients with PFFD and would be the doctor to perform "the big operation," as it had come to be known. I liked him; he called me "peanut" or "Miss Emily" and always had a different stuffed animal with him that he let me hold and chatter to. He had a pleasant smile. He grew up in Tennessee and had a soft southern accent.

Dr. Elliot recommended a repeat osteotomy (the earlier one had not held), together with amputation of the left foot and the insertion of a permanent plate in the left hip area. I liked the way he talked to me—not just to Mom and Dad—even though his explanations were beyond me. I did understand "hip" and "plate." For a long time, I imagined one of our nice china dinner plates embedded in my hip, the kind that were used only at Christmas and Easter. It gave me comfort to think of the plate there, as if the doctors had been kind enough to leave behind something from home after they cut me open and started moving things around and putting bones into their proper place.

Dr. Elliot explained that the only way to effectively manage PFFD was through amputation. The percentage of bone shortening is progressive. For example, if the defective femur is 50 percent shorter than the other, as both legs grow, this discrepancy will persist. The body stays geometrically aligned, maintaining its given shape as if asymmetry had been the plan all along.

There are various levels of severity with PFFD, ranked from A to D using the Aitken classification; a grade D indicates the most severe case with the most potential ambulatory problems. I had a grade B, and with it came associated fibular hemimelia (a term that includes fibular abnormalities, limb-length discrepancy, and other related issues). My knee joint had a ring meniscus instead of one that was semicircular and was therefore unstable. The only way to get the solid, weight-bearing segment required for walking in a prosthesis was, as Dr. Elliot recently explained to me, "early ablation or removal of the foot by ankle disarticulation." Essentially, as I later told kids at school, "my foot got sawed off"—and this wasn't so far from the truth. After the procedure of Syme's amputation (named for James Syme, who invented this method of amputation in 1843), I would be left with a weight-bearing stump that, with the help of an artificial leg, would have to do the job that the original "birth leg" was unable to perform.

On May 26, 1978, a few months before my fourth birthday, I had the repeat osteotomy, and my left foot was amputated to ensure a chance for a better-fitting and more aesthetic prosthesis in the future.

The nurses sang a song from the musical *Annie* as the anesthesiologist fitted the clear plastic mask over my face in the operating room and I began to count backward slowly from ten. The mask was like a toxic flower, and with my nose pushed deep into its dull, gray-colored petals, I was being forced to inhale its dangerous scent. The anesthesiologist stared down at me as the flower-venom disintegrated in my mouth. I was already too tired and too heavy to struggle. "Good job, good girl," the doctor said, and the notes of "Tomorrow" faded into silence. My breathing slowed. My muscles loosened. The anesthesiologist's big hands held the mask to my face. His nose was round and slightly red; sweat leaked out from the edge of his blue cap. I would never be able to snorkel or dive without thinking of that mask. Having plastic in my mouth or over my nose always makes me feel as if I am about to inhale a substance that will put me to sleep and when I wake up part of my body might be missing, gone forever. The nurses' blue caps blurred together, and all the voices stopped. I never got past the number seven before I was completely asleep, floating in a dreamless oblivion.

I regained consciousness in the recovery room with my head over a plastic bowl, vomiting. Recovery is a misnomer for this room, as little recovery happens here. What happens instead is discovery: What's been taken, what's been fixed, what's in a cast, where does it hurt?

I looked down at my body. My left leg looked like a rounded, bat-like object, covered in plaster. The foot was gone. I looked around: Maybe it was nearby, maybe in the next bed. No. When I turned my head, the world spun a bit; when objects were clear again, I saw, on either side of me, beds with side rails holding sleeping kids wearing casts that were slightly different from mine. The girl next to me woke up and vomited, too. She looked at me, bewildered, and started to cry. The sharp odor of her vomit was a sting in the air. Two nurses appeared to comfort us and wipe our mouths. I wanted my mother. When I tried to sit up, I realized I could not bend at the waist. I put my hands on my stomach: plaster there, too. I tried to shift my weight but could not. I could not bring my legs together; I could hardly move. Now I was angry as well as confused.

"What's this?" I asked, batting at one of the nurse's arms as she helped lift me onto a rolling stretcher.

"That's your cast, honey. You're going to get all better now." I knew she was lying. I was trapped again inside those walls of thick plaster.

As the nurses wheeled me from recovery back to my room and my waiting parents, I kept screaming, "Let me out of this brick house!" Even though it hurt to do so, I pounded my fists on the body cast, trying to break it open. I continued throwing a fit and did my usual act of resistance: repeatedly pulling out the IV and then wailing and crying when it had to be reinserted.

Before the surgery, a different nurse had tried to explain what was about to happen to my body by using a stuffed doll with one leg, but the doll didn't look right and I didn't want to play with her. When the nurses left, Dr. Elliot sat next to me on the hospital bed and showed me a small picture book that told the story of a girl's amputation.

"See this pretty little girl, she's just like you," he said. I still didn't recognize myself as the girl with the bandaged half-leg; my leg was going to be *wooden*. I figured Dr. Elliot just hadn't understood what was happening to me. But when he asked, "Do you understand, Emily?" I nodded and smiled. I wanted to be nice to him. I knew he was trying to help me, and I didn't want to tell him he was wrong.

I was hospitalized for ten days. After my amputation, I felt that Dr. Elliot had betrayed me, particularly when I began to have phantom limb pains. He had told Mom that I would most likely not experience these, because I was so young and might not yet have a conscious sense of my body's contours.

It is generally thought that pain "memories" cause these mysterious but powerful pains. "Body mapping" exists in the brain so that even when a part of the body is removed, the map, or "energy body," remains. Phantom pain results when the brain sends ever more persistent messages to the limbs that have been severed or removed. The nerves are compelled to send messages from the foot to the brain and back. When a part is removed and the communication stops, they continue to transmit a false message. The body searches for the missing part, desperate for it to reappear as if from a dense fog. When the body fails to locate the missing piece, it responds to the perceived emergency by sending signals of intense pain, as if this could call the limbs back home. Pain like the voice of a lost person, alone in the woods, afraid of the dark and screaming.

At first I felt sharp, stabbing sensations at the bottom of my stump, as if the foot were still there but had simply fallen asleep and now had begun to wake up. Later, between dosages of pain medication, it felt as though the left leg were trapped under heavy bricks, possibly under the body cast, which I insisted on referring to as "the brick house." I was starting to worry that I'd end up in one of these plaster houses every year.

The site of the amputation itched and ached, and I could not get to it. "My foot, my foot," I said to Mom, as if she could get it for me as easily as a glass of water or a snack. "Where's my foot?" I asked her, and several times, in my sleep, I shouted simply, "Foot!" as if I had suddenly come upon it like a unique flower or plant in the woods that I had not been expecting to find. The disappearance of a foot seemed impossible, preposterous, although I had been told many times that it was going to happen.

Mom rubbed the air above the sheet where my foot used to be, which helped a bit, as this maintained the illusion that the foot was still physically present and could therefore be touched and soothed. As wounds drained, a small bag next to my waist collected the old blood until the bag was changed.

An essential part of healing and postoperative recovery was physical therapy, which I attended daily, much to my resistance and dismay. When my therapist, Ms. Sharon, put me on the slant board to send blood to the wound and assist in healing and circulation, I screamed and wailed. She was a short, strong woman with extremely soft hands. Her hair was like a curly gray ball on top of her head. She appeared to me then as the oldest woman I'd ever seen or known, and I was afraid of her. Although she was gentle with me, Ms. Sharon did not tolerate my frequent fits of temper; she simply waited for me to finish screaming, and then it was back to work. "C'mon, little girl," she'd say. "You can do it, little button. You have got to do it." When she brought me down off the board, I struck her with my fists. She let me get in a few punches, and then back on the slant board I went.

In the gymnasium were other people with different ailments going through their own torturous physical exercises. The worst to watch were the kids with severe burns who howled as they rode tricycles across the floor. They needed to move and stretch their skin to keep it from tightening, and their therapists pushed them forward when they stopped, urging them on. Down and up I went on the slant board, watching the burn victims ride in painful, screaming circles and adding a few screeches and howls of my own. Our shouts and cries echoed in the gymnasium as if we were kids in a horror house, being forced to watch some terrible, frightening film.

When my anger at Dr. Elliot and the brick house was dulled temporarily by pain medication and total exhaustion from physical therapy sessions, Mom took me for wagon rides up and down the white hospital hallways that smelled like glass cleaner and rubbing alcohol. There were blue lions painted on the ceiling so you had something to look at when you were being wheeled somewhere on your back, which was a lot: to physical therapy, to X-rays, to surgery. You could really only count the lions on wagon rides. When a person was being wheeled anywhere else, the rolling beds always moved too quickly, and the lions' bodies and manes became blue stripes along the white ceiling.

I was placed deliberately in the oncology unit so that I would have a private room and Mom could stay the night on a cot. During my other surgery, she had slept in a straight-backed chair in the orthopedic ward. Colorful drawings by the sick children in the ward covered the walls. I watched bald kids as they walked down the halls, wheeling an IV pole with one hand. They looked like girls and boys who had suddenly aged and lost all their hair, even though their bodies remained small and childlike.

Whenever I saw Dr. Elliot, I threw something at him—a toy, a pillow, a book. Once, before Mom could get hold of me, I overturned my food tray on his lap when he drew a chair up next to the bed to talk to me. I was happy to see him get drenched with milk; a small pile of mashed potatoes stuck to his shirtsleeves, and blobs of green, inedible Jell-O landed on his shoes. "It *hurts,*" I told him.

The phantom limb sensations worsened. The pain was like nothing I had ever known—it was as strange and strong and foreign as a terrified scream in a voice you don't recognize. The ache was painful, yet it was beyond pain: It was the hollow feeling of loss—physical, yes, but a more whole body feeling, as if a cave had been gouged deep in my leg somewhere, and air was blowing—howling—through it. It was like the pain of nostalgia—vague but omnipresent, attached to everything but nothing in particular. The sensation of complete loss.

When the pains came, Mom would rub the "ghost" of my foot for hours. Her dark hair fell into her worried face, and sometimes she hummed songs she'd once used to rock me to sleep: "Count Your Blessings" and "Do Lord." I watched her fingers move through the air above my foot, trying to recapture the spirit and coax back the presence of something that was already gone. I had stopped calling out for the foot—I knew now it was lost for good, even if the nerves continued to transmit false messages of its existence to the brain.

She sang: "When upon life's burdens you are tempest tossed, when you are discouraged thinking all is lost . . ." It was a paradoxical feeling of trying to reattach something while simultaneously trying to set it, once and for all, free. "Count your many blessings, name them one by one. And it will surprise you what the Lord has done. . . ." It was painful. It was impossible. I felt the presence of my lost foot when I wiggled the bottom of my stump as if I were wiggling toes. "Do Lord, oh do Lord, oh do you remember me?"

Misshapen as it was, that foot had been mine, and I had learned to live with it. For example, when Dad carried me on his shoulders, holding me at my ankles, he clasped one foot close to his shoulder, and the other one—the shorter one—he held tightly, close to his cheek, so I wouldn't tip to the side. I was used to wearing my brace on the outside of my clothes; I had learned to stand up and sit down. Just when I had gotten used to it, the body had changed.

I never fully understood the gravity of what was going on or what was at stake during the operations. Nothing at that age seems permanent; a person believes that everything can be fixed. What I knew was that Mom slept in a cot she made up in the morning before the nurses came around; people were nice to me; the baby with cancer whose room was next to mine had wispy, angel-like hair. I liked worrying about her. Cancer was far worse than anything I had or ever would have. I was told it could kill you.

Every once in a while, floating in a drugged and uncomfortable sleep, I saw the shadow of Dr. Elliot in the room. I felt his cool hand on my forehead and sometimes some light pressure on the cast. I caught a glimpse of the dark shelf of hair over his head.

For years after my amputation, I had a couple of horrible, recurring dreams. One was of a trash bin for amputated limbs—a huge, green-sided metal bin big enough to fit several people inside. Nurses and doctors I had never met had the job of dumping the newly severed parts; their green uniforms matched the bin. Inside were piles of bare, amputated feet, hands, entire legs and arms, all floating in blood. I never imagined that the limbs might be wrapped up or wiped clean. This implied effort, and I thought that amputations involved a simple hand saw that moved back and forth through the bone until something fell off, as if severing a part of the body were not so different from felling a tree. Later I would learn that there was a specific term for amputated specimens like mine—medical waste—and that it was disposed of in a specific way: It was burned. Trash from waiting room wastebaskets was combined with blood-soaked bandages, culture dishes, needles, swabs, used surgical gloves, scalpels, and limbs and organs from the operating room, and everything was incinerated in a special receptacle at the hospital designed specifically for this purpose.

In the dream, I am always four years old. I stand on a stool in front of the bin, sorting through the floating body parts with my bare hands, trying to find the one foot among the many that is mine.

Plagued by nightmares and sometimes by pain, I woke up in my hospital bed and tried to orient myself. I looked at the glass of water on the table next to me, at my body, prone and encased in plaster, and at Mom's face. She was always asleep, her blanketed back moving up and down with her breath. Eventually I went back to sleep, soothed by the familiarity of my mother's body and the objects in the room.

The body cast was hot and uncomfortable during the summer. The smells were horrible. Every day, Mom gave me a sponge bath and directed a small fan or cool air from a hair dryer down the cast's narrow top opening. It felt delicious to feel air move inside that closed space, but it did little to alleviate the mix of smells—dried sweat, crusted blood, shit—that wafted up from the stale, gluey air trapped against my skin.

In addition to the heat and smell, the logistics of the cast were a challenge. I had to go to the bathroom through a small square—like a trapdoor—between my stiff, separated legs. If I needed to use the toilet at night, I had to shout and wake up my parents. Sometimes I peed in the cast and endured the awful smell until it faded into the others.

Mom "petaled" my cast—an old technique she had learned in nursing school. She cut strips of adhesive tape, each about the size of a Band-Aid, and put half of the strip outside the cast and half inside. Petaling created a smooth surface at the rough edges of the cast. After the tape had been soiled by shit and urine, it was simply peeled off and discarded. "It was like laying the petals of a flower," Mom explained. "Although it was never going to smell like a flower down there, it did smell better and the cast didn't scrape against your skin."

I liked to go on long drives in our yellow station wagon. That way, I could still cover distances, even though I was immobile. That summer, when we drove to Illinois to visit my aunt, uncle, and cousins, I sat propped up on pillows in the back of the station wagon and watched through the windows as the land rolled away in reverse, changing from rocky and hilly to flat fields decorated with silos. In the distance, the land met the sky in a smooth line. Andy handed me treats and books over the middle seats that he was happy to have to himself for a change.

When we arrived in Illinois, the body cast had been on for several weeks, and Mom insisted on combing out the tangles in my long hair, which she'd arranged in a high, messy bun. She propped me up against the couch in my aunt and uncle's living room and tried to distract me by playing cartoons on television and offering sweets.

"Maybe we should just cut her hair," Dad said, watching as I screamed and protested. "It sounds really painful." At this, I howled louder. I was definitely in favor of a haircut. Who cared what I looked like? This painful process didn't seem worth it.

"No way," Mom replied, spraying my hair with more detangler. "I won't cut her hair." When she was ten years old, her mother had open heart surgery, and Mom went to live temporarily with her aunt and uncle. The first thing her aunt did was take her to the town barber to have her waist-length hair cut short so that it would be easier to care for. She'd hated it, she said, because she'd felt like a boy when she wanted to be a little girl. "She's keeping all of this," Mom said, fingering a strand of my hair and preparing to rake out a tangle. Dad shrugged and left the room.

"Ready?" Mom said cheerily, picking up her comb. "Almost done!" I groaned as she handed me a butterscotch candy.

The June air was sweltering hot. I heard the shouts and giggles of Andy and my cousins Erica, Beth, and Sarah as they played in the backyard. Periodically, the screen door would screech open and then close again as one of them ran in to check on me. I heard the deep tones of Uncle Aaron's voice as he talked to Dad. I heard the clink of ice as it melted down in their Manhattans.

After all the knots were out, Mom washed my hair in the kitchen sink; gentle as she'd tried to be, my scalp stung. The comb moved smoothly through my wet hair. "See," she said, squeezing the ends of my hair with a towel. "All better." I glared at her.

Dad carried me out to the back porch so I could sit on the patio, propped up on pillows. I looked out over the yard and watched the fireflies bob and spin in the thick, early evening air. I put my hands in my sweet-smelling hair as it dried, wavy and heavy. I smelled of sweat on clean but sticky skin. These smells of summer temporarily masked the odors wafting up from the cast, which would be on for another four weeks. My cousins took turns drawing on it; they signed their names under their creations and then passed the pen to the next girl who wanted to leave her mark on the brick house.

Sarah caught a firefly and pulled off its blinking back. I loved those lightning bugs because even when they were dismembered, part of them lived on. There was no pain to imagine, no struggle to witness; there was only light that gradually and beautifully faded. Sarah bent her dark head over my hand and attached the firefly's lit back. Dulling quickly, it balanced on my sweaty finger, a ringless jewel.

The brick house came off on my fourth birthday. Afterward, I wore a walking cast, a cone of plaster that extended past the edge of my stump. I walked on this for a while as the healing was completed.

When this second cast was removed, physical therapy was required to restrengthen the atrophied muscles. Mom helped me do the exercises in the bathtub, because warm water helped the muscles relax, making them easier to flex and stretch. "Kick, one-two-three, kick," Mom said as my splashes dampened her blouse and a rubber duck floated to the far reaches of the tub. She drew a smiley face on the end of the stump with bath paints and put a doll's skirt on it, and I called it Super Stump. Super Stump loved to fly around, particularly in Andy's face. She got me in trouble a few times, but I was proud of her. Sometimes I would bend her up to my mouth (my knee was still functional) and sing into the heel as if it were a microphone. Andy and I both learned to balance a spoon lengthwise on the end of Super Stump. We loved showing our friends this cool trick. I felt that my leg made me different and special and interesting to other kids. Instead of being the dorky kid sister, I was a novelty. "Hey, watch this," Andy would say, and off came my leg and out came the spoon, followed by the oohs and aahs as it trembled on top of the line of stitches at the bottom of my stump.

But how to *explain* what had happened to me? Nobody understood about PFFD, least of all me. When kids asked, "What happened to your leg?" I replied, "A dragon bit it off." I thought this was genius—what a glamorous tale! What a story I had! I told everybody this, embellishing it more each time (the dragon challenged me to a duel, and I lost; the prince threw me out of the castle, and the dragon attacked me) until Mom told me to stop. She said that it wasn't appropriate, that I was *lying.*

I didn't get the artificial leg as originally planned. In October, Dad noticed a bump on my left hip and made an appointment with Dr. Elliot. After several X-rays, Dr. Elliot, looking pale and visibly shaken, reported the news. "This has never happened to me before," he explained. The plate had failed to heal; the "screw" that had been inserted into the hip plate was floating around and had broken in the socket. He told us to come back the next day while he came up with an alternative plan. Mom always wondered if this problem had been caused by the walking cast, which had not been connected to my hip and slumped to the floor when I sat down.

Dr. Elliot recommended a hip surgery in October that would take out the screw (embedded in the bone) and the plate. This would be followed by three to six weeks of traction in the hospital to keep tension on the leg. The surgery took about six hours; after four hours, Dr. Elliot appeared in the waiting room and told my parents that there would be no need for traction, as he could do a bone graft on the crest of the hip and place pins in the bone that would then be removed in three to four weeks.

During this long surgery that my parents found difficult to sign off on, Dad had refused to go to the hospital chapel with Mom. Instead, he walked around on different floors of the hospital, poking his head into the rooms of other patients and asking, "How's it going in there? Everyone okay?" He told me that he'd had no mind for prayer that day. "I just kept moving around," he said. "It was the only thing that made any sense."

Mom tells me, "Dad and I were the only ones left in the waiting room when Dr. Elliot came to get us. We were so happy that you were going to be in a body cast, which sounds strange—to want your child in another body cast—but it was so much better than traction." The hip spica body cast would be on for seven more weeks, scheduled to come off just after Thanksgiving. My legs were separated again by the metal rod and also by metal pins through the femur bone; like anchors, they held everything in place.

That Halloween, I was Little Red Riding Hood and Mom was Groucho Marx. The rounded edge of the cast stuck out from beneath my red dress, and I wore a black felt boot on my right foot. Our eyes were hidden: mine in a red mask, Mom's in black plastic glasses attached to a false rubber nose. Mom carried me on her hip around the neighborhood, collecting candy. "We were a hit!" she said.

Before I left the hospital and returned to preschool, Ms. Sharon searched through her supply closet and found an old walker that looked like pipes that had been soldered together. "That thing was impenetrable," Mom tells me. "Like a metal tank. If some kid ran into you, they'd probably regret it." Dad used the bicycle seat from my first makeshift walker and covered it in a new layer of sheepskin so my butt wouldn't get sore from so much sitting.

The pipe walker, or "the tank," as we called it, was great for protection from other kids who might collide with me during the chaos of preschool, but it was so heavy that I could not move it alone. The teacher or several kids together had to push me around the schoolroom.

At home, Mom gave me a small, round platform with wheels attached. Lying on my plastered stomach, I pushed myself forward and backward with my hands. I looked like a white plaster beetle with my back legs immobilized and stiff and my hands scurrying like small feet along the ground. I felt mobile once again after the disappointment of not getting the leg and being forced to move around in the tank while wearing another body cast. A few hours of fast forward motion across the kitchen linoleum made the situation feel more bearable.

The best part of the scooter was being able to play with Andy again, not just indoors but outside, too. After a snowfall, he suggested projects that we could both do at ground level; we built miniature snowmen and shallow forts in the snow. Then one day he dared me to a race—he would crawl, and I would push. We weren't even supposed to be outside without supervision—but we didn't care. It was a beautiful November day. The sunshine was luminous against the white, melting snow, and the wet ground smelled fragrant, almost springlike.

When Mom thought we were napping, Andy quietly crept outside and I followed on the scooter. We started the race on the long concrete walk that ran the length of our downward-sloping backyard and had just been cleared that morning of fresh snow. In the middle of my descent, I hit a hidden patch of ice and the scooter slid out from underneath me. I skid face first on the concrete, knocking out a tooth. Catapulting into the alley, I bumped one of the pins and landed on my back. The force of the jostled pin hurt so terribly that I threw up on the front of the cast.

Stunned, I looked up into the branches of the snow-covered trees. Wet snow crystals dropped on my face when the wind shook the branches. Andy was screaming my name, but his voice disappeared into the cold ground. I could taste blood and feel it, fast and wet, filling my mouth. I heard Mom's shouts and hurried steps down the path. I wanted to move, but I could not. Sun moved over the snowy branches, and then the whole sky exploded into a glowing, sparkling white.

After everything was healed and my tooth was spirited away by the tooth fairy in exchange for a one-dollar bill, the cast was cut open and the pins were removed. I knew it was going to hurt, but when Dr. Elliot pulled each of them out—quickly, one after the other—I had never felt anything like it. It felt as if the tissue and bone were being yanked out at once or the body was being forcibly turned inside out. I gritted my teeth, determined not to cry out. "Brave girl," said the assisting nurse. "What a brave girl," she said again, wiping my sweaty forehead with a cool towel. Those words of praise made all the pain worthwhile. Bravery in these situations was a virtue; it set me apart and made me feel proud.

The healing stump was wrapped in an Ace bandage, and I used crutches at home, but at preschool I continued to use the tank.

I wore long jumpers to cover the Ace bandage, but I was known for plunking my stump out in public when it itched. Singing in the church choir, I often sat down and started scratching, with my jumper hitched up around my waist. Mom and I had a discussion she called "stump etiquette."

"Don't plunk your stump," she told me.

"It itches," I said. "I itch."

"We don't itch ourselves in public."

"*You* don't itch! *I* do."

"It's not ladylike."

"I'm not a lady," I replied. And I didn't feel like one. I had walked with a tank; I wanted to be gritty and strong; if something itched, it made sense to scratch it.

"Well," Mom said, "soon you'll have a new leg. A prosthesis." That word sounded awkward coming out of her mouth, as if she were trying to hiss like a snake. This made me giggle. She continued, "And then things will be different. Things will be better." After the healing process was complete, I would be fitted for my first artificial leg. I'd heard this story before and had ended up in a cast.

My parents showed me pictures of what this newest part of my body would look like: My left leg would be made of shiny, light brown wood.

"When you grow," Dad said, pointing at the area where foot and ankle met, "we'll put something extra here, to make it longer, so you can have this leg for a long time."

The SACH, or Solid Ankle Cushion Heel foot, was a flexible rubber shell that fit around a wooden core. When I took a step forward, the heel of the foot would compress and the toe area would bend. As I grew, length could be added at the ankle and the foot screwed back on again with a thick bolt that was tightened or loosened by the prosthetist. Essentially, the leg would grow with me, only the prosthetist would be responsible for its growth.

"Will it be like the big table?" I asked.

Dad waited for a moment and then seemed to understand. "That's it," he replied. Whenever we had big dinners at Christmas and Thanksgiving, the oak table in the dining room was pulled apart and a piece of wood sandwiched in to make room for more people.

"My leg is like a table," I said, giggling.

"No, it will be a leg," Mom said with a serious look on her face. "You're going to love it." She suddenly looked enthusiastic. I wasn't sure I trusted her smile. "We're going to make it work."

I would be disappointed with the SACH foot. It was the thinnest foot around, but it was still bigger than my right foot and wasn't terribly functional. Only after my left hip and stump began to ache from the impact of running, skipping, and jumping rope did we learn that it was designed, according to the prosthetic company, for "moderately active to less active amputees." In short, I would be too active for that first foot.

At the time, as I looked at pictures of SACH feet, they looked all right to me. I didn't understand anything about compression, but the foot and even the leg itself reminded me a bit of Barbie's long, slim legs and sleek feet without toes or veins. A clean look.

"You'll learn how to walk with the new leg," Mom said. "It might be difficult at first, but you'll learn. Okay?"

"Okay," I replied.

Dad nodded. "That's right," Mom said.

For a few weeks, my stump, when it was briefly free of the Ace bandage, was a red and shriveled thing, like a mutilated, blood-soaked baseball bat. The skin smelled rank, and the bones inside felt like noodles. Noodle bones. I had a stuffed dog named Feather at the time, a beanbag dog, and his flexible back and body seemed more substantial than the bone that would fit into the artificial leg, but I was tired of the crutches and the walker. If Mom and Dad said it would work, then I believed them.

These were my first real memories of my body. They were already memories of a body that would be no more, that was on its way out, disappearing. I remember little of a flesh-and-blood foot, just isolated moments and then the memory of the loss. What I remember most is being told how and when I was going to lose the foot and what would happen next. I thought of myself as linked to Super Stump, the stump I'd been given, the way I could move the muscles on the bottom and the side; the way it was rounded like the end of a bat; the way I could bend it like a length of flexible tubing and fold it across my right leg in order to sit cross-legged on the floor. That was my body. At this young age, I simply accepted the body as it was, while also feeling anxious to be more mobile, to really *move.*

Chapter Three

A PIRATE'S TREASURE

I crouched on the edge of the pool platform, preparing to dive. The smell of the pool was deep and dark, not unlike the smell of the room where Communion vestments were kept at church. When I pulled out the small, cloth-covered box full of wine and wafers that Dad used to take Communion to older parishioners—we called them "shut-ins"—who could not make the journey to Sunday services, it felt like encountering some dusty secret; the bottom of each thimble-size wine goblet was tinted red and smelled vaguely of vinegar. These odors and stains suggested that the shadow of something holy remained, some crucial remnant had been left behind for the next user to divine and ingest, linking all the communicants to one another.

On that day of my first dive, there was something secret about the water, although it was clear and emitted the scrubbed-clean smell of bleach and chlorine. I had seen many people dive off this same ledge, and today it was my turn. Without my glasses, the black lane markers were blurry; they looked like slow-moving caterpillars under the rocking motion of the water as people getting in and out of the pool disrupted it. My private swimming teacher, Ann, stood at my side, coaching me.

I tipped back and forth on my right leg until I could balance in a crouched position; the blue flipper on my right foot squeaked against the wet tiles. I looked up and noticed people staring at me in my blue one-piece swimsuit, with my stump hanging stiffly next to my body like a kickstand. I looked back at the water and took a deep breath.

"Hold the stump close to your side," Ann said. "Put your arms over your head. That's right. You've got it."

I wanted to dive to a specific point in the water, to the middle of one of the black caterpillar lines, as if there were something special there for me to find. I steadied myself, hunched over, and finally dived into the water. My head went under first, then the cool water closed over my back, my butt, and finally my right leg and my stump. I felt as slippery and slick as the tiny rainbow trout Dad taught me to throw back into the river after we brought them up, wriggling, from the ends of our fishing rods. I felt absorbed, taken under, and enveloped; the water was a cool hand guiding me forward. My body felt light and remarkably even, its asymmetry balanced and supported by the softness of the water.

When I came up for air, I heard Ann clapping. The applause echoed against the pool walls, and I hoped that all the people who had been staring at me were listening to this praise. I began to swim, first freestyle and then the breaststroke; I had been practicing both moves all summer. The fin on my right foot made me feel like a fish cutting gracefully through the water, headed to the other side of the pool. When I flipped over to my back, I heard the tide of my breath in my head, powerful and rhythmic as a wave; my single foot was strong enough to move me through the water. The stump didn't do much, merely bobbed and floated like a buoy. The right leg took over on its behalf, compensating, kicking, and shearing the blue water. I was dividing a space with my body versus being divided: by a surgeon, by a prosthetist, by a wooden leg that was removed each night and lay by my bed until morning.

After reaching the other side of the pool, I lifted my head, triumphant. I hoisted myself onto the ledge. A little girl who was walking past stopped abruptly. Water dripped from the ends of her hair as she stood staring at me until a woman steered her away by her wet shoulders.

"Great," Ann said, putting her warm hand on my back. "You did great."

I loved to dive. I progressed steadily in ability until I could do jumps off the springboard, hopping up the first step and then crawling out to crouch carefully at the edge of the board, maintaining my balance. Just once I would plummet off the high board, letting every person in the pool have their moment to stare at me, the one-legged girl descending in a smooth arc into the water. I felt powerful, and I thought about my body in a new way, although the high dive itself had absolutely terrified me and I never did it again. Later, I would understand that learning to dive was my first experience of my body as capable of powerful, fluid, and beautiful motion. In those moments when I rounded my back, tucked my chin, and tipped gracefully into the smooth, accepting water, I was aware of the song that a body creates when it is released for just a few moments from its regular rules and restrictions and from the expectations of the person who lives with it. I felt the beauty of movement when the person who inhabits his or her unique form is perfectly content to do so, as if it were unimaginable being any other way.

At that time, a photo was taken of me with another amputee who was in her early thirties. We stood against a tile wall in the locker room, smiling, sharing just two full legs between us. I was thrilled to meet someone who was like me. She had long brown hair, soft-looking skin, and a bright smile. After Ann took our picture, the two of us put on our wooden legs. Mine was newer and shinier than hers, but they were similar models. Both had metal hinges on the outside of the wood; both were suspended from our bodies by a cloth strap that buckled just above the pelvis on the left side of the body.

Years later, when I looked at that photograph, I felt horror at my body and particularly at the woman's. By that time, I was used to seeing models in fashion magazines and judging my own appearance by the ways in which it compared with—and fell short of—theirs. *Who would ever want this woman?* I found myself thinking, and by *want* I meant *love,* as if these two expressions of desire were interchangeable. In the photograph, both of us were beaming. *What does she have to be so happy about?* I wondered bitterly, although arguably she and I shared a similar fate. I looked over at my younger self, who was wearing a similar genuine smile, who would grow up to be a similar disabled woman. Although I destroyed the photograph, I often thought about the woman standing next to me and wondered what had happened to her: *Did she marry, did she have children, did she love her life, did somebody love her?*

Two and half years earlier, in January 1979, I had finally received my first wooden leg. For my first fitting, I stood barefoot on the dirty floor of the changing room while the prosthetist took measurements of my stump. The stink of the healing wounds was finally gone; the limb was clean. Now that the left foot had been removed, or "disarticulated"—the sharp sound of the word matching the rough nature of the action itself—I had my natural heel at the end of the short leg.

For two months before the fitting, I wore a walking cast that looked like a pirate's peg leg; it began at my hip and narrowed to a cone of hollow plaster that extended past the end of my stump. It looked like an ice-covered tree limb and was fitted at the bottom with a rubber knob.

"For traction," Dr. Elliot told me, pointing at the knob as he helped me put on the cast in the examination room.

"So you don't slip and fall," Mom said. I leaned my weight on the cast and took a few stiff-legged steps.

Dr. Elliot saluted me and said in his best "pirate" voice, "Harrr . . . who goes there, missy?"

"Harrr," I replied, and bared my teeth in a piratelike grin.

He and I laughed. Mom looked pale.

As we walked through the hospital corridor on our way to the parking lot, I asked Mom if I could get an eye patch to complete my pirate outfit. She refused. "You are not a pirate," she said. The tone of her voice warned me not to push it.

Dr. Elliot's pirate image stayed with me long after I stopped using the cast and began walking with a wooden leg. I envisioned myself as the solo sea-weary girl preparing to embark on a grand adventure. I wanted to battle foes and fight for the underdog; I would be a combination of guts and glam, beauty and strength, with my unique body—like a one-of-a-kind sailing ship designed to withstand dangerous waters—propelling me into the unknown world.

Rinehart Schmidt, my first prosthetist, had an office on a busy street in Denver near the Capitol building. It was next door to a bar and grill; the changing rooms, which were brown and windowless, always smelled of French fries and frying hamburgers. The bathroom was in the corner of the back room, where limbs-in-progress and other prosthetic parts—feet, calves, hands—were kept propped up on plaster pedestals or leaning against walls. Saws, hammers, screwdrivers, and other metal objects were scattered over two long worktables that ran the length of the room. A dusty transistor radio atop an old refrigerator was always tuned to a country music station. The toilet seat in the closet-size bathroom was bumpy and uneven, as dried plaster had been spilled on it and never cleaned up; there was no mirror on the wall and no soap for your hands on the sink. Often I had to yell through the door and ask Schmidt to bring me a roll of toilet paper that always smelled like cigarette smoke after he cracked open the door and tossed it through to where I waited on "the john," as he called it. Through the bathroom wall, I heard the clink of dishes being washed at the restaurant next door.

Schmidt was a short, wrinkled man nearing retirement. While he was making adjustments to the leg, he often smoked cigars or cigarettes, letting one or the other dangle from his mouth. When Mom asked me what I thought of him, I replied, "He's older than God."

Schmidt's bald head sweated constantly. A single piece of white hair swept over the dome of his freckled head. Sweat dripped from the end of his hair onto his cheek or rolled off his long nose and landed, trembling, on the edge of his lip. The handkerchief kept in his lab coat was covered in yellow and black stains and clumps of dried plaster, but he wiped his sweaty forehead with it anyway. The first time I met Schmidt, he cuffed me lightly on the shoulder and said, "Who's looking pretty today?" He had fat fingers, and his palms were wide and rough feeling, with deep, painful-looking cracks, as if he'd been rubbing them with sandpaper.

"Let's see what we have here," he said. Standing on one leg, I leaned against the examination table. Schmidt sat on a low stool with wheels and examined my stump, gently tracing my new scars with the callused pads of his fingers. The scars on my hip were bumpy and sometimes slightly tender. *What* did *we have here?* I wondered, and felt nervous. I stared at the top of Schmidt's head; I watched to see if his eyebrows raised at all, trying to track an expression. "Hmmm," he said, and looked up at me, grinning. I smiled back, hoping this exchange was a sign that things were okay, that what we had here was good.

Schmidt cupped the bottom of the stump in his palm and pushed lightly, then harder, watching me, then harder still until he saw me wince. "Good for weight bearing," he said, and stood up. "We've got this little bone on the edge here," he said, running his thumb over my original ankle bone—it looked like a little marble embedded in the skin. "That will be tricky. Could cause problems."

"What kinds of problems?" Dad asked. He stood next to me with his arms crossed.

"We just make sure there's no pressure there—we hollow out that part of the socket. Otherwise"—he rubbed his hands together—"there's friction, then sores and pain. Can't have that." Schmidt ran his hands once more along the length of my stump and then rolled on his stool to the cabinet in the corner, leaving the odor of stale smoke in his wake. "It's a good one," he announced while rummaging through a drawer. He nodded over his shoulder at me and then at Dad, who said, "Okay!" in a bright voice. I nodded, too, relieved, although I wondered what a bad stump would look like. Was it possible to move easily from bad to good? If so, how could I make sure that my stump stayed on the good side of things?

Schmidt rolled back over with measuring tape. Dad and I watched as he wrapped the tape around the stump in five different places: at the fattest point near my hip; then in the middle, where it narrowed slightly; then at the lowest point where it tapered to the heel. As he worked his way down, he recorded each measurement on a piece of paper folded over his knee. Leaning over to get a closer look, I saw a light pencil outline of a stump with blank spaces next to it for the numbers. His touch was light and quick. After he measured the circumference of my right thigh, I hopped up on the examination table and waited. The backs of my legs stuck to the table, as the rooms were always too warm and badly ventilated—not a window or a fan in sight. I was reminded of summer cross-country trips in our station wagon with its sticky vinyl seats.

Schmidt disappeared from the room for several minutes and returned with a bucket in one hand. Rolls of white plaster of paris were wrapped around both his arms, from the wrists to the elbows. He sloshed water all over the floor as he moved to set the bucket on the plastic sheet. He shook the rolls of plaster from his arms. I stood still, awaiting instructions.

"Now we'll make the mold," he said, and dunked one roll of plaster into the bucket, where it quickly softened and expanded in the water.

Before Schmidt could make the main part of the leg—called the socket—he first needed to make a cast. After the stump was covered with a thin, soft cloth called the cast sock, it was encased in long strips of wet plaster. When the cast was complete, the prosthetist's hands would be white up to his elbows, the grainy plaster embedded beneath his fingernails.

Schmidt brought out the rolls, dripping wet. Seated on the table, I held the cast sock up in front and back. He wrapped the warm, wet strips around and around my stump, all the way down to the rounded end. After wrapping the heel a few more times, he gave it a pat, which tickled a bit. He smoothed the plaster around the small ankle bone as if he were molding clay or Silly Putty. As he worked, I sometimes felt stabs of pain, especially as the wet strips became heavier and heavier, but I said nothing. While in the hospital, I was constantly commended for being brave, for not crying. I wasn't about to upset that trend now. The prospect of this cast did not upset me; it would be removed in twenty minutes instead of six or eight weeks, and there would be no crutches, no walkers, no tank, no scooter, and no Ace bandages.

"Now hold the stump away from your body to let it dry," Schmidt said. He left the room while the warm plaster cooled. I leaned back against the table, and Dad and I stared down at the mummified stump, not saying a word. We listened to Schmidt bellowing the words to a country song in the other room. The plaster finally set, and the cast was stiff enough to remove.

"A-ha!" Schmidt exclaimed as he twisted the cast off gently. It resembled a snakeskin newly shed. Using a pencil, Schmidt made several marks on the outside of the mold. "This is the house for the residual limb," he said, tapping it with his index finger. He looked up at me. "Like a little house."

I didn't know what residual meant, but I understood that my stump would live in that house made of plaster and that's how I would walk. It was another type of brick house, but unlike the other one that had imprisoned me, this one, made of wood and metal, would set me free. The mold reminded me of a gingerbread house, the way you'd put the wet pieces of cake together and wait for them to dry into something solid, something real, something that could be called by name.

"Now we can make the leg," Schmidt said.

"Using that as a model?" Dad asked, clarifying.

"Yes, for the socket." Schmidt looked at me. "The little house. Now, the metal hinges at the sides of the socket will mimic the motion of a knee." He moved his hand back and forth through the air. "It's a simple motion, simple system." He stood up and opened and shut the door of the exam room with his plaster-covered hands, leaving two white handprints on the door. "The knee is like a hinge," he said. "Just like a door hinge."

After Schmidt left the room, Dad pushed the door back and forth. "That makes sense," he said.

While we were making another appointment for the next week in the "reception area," which was a tiny front room with a smelly old couch, a few chairs, and a pile of outdated *Time* magazines stacked on a dusty table, the bell on the door rang. For a few moments, the open door let the sounds of traffic rush in. As Schmidt flipped through the waterlogged appointment book, I turned around and saw a man who was very tall and looked older than Dad, but not as old as Schmidt. His dark, wavy hair was streaked with silver, and his leathery skin made him look like the ranchers who attended Dad's church. He wore khaki shorts; his right leg was shiny and wooden with bright metal hinges where a normal person's knee would be. When he walked, his foot swung out to the side. It was an odd, awkward movement, as though the fake leg might fly off his body at any moment. The leg made noises like a squeaky door as the man came closer. Was I going to look and sound like that when I walked?

I looked up at Dad and saw that all the color had drained from his face. His eyes looked wide behind his glasses; one of the lenses was smudged with a bit of white plaster. The hinges of the man's leg made a scraping sound as he crouched in front of me. I thought he looked like a robot, and not a very modern one. I knew it was rude to stare, so I looked at his face, my mouth partly open. His face and neck were sweating. "High-five, little lady," he said, and held out his tanned, perfect hand. When he smiled his teeth were white and even. I slapped his warm hand and giggled.

"Good luck!" he called to us as we left the building.

Driving back from Denver to Laramie, a three-hour drive, I asked Dad, "What did Schmidt mean by a good one?"

"He meant that your stump is healthy and looks strong."

"Really?"

"Yes. It all healed perfectly."

Healthy and strong was good. I felt proud, as if I had had something to do with how well I had healed. It meant that I wouldn't walk like that nice man I'd met on the way out of the office. I felt better, although I hadn't realized until that moment how unsettled I'd felt.

"What does 'residull' mean?"

"You mean 'residual'?" Dad was silent for a moment. "It means what's left after something is taken, goes away. What's left over."

"Like leftovers?"

"I guess so."

Residual. What's left when something's taken away. This strange word that I had never heard before and didn't completely understand made me sad. I looked out the window and watched as a truck barreled past us on a steep hill. As we passed Abe Lincoln's monument on I-80, I stared into his bronze, deeply lined face until our car was too far away for me to see him. As soon as I had the leg, I was going to walk right up to that monument. No walkers or scooters or casts or crutches. Just me and my good and healthy stump.

I would remember this experience later. The words themselves, "residual limb," implied lack and also—to my mind—held within them a kind of mythic power. They were labels for the body, albeit ones I didn't initially or immediately understand. Even so, in that moment in the car, I had already resolved to overcome those labels—to prove even the words wrong.

A few weeks later, Dad and I returned to Schmidt's office. "Ready to get rid of those?" Dad asked, pointing at my crutches. I nodded.

"There she is," Schmidt said as we walked in the door. He stood in the reception area with the leg in his arms and a cigarette dangling from his lips.

Leaning forward to balance my weight on the crutches, I took the leg and held it in my hands. I felt inside the molded plastic socket—it was perfectly smooth. I ran my fingers over the orange, toeless foot. The wooden calf looked solid and flawless. The buckle on the canvas waist strap was silver and shiny. There was a barely visible line where the foot met the ankle. The metal hinges on each side looked sleek and mechanical. The leg was made especially for me. It was mine. Now I could walk like other kids; I could have adventures, no longer bound by any cast. "I want to wear it," I said. Schmidt carried the leg into the changing room, and Dad and I followed.

That afternoon, I walked the runway with the prosthesis. I had discovered a treasure: this new body of mine, this new wooden leg.

Dad and Schmidt clapped and cheered as I went back and forth across the thin strip of linoleum that ran the length of the front room. The leg made either a loud thump or a crack each time I swung it through, as if my forward motion—at last!—were special enough to make its own sound.

"How does it feel?" Schmidt asked.

"Weird," I said. He looked at me. "But good." It wasn't like walking with a cast at all. The leg felt like a part of me, like an extension of my flesh-and-blood stump; it *was* me. It did feel strange at first—and heavy—but soon it felt natural, as if the body filled it exactly the way it should.

"Does it hurt anywhere?"

I shook my head. "Well, it kind of rubs on the side, but it's okay." *Don't take it away,* I thought. "It's okay," I repeated.

"Show me where it rubs," Schmidt said, and I pointed. "Ah," he said, and marked that area with a red grease pencil. I watched him. "Don't worry, it will rinse off," he said. I unbuckled the strap and slipped off the leg. Schmidt moved his hands over my stump, checking skin temperature as a gauge of irritation. "Come with me," he said, and Dad bent down so I could hop up on his back. I wanted to see where my leg was going.

We walked to the back room, where Schmidt set the leg on a pedestal and used an electrically powered router—like a long arm fitted with a metal tip—to grind out those places where I'd felt pressure on my stump. Dust spun out everywhere as the socket was modified. "Makes good dust!" Schmidt shouted.

Back on the runway, I put on the leg and took a few steps.

"Better?" Schmidt asked. I nodded.

I used the bars along the runway to steady me when my balance faltered. "It will help your limp if you imagine swinging the leg through as smoothly as possible," Schmidt advised. I imagined the pendulum in a grandfather clock swinging gracefully and evenly as it marked each second. I took a few more steps. "Good," he said. "Much better."

I looked at Dad. "Looks great!" he said. "Wow."

Schmidt periodically leapt out in front of me and bent to make an adjustment, asking again about pressure points and turning the left foot in and then out again to match the position of my right foot. "You don't want to look pigeon-toed!" he warned. I thought of a car race I'd seen on television, when a mechanic ran out to fix the cars after an accident to get them up and racing again. I thought of designers nipping a hem or adjusting a belt on a model before a fashion show. I was pleased with both of these associations—divided, as they were, between rugged and lovely—and I was absolutely thrilled with my new leg. After a while, I no longer needed the bars.

"Look at that. Look at her go," said Schmidt. He watched me carefully, clearly admiring his handiwork. *I'm going,* I thought. *Here I go.* Dad looked as if he were about to burst into tears or laughter or both at once.

"I want to go faster," I said, looking at Schmidt. "How fast can I go?"

He took the cigarette out of his mouth and said, "You go as fast as you want to." I hugged him, cigarette and body odor and all. Dad laughed.

After that, I walked everywhere until I was sore and exhausted. I did not allow the leg to be removed from my sight. At night, I slept with my arm slung around it, and if I slipped out of it to watch television at night, I made sure to keep a hand on the foot, the ankle, or the strap. If I hopped off to the bathroom, I instructed Andy to look after it, as if the leg might walk away on its own. Although I later went through periods of being cavalier about my prosthesis—tossing it about or throwing it down the stairs to watch it bend at weird angles like some kind of strange, anatomical Slinky—much of the time I guarded it as fiercely as I did during the days when it first was mine.

Initially, everything about the new leg seemed miraculous. Not only was it much prettier and more interesting then my flesh-and-blood leg, but it had freed me.

The leg slowly revealed itself to be far from perfect. The waist strap chafed against my hips and made my right leg go numb if I sat still for too long. I often dropped the strap into the toilet when I was in a hurry. The metal hinges ripped my clothes. The cheap silver buckle tarnished quickly. I liked the look of the leg's slick wood, but I could not sit in a smooth chair without sliding out of it. The SACH foot soon had its share of grass stains and dirt smudges that looked like bruises; after a while, the initial bounce disappeared, and it felt like walking on a block of wood.

"Those feet are not free," Dad reminded me, pointing out the most recent, permanent stain.

"Uh-huh," I said, but I didn't want to be careful while playing outside. I wanted to be active and adventurous.

During the summer, the socket was incredibly hot; the thin fabric stump sock was wet and stinking at the end of the day. I used to dare myself to smell it, amazed that such horrific odor was produced by my body. The metal hinges on either side burned me when I touched them after being out in the sun.

Dad oiled the hinges with WD-40 when they became stiff and creaky in the winter. I hopped up on the thick rope swing that hung from the garage rafters and moved back and forth through the air. My arm muscles strained as I rose higher and higher, leaning back to create more momentum. I felt as though I had two bodies: the one on the swing with its right leg pumping and straightening and the other body that needed the leg to walk and run, the one with the artificial part that was being oiled and tended to as I looked on. I was comfortable with both embodiments. After they were oiled, the leg's hinges leaked frequently, and I left a greasy mark on my clothes, car seats, bedsheets, or the couch—anywhere I sat down.

While visiting my cousins one summer, I left my leg unattended at the public pool for just a moment to show Erica, Sarah, and Beth how well I could dive, and when I resurfaced and found that it had disappeared, I became hysterical. Erica and Beth stayed with me while Sarah shot into action, as was her way. She roamed the pool area and the locker rooms until she tracked down the thief and shook him down. Carrying it carefully in her arms, her steps sure and steady, Sarah returned the leg to me.

I frantically wiped down the socket and the hinges with my beach towel, as if to remove the mark that this foreign handler—this thief—had left on a part of my body. "He does that again," Sarah promised, "and I'll make his nose bleed." I nodded, thankful and vindicated. We never had problems at the pool again, although one of my cousins would always work on her tan in order to stand watch over the leg where it leaned against a plastic pool chair, completely covered by a beach towel. When I was ready to get out, the wrapped prosthesis was brought like an offering to the edge of the pool. I dried the stump as quickly as I could and slipped on the sock, my hands sometimes shaking. I didn't like strangers staring at my body, at my deformity, although I was perfectly comfortable having my leg off around friends and family. I shoved the stump into the sun-warmed socket, buckled the strap, and tied the towel around my waist to cover my lower half. Immediately I felt better, like any another girl having just finished her swim.

At slumber parties, I clung to the leg inside my sleeping bag with both arms wrapped around it as if it were a favorite stuffed animal, a beloved pet, or, much later, a lover; as an adult, on overnight train trips, I zipped it into my coat and used it as an uncomfortable but functional headrest, wrapping both my arms around it to hold it firmly in place. If anyone tried to take my leg—as a joke, as a way of being cruel—he or she would have to take me with it.

Years later, when I began doing research into the history of prosthetics, one of the first images I came across was that of Captain

Hook; one of the oldest images of a disabled person, this villain gestures with his hook-hand, his evil eyes narrowed in mischief. How, I wondered, had the idea of being a pirate ever comforted me?

Soon after, I had a vivid dream. I was on a pirate ship, being forced to walk the plank in my first wooden leg, with my blue flipper on my right foot; neither fit me properly, because in the dream I inhabit my adult body. Schmidt was there, too. He stood on deck with a heavy-looking wooden treasure chest balanced in his arms, telling me to come back, that it was dangerous, that he had a special gift for me that he couldn't hold on to much longer, but I hobbled on, dragging my left leg and then the right one in its ill-fitting flipper, unable to stop myself, wanting to feel the freedom of diving in the water. At the very end of the plank, I turned around and held out my hands for help, but it was too late; the heel of the SACH foot had gone over the edge of the plank without my realizing it, and I fell backward. Once in the water, the prosthesis dragged me down, fell off, and disappeared. The flipper came off, too, and I could not kick hard enough with my right foot to move anywhere. I was trapped underwater as the contents of the treasure chest, thrown overboard, emptied around me. Suddenly coins were everywhere; they shot into the water and whizzed past my face. I grabbed at them, and they made a dull clink against my fingertips. As I failed to capture a single one, the coins floated down and away, entirely useless and inaccessible to me, but still holding the promise of riches, gleaming and glittering gold.

Chapter Four

POSTER CHILD

In 1980, I was chosen as the March of Dimes poster child for the Medicine Bow chapter of Albany County, Wyoming. Reporters from the *Laramie Boomerang* took pictures of me playing ball, climbing a rope, and doing jumping jacks in gym class. Photos were snapped as I strolled around in public parks, fed ducks, and sat beneath evergreen trees. Reporters were invited to document my participation in "Jump Rope for Life," a program to raise heart health awareness that was held each year at my elementary school.

When the photographers came to my house to take the official publicity photographs for the March of Dimes fund-raising and promotional materials, I wore a long-sleeved, blue velour shirt with a matching calf-length skirt and a gold necklace with the initial "E." On my right wrist, I wore the silver charm bracelet my grandmother had given me as a birthday gift the year before. It bore two charms: The first was a silver disk with the date of my baptism engraved into one side and my full name engraved into the other; the second was a tiny silver angel dangling from the bracelet by one thin wing. Mom fixed my long hair into two high pigtails and tied bows at the top of each with white ribbon.

I sat in front of the Christmas tree with my legs stretched out in front of me. I wore black Mary Jane shoes and thick white tights. With my hands folded neatly in my lap, I smiled up at my parents, at the reporter from the *Laramie Boomerang,* and at the March of Dimes representative, blinking into the camera flash and trying to keep my back straight.

While Mom and Dad were busy chatting with the reporter, who had come for a human interest story, Andy shook the biggest Christmas gifts piled against the back wall behind the tree to try to detect what was inside. I heard rustling behind me each time he picked up a wrapped package. Once I heard a shaking and then a jingle before the sounds stopped abruptly. I knew that was my gift; I'd asked for a plastic piano shaped like a dinosaur—Pianosaurus Rex.

I did everything the reporters and photographers asked of me. I stood up; I sat down again. I sat on the couch; I stood by the window; I posed in front of the oil painting of the Rocky Mountains that hung on the living room wall.

After the photo session, the living room with its pale blue love seat, gold fabric couch, antique rocker, and huge oak stereo looked as if it were under bright lights. I felt as though I had been changed into a new and exciting person. I felt famous; I felt singled out and special; *and* I knew what I was getting for Christmas. The camera flashes exploded like stars in my vision. I blinked again and again, waiting for the white flashes to recede.

Throughout that year and into the next, I made many public appearances as the poster child for the nation's leading organization dedicated to improving the health of babies by preventing birth defects. At each of them, I showed off my sleek wooden leg as if it were the latest fashion accessory. The newspaper headlines ran: DISABLED GIRL IS ACTIVE IN SPORTS; ALBANY COUNTY'S RAPP ATTENDS BUILDING DEDICATION; POSTER CHILD BUILDS HEART AND SOUL IN ANNUAL JUMP-A-THON. My six-year-old grin beamed beneath the March of Dimes motto: "Help Prevent Birth Defects." There were posters of me on the walls of Slade Elementary School. I attended luncheons at the Chamber of Commerce; I joined the Handicapped Ski Program in Winter Park, Colorado; I visited the governor in his Cheyenne mansion.

At church functions, at rodeos, and at other community venues and events, I spoke to crowds both large and small about how normal my life was and how happy I was—all in an effort to raise awareness and money for an organization designed to fund research that would prevent congenital birth defects similar to my own. I made proximal focal femoral deficiency sound attractive and deliciously unique. My speeches began something like this: "I might have one leg, but I'm not disabled." I explained myself away with a great deal of youthful zeal and confidence. "I was born with a different body," I said, "but it hasn't stopped me. If you believe in yourself, you can do anything."

Adults often asked, "How does it feel to be disabled?"

"I don't feel different," I replied, and I meant it. "I'm just like anyone else."

Kids asked me, "What things can you do with an artificial leg?"

"I can walk and run and ride a bike," I replied. "All kinds of things. I swim, too."

"Is there anything you can't do?"

"No," I said proudly, and at the age of six, I truly believed it. "Nothing." The applause was immediate.

I felt like the winner of a beauty contest, although I had received my title for an attribute that was certainly not coveted by others. I didn't care, because I loved the attention. I felt like a star.

People told me, "You're such an inspiration," and, "You're so brave." I believed them. I thought that as long as I was inspiring and fantastic, as long as I compensated for the missing leg by being smart, cute, intelligent, and fun, I would have a normal life. I would survive in the world. I even thought, for a long time, that it would be easy.

I had my fourth surgery over Christmas break, shortly after the March of Dimes publicity photographs were taken. My left knee was fused in order to ensure a better fit in the prosthesis. Although I was managing quite well in the leg, the stump's ability to bend often made me trip and fall forward. Dr. Elliot called it my "football knee." I had ruined countless pairs of "church tights" this way, and it was embarrassing to lose my balance and tumble to the floor.

I had been promised that I would be able to run, so I ran everywhere, even if it meant falling over in midstride and tearing my clothes.

My left knee was fused through epiphysiodesis, an operation that creates a premature closing of an epiphyseal plate, resulting in the cessation of bone growth. The epiphysis is a part of a bone, often the end of a long bone, that initially develops separated from the main portion (the bone shaft) by cartilage. Scraping this layer of cartilage creates a bridge of bone that arrests growth. Not only would a fused knee make the residual limb more stable, but on an aesthetic level, if growth was stopped now, then my artificial and natural knees would line up, creating both greater ease of motion and a more realistic illusion of two normal legs.

When I woke up in the recovery room after the operation, I saw two bright yellow reindeer ornaments dangling above my bed. I reached up for them and saw that I had two hands as well, even though only one hand was in the air. Double vision. Looking down at my body, I saw two torsos covered in plaster. A body cast again. After vomiting, I felt better, and the double vision gradually disappeared, but I was back in a body cast and extremely unhappy about it.

"What is this?" I asked Dr. Elliot. "I thought body casts were over."

"Peanut, this is the last time you'll be in a big cast."

I desperately wanted to believe him. "The very last time?"

"Yep."

"You promise?"

"Yes, I do. No more body casts."

Mom stayed with me in the hospital. We did puzzles, ate oyster crackers, and watched ridiculous daytime television. It was Advent, so Dad read aloud the different versions of Jesus's birth in the Gospels. A nurse hung the reindeer ornament over my bed. He had brown beads for eyes and a red saddle stitched on his soft felt back; his black felt antlers were long and curved.

After my release from the hospital, I spent much of the holiday on my back, looking up through the branches of the Christmas tree at the twinkling edges of the ornaments. While I unwrapped presents, our dog, Muffin, stood on my cast, growling playfully and pulling on the bows with her little yellow teeth.

"Hey, look. A piñata," Andy said one night when he brought me a Christmas cookie. He held it in front of me, but when I tried to grab it, he snatched it away. Drumming his fingers on the cast, he asked, "If I hit you, what will come out?"

"Not candy," I said. "Poop, maybe."

"You're gross," he said.

"Give me that," I said, and he gave me the cookie.

Operations were scheduled during holiday breaks so I would not miss school. Christmas in the hospital was wonderful; there were carolers, candy stripers, festive decorations, and special meals. The Lutheran bishop of the Rocky Mountain Synod brought me a red poinsettia plant and blessed me with his hands. I was given a music box that played "Silent Night" as three painted porcelain angels moved in a circle; one of them held a silver star in the air, her smooth bare feet soaring high above the others' heads. I rang in the New Year with a new cast and a new scar.

I believed that something magical happened within the walled fortress of my casts. Bones dwelled, alone and unwatched, for weeks at a time inside those dark caves of plaster. I was sure that when the scars were finally exposed, secrets would be disclosed and conspiracies revealed.

The room where casts were removed smelled like rubbing alcohol. The tools were hard and slick looking, reflective as a room full of sharp knives. The electric cast cutter, held in the doctor's hands, whizzed and whined as it spun, moving closer and closer to me. Sometimes my casts were covered with pictures and signatures, food, and other stains—images and smells I had lived with for six or eight weeks. I had a particular attachment to a drawing of Linus and his blanket that a nurse had drawn on my upper thigh; I was sad to see him go, sliced in half under the doctor's hands. As the saw made contact with the stiff plaster, the vibrations shook the skin first, tickling it, teasing it. But soon the quakes felt electric and unstoppable. They rattled the twined fibers of the bones, making sure they were set and healed. As it broke apart, the cast made a terrifying noise, like thick layers of winter lake ice thawing and cracking in spring's first bright sunshine. It felt like being trapped in a building that was coming apart all around you. The friction of the cutter against the cast produced a burning smell. Shards of plaster floated into the air, and the doctor's hair and mine would be clotted with white specks that looked like tiny plastic snowflakes.

A nurse sliced away the dirty, smelly cloth between the skin and the plaster and used a flat, tonguelike object to gently scrape off bits of dead skin. The stump was then washed with soapy water to clean the stinking skin and relax the atrophied muscles that had been trapped and immobile for so long. I thought of Lazarus, the sick man who had been wrapped in cloth and entombed in stone before he was raised to life again by Jesus. Risen again but altered how? I watched the nurse carefully, waiting to see how the stump had changed this time.

I never understood why the cast didn't fall away to expose a twisted mess of bone or something sinister and dangerous, something that would rise up and tell a story of danger and intrigue. Instead, a shrunken, meek-looking red stump appeared with a ripe odor and flaky skin that itched for weeks. After the smell disappeared and the wound healed, there was the scar: a secret sign that I wore like a hidden badge.

I was fascinated by the changing landscape of my body. I collected scars the way I collected storybooks or memorized Bible verses. The smooth white holes where the metal pins had held me together were proof that a dragon *had* bitten me. After the knee fusion, a crisscross pattern ran the length of my stump and resembled the stitching on a football; a half-moon of stitches above the heel looked like a crooked smile. The scars on my left hip were thick and lumpy, like bread that hadn't risen properly.

I loved my scars and their stories. I felt them with my hands and told them who they were: this one from a dragon, this one from a battle. They eventually went from red and angry looking to smooth and silvery white, the skin so shiny that it was almost reflective. After several months, the tender marks lost sensation. I could press my fingernail into them, but there was no feeling—the skin had fallen silent.

When I got older, I no longer found it necessary to tell myself stories about how my body came to be, I simply got up in the morning and put it together. It just was. A few buckles and straps, and the body seemed to fall together like magic or by accident. Any story of the body that a scar might tell was sealed off and silenced—a mystery.

I was in the full body cast for six weeks and used the tank again at school, although this time I was strong enough to push myself around without help. At first, Mom took me home during lunchtime, until Mrs. Nicolas, my first-grade teacher, offered to learn how to use the bedpan, allowing me to stay at school for the entire day.

In the teachers' bathroom, Mom showed her how to assist me: I was lowered onto my back, and the bedpan was positioned directly under the small hole between my legs. After I'd done my business, I was wiped off, lifted up, and positioned inside the tank. Mom made me special underpants to ease this process; she slit a pair of women's underwear up the side and then sewed Velcro at the seams so they could be removed easily. I wore long corduroy jumpers so I could sit in my walker or on pillows without being completely exposed.

Each year before school began, Mom met with my teachers. She told them that she did not want me to be treated as a handicapped child, as the term was then; she wanted them to know that she and my father had the same expectations for me that they would have for any other child. She told them, "We do not call Emily handicapped. We say that she was born with one leg shorter than the other and wears an artificial leg. She may have some limitations, but she is not handicapped." She was firm in this. "You are just the same as everyone else," she always told me. "Don't ever think you're not."

And I didn't feel handicapped. I have a vivid memory of watching a line of students move down the dark hallway to their separate room. They were the "special education" students—the "less than" students, as some kids called them—and they were always hidden away, shuffled out of sight, and forbidden to be a part of the regular classroom. I stood there in my body cast with my iron pipe walker, feeling grateful that I was not handicapped as those poor kids were.

In 1981, in addition to being the poster child and wearing the body cast for part of the year, I enjoyed singing in the choir at church, became a Camp Fire Girls Bluebird, loved to read and memorize stories and poems, and adored first grade. This, according to the family Christmas letter. "Throughout all this," Mom and Dad wrote, "Emily has been a real trooper."

I liked being described as a trooper. I saw myself as strong, able, and special because I could withstand situations other people assured me were extraordinary.

"How do you get around so well? How do you do it?" people would ask.

"I just do it," I chirped back, but inside I knew it was because I was amazing and brave. How else could I have survived all those operations and still be such a happy little girl? The word "disabled" rarely crossed my mind.

As a result of all the attention and the March of Dimes publicity, I was very proud of being singled out for having a fake leg. It was almost as if being recognized for having a disability made me feel somehow normal. As if the fact of people paying greater attention to the leg made it seem less like an insidious flaw and more like a conversation starter, a special attribute, or a sign of grace bestowed upon me and me alone. While I was the poster child, the word "disability" seemed to have little to do with my different body and much more to do with the way I was treated like a princess. The word felt like a description that conferred a kind of status, the way the word "beautiful" or "brilliant" might. I felt special, interesting, extraordinary, and *better* than the average girl. My disability brought me attention; it brought me friends, and most of all, I thought, it brought me love.

I was proud of my disability when it afforded admiration and attention, but when it required that I ask for help, I felt ashamed. While I was growing up, my severe nearsightedness felt just as limiting as my artificial leg, if not more so. As myopia was something I shared with other kids, it didn't attract special attention, either, and this was another mark against it. My leg was fun; at summer camp, after I discovered a big ant in the socket one morning, I had a crowd of girls watching me after wake-up call, waiting eagerly to see what I might find.

One night at camp I woke up, dying to pee. I reached out to the floor near my bottom bunk and couldn't find my glasses. I couldn't see well enough to go anywhere. Just before I woke my counselor to ask for help, I stopped myself. My leg was cool and set me apart—everyone was amazed by the amount of physical things I could do in it—but being unable to see and walk at the same time seemed debilitating and therefore embarrassing. I thought of myself as the poster child, as the girl whose smiling face was plastered on posters around town. Blindness called forth images of people with black sunglasses, people who used canes or their hands to search for their way. This was the first image that sprang to mind—in addition to the Bible verse about "the blind leading the blind." In a moment of panic, I went with the most convenient, accepted description of blind people: I saw them as helpless.

I groped everywhere, searching for my glasses, able to see shapes but no colors. My search was unsuccessful, and I finally peed in my sleeping bag. In the morning, I found my glasses far under the bunk, pressed against the cabin wall. Too ashamed to admit what had happened, I rolled up the bag during the day to mask the smell and slept in it all week.

My parents, both with excellent vision throughout their lives, had two kids who cried before reading the distance chart, knowing that our glasses would get thicker and heavier when we couldn't identify the numbers and letters correctly. Andy began wearing glasses at age four, and I got my first pair at age six. Our vision worsened quickly as we aged.

To compensate for our poor vision, we developed excellent hearing. We heard whispered words between our parents in the front seat of the car: discussions about birthday presents or other things we weren't supposed to hear. Both of us could make out bits of conversations at dinner parties by pressing one ear to the floor above the living room, where the adults sat for dessert after dinner. We were like bats, we said. Bat-kids. We had contests about who could hear the best. Andy—whose eyesight was worse than mine—always won.

When he was ten years old, Andy discovered that he could not see at night. He'd been on a Boy Scout camping trip and was somehow separated from the others during a hike. He wandered for a while, confused and afraid as the sun went down. He spent hours sitting in darkness, shivering with cold and fear, until he was found.

"I just couldn't see anything," he told us. The lenses in his glasses looked thick as crystal tumblers; they made his eyes look huge and were so heavy, they constantly crept down his nose.

The autumn after the camp episode, Andy was sent to Dr. Leland, an ophthalmologist in Cheyenne; he was a thin, friendly man with slight, sloping shoulders and short tufts of gray hair over his ears.

Mom, Dad, and I sat in the waiting room as Andy had the Humphrey field test to determine if he was in fact going blind. He has never seen, and never will see, stars.

For once, the situation of potential physical danger was reversed. How many times, I found myself wondering for the first time, had

Andy been stranded in a waiting room like this one, stuck with a pile of crappy magazines and the prospect of hours spent waiting, with no possible means of escape or relief? It wasn't just prosthetic fittings, but trips to the hospital, trips to the physical therapist, and trips to the eye doctor for both of us. When I had surgery, it was literally weeks of sitting around with an unhappy sister in a series of sterile hospital rooms, surrounded by sick people and anxious parents, well-wishers who would come in the room to visit me and never him.

I was fresh from my own intensive examination, which was something I dreaded all year. All parts of my body above the waist were extremely sensitive to intrusion. I was known for my furious blinking, and it took ages to get the eyedrops in. After so many surgeries, I felt that anything from the waist up should be decidedly off limits.

Once a year at my appointment, Dr. Leland got out a light that was so enormous and bright, it looked like something you'd use to explore a cave that was particularly deep and dark. He held my eyelid open and peered deeply into my eye until all I could see were thin red lines snaking away in all directions, the way hiking trails were traced on maps we used during summers in the Rocky Mountains. I felt as though Dr. Leland were trying to blind me; in the meantime, Andy's tests were meant to determine exactly that.

"I'm the one who might go *blind,*" he had said before his test.

I remembered my own moment of panic at camp and the image of the blind person that I had been so reluctant to be associated with. "No, you won't," I said as he left the room with a nurse.

Are you afraid? I wanted to ask, and also, *What am I supposed to do while I wait?*

It was intolerable to watch my parents fidget while they waited for Andy's test results. I now had an idea of what they did while I was in surgery, something I had never seriously thought about before. Dad tapped the wooden armrest of the waiting room chair and leaned back and forth over his knees, sighing, biting his lip, rubbing his hands together. Mom sat next to him with her legs crossed, flipping through a magazine so quickly that I knew she wasn't even attempting to read it. How did Andy stand it? After a few minutes of watching this, I simply couldn't bear it any longer. I stood up and said I was going outside.

I sat on a bench under a tree outside the office for the next thirty minutes, and nobody came to get me. After a while, I took off the square plastic glasses designed to protect the eyes after dilation. The air was cool, and the light was fading quickly.

I wondered: *What if Andy really went blind and became the poster child?* The idea of this repulsed me, which was a surprise; why such a reaction, when I was so proud of the status that the March of Dimes had afforded me? I imagined Andy beating the floor with a cane, searching for a curb or a door. It had never occurred to me that a blind girl or boy might be chosen as the poster child. When I thought of disability, I thought only of my leg and the attention I received for being different. As I imagined my brother as disabled, for once getting outside of myself, I realized something: I would pity him, and that meant people pitied me; I was not so special after all. Could it be possible that hidden in people's compliments was revulsion, even disgust? As soon as I had the thought—maybe being the poster child was not so terrific—I pushed it aside. Of course it was, I thought. I reminded myself that I had been *chosen.* I was special; my picture appeared in the paper all the time.

When I finally returned to the office, there was Andy, looking dazed and silly with his dilation glasses on. His hair was rumpled and stuck up on top of his head in a peak. There were sweat stains under his chubby arms. He would not go blind, at least not yet. But he would have to come back and have this same test every year for the rest of his life.

"Where are *your* glasses?" he said. "You have to wear them after your eyes get drops."

"Right here," I said, and put them on. I didn't need them anymore, but I wore them until he took his off.

As I fell asleep in the backseat on the drive home, I realized how terrible Andy must have felt all these years, waiting for me in cold, sterile rooms or in the homes of people who were probably inordinately, strangely nice to him. This new knowledge, rather than make me more tolerant of him and appreciative of his patience, enraged me. *How dare he make me feel guilty? How dare he be so kind?* How would I ever repay his fierce desire to be good, to help? Sometimes I was not even this charitable but simply resented that he might have a problem that would usurp mine and take away the attention I had claimed from my parents since the day I was born. Still, I wanted to tell him now that I knew how he felt. Did he think he knew how I felt? Did it matter? These were the thoughts that occupied my mind as I drifted off to sleep.

I woke up when we were right outside the Laramie city limits. Out the car's window, I watched a train rattling over the tracks. The long black cars were like dark stitches sewing up the land. The conductor blew the whistle: a sweet, hollow, lonesome sound. There was something proud and human in the noise that took away its desperation on this chilly night. It suggested to me that life was worth getting on with: Trains kept moving, new nights fell, parents drove their kids home in the dark, with everybody inside healthy for the moment. There was the knowledge that other people, tucked in their beds or riding in cars, heard the same note as the train crossed its wide territory and that somewhere, inside a lit and heated home, someone else was listening, too. It was the sound of the cold when all you know is warmth and all you hear is a single note rippling heavily over the flat, dusty plains.

My father was not the first "Reverend" listed in the Laramie phone book, but he always seemed to be the only one at home. People heading through town on Interstate 80 who needed food, money, or solace used to look up our telephone number or just show up at the house on Mitchell Street. Dad or Mom might offer them a meal or a shower, maybe some money for gas or food. I might be instructed to put clean, folded towels in the bathroom while the visitor had a cup of coffee in the kitchen. Sometimes the phone rang in the middle of the night, and I heard Dad's Volkswagen Bug revving up in the garage, headed somewhere.

We referred to these people who appeared at our door asking for help as "transients." "They're on their way from one place to another, and they landed here in between," Dad explained. Their coats often looked dirty and battered, with the cheap filling sticking out in white tufts; their hair might be greasy and smell of car exhaust; sometimes there would be an old car running noisily in the driveway with the faces of children peering through the windows.

If Dad was at church, Mom answered the door to a man or woman who stood awkwardly on the landing between the first and second floors, in front of the hall tree that was loaded with coats, hats, and scarves. Often a child was sent to the door to ask for money or food while the parents waited in the car or on the street corner. Andy and I were instructed to stay put, so we huddled at the top of the stairs, peering down. I remember one man held his hat in front of him as if he were paying his respects at a funeral.

"How come those people end up like that?" I asked Mom once when she came back upstairs. "Why are they so poor?" She opened her purse and pulled out a ten-dollar bill.

"That's a lot of money!" I whined.

"Be still," she said, and returned to the front door. Her curled hair was flat at the back of her head; she'd been sitting on the couch watching television with Andy and me. She passed the money across the doorway. A male hand thrust out, and she shook it, nodded awkwardly, and said, "Good-bye," in a strange, stiff voice.

"Brrr," she said, pulling an afghan tighter around her slim shoulders. Before she shut the door, the lights from the car illuminated her pale face for just a moment.

"What's the matter with that guy? What'd he do?" I asked. The people Mom and Dad helped looked unlucky; they seemed to define this word. I was confused by the space that money had crossed, from my mother's hand to another's. It was such a short distance, yet both people seemed to be reaching out, or was it away? The transients disrupted my safe space with an air of desperation and resignation that I found almost toxic. I wanted to clear the air.

"Why are they so poor, those people?" I asked. "What's the matter with them?"

"They just are," Andy said. "It's not their fault." He looked at Mom for confirmation, and she nodded as she came up the stairs. I didn't buy it.

"It's just what happens," she said. "They didn't do anything wrong. They just need a little extra help."

"People need help sometimes," Andy offered. "They're poor, Emily."

"That's right," Mom said, looking at me. "Listen to your brother."

When I asked Dad about our visitors, he said, "Oh, they're not so poor. They're doing all right. Something good is bound to happen to them at some point." This boundless, unfounded optimism seemed like an even more ridiculous answer in my mind, as much as I wanted to believe it.

I did not feel benevolence toward the people who came to our door asking for help. There was a song I had learned at Sunday school—"And they'll know we are Christians by our love, by our love"—but I did not feel loving toward those who were needy. Unlike the rest of my family, I did not feel kind or obligated to offer any assistance. What I knew about the body was that it could be harmed, wounded, and dismantled. I had been told that my disability was the result of an accident that had "just happened" long before my birth, the effect of which—the shorter leg—was discovered only when I was born. This always confused me: When exactly had the accident happened? During the first week of life inside my mother? The first month, the third? Hours before I came into the world? Minutes after? Was I floating around in the womb and then suddenly the leg was twisted, made deficient, just like that? What was the cause that had produced this undesirable effect? Who did it? Was it God, whom I thanked in Sunday school songs for "making me me"? Was it Mom's fault? Mine? Nobody had answers to these questions, and I grew tired of asking them and thinking about them. When, why, how? Nobody knew. I would have to be content with this: A mysterious, random accident had created the body I now inhabited.

Unhappy with this paltry explanation, I had decided that my days of accidents were over; I simply would not be having any more. The sight of those needy families and individuals made me uncomfortable because they held out the very real possibility that my life might carry with it a string of unforeseen and undesirable events. How many was one person allotted by God or who or whatever decided? I convinced myself that the people my family helped because it was "the Christian thing to do" had done some grievous wrong to end up as they did. They must have some bad habit or personal flaw that landed them, desperate, at somebody's door. That, I assured myself, would certainly never happen to me. I was the poster child, destined for much better things. But lurking behind this confidence was fear, however fleeting: I would not be the poster child forever; I would not be a *child* forever. After my term ended and another little girl or boy appeared in the papers and on the posters, then who would I be? What would happen when I grew up, became a woman, became a mother? At the age of six, I did not engage these questions deeply; it would be years before I engaged them at all.

Being the poster child certainly did not exempt me from more operations. Two years later, during Christmas break in the third grade, I had a repeat epiphysiodesis. My femur was still growing; Dr. Elliot was concerned that if it grew any longer, I would have difficulty walking well in a prosthesis. After the surgery, I was not in a body cast but was instead given a leg cast and crutches.

The day before the operation, I was walking back from lunch with some friends. Wearing our moon boots, we had to be careful not to slip and fall on the pools of melted snow in the hallways.

"Aren't you scared?" one girl asked.

"No," I said. They looked at me with slightly stricken, amazed faces, as if they were gazing at a religious shrine in which I was the main attraction. I straightened with pride; I could see they were in awe. "It's just the hospital. What's there to be afraid of?" I said, as if I were explaining why it was silly to be afraid of an innocuous animal at the zoo.

I wasn't afraid. Although I remember pain from my surgeries, the thing I remember most is attention: undivided, concerned, and concentrated. It was a vain little girl's dream. Because I felt so pampered and attended to, I rarely felt implicated in the danger of the procedures.

"You'll be just fine," Mom always told me before operations. "These doctors know what they're doing." How did I know she lay awake, sleepless, nearly every night for a week before the surgery? I didn't notice the bags underneath her eyes. What I noticed was her presence and her reassurance, both of which I expected and demanded.

In the hospital, I ruled. Not only did my parents cater to my every need and desire, but visitors and friends came with gifts and good wishes. I held court from my post in the orthopedic ward. I reveled in the hospital's busy atmosphere, its citylike noises: the traffic of nurses through the hallways; the slide of metal rings over metal rods as room-dividing curtains were opened and closed; constant sports talk radio or easy listening tunes at the nurses' station; kids playing games in their rooms; the clip of a pair of dress shoes past my half-open door; a low and layered murmur of voices complicated by the occasional bright outburst of deep laughter or a wild and confused scream. Too young to fully understand the long-term effects these surgeries would have on my life and too accustomed to operations to be overly phased by them, I practically looked forward to stints in the hospital. Here I reigned, the redheaded queen: bubbly, happy, and brave. I felt at home in those rooms and corridors, as if this were my rightful home all along.

As a young adult, when I went to orthopedic appointments and sat in the waiting room by myself, I watched the mothers of Dr. Elliot's patients. They looked at me carefully. Perhaps they were wondering about their child's future: how she would walk, how she would move, how she would manage the everyday stresses and trials of the world. I felt so implicated in those mothers' pain, I wanted to weep. I kept my eyes focused on the wall, waiting for the receptionist to call me back to the exam room; I felt the stares of the women breaking me down. I felt them itching to ask me questions as their own misshapen children played on the floor with blocks and dolls. The mothers practically glittered with fear, with helplessness, with a defiant love that would never give in to shame, and with a fierce optimism that was practically a sound—like white noise—in the waiting room. I thought of my own mother. How little I had appreciated her, how alone she must have felt in her fear.

When I was more conscious of everything Mom had to deal with, I wondered if she resented having such a difficult girl for a daughter; I wondered if she'd wished for a different kind of life, a different kind of child. I knew that I wanted to have two children—both girls—and I had already selected their names and professions: Cassandra would become a ballerina, and Sonya would be an opera singer. I asked Mom what she'd wished for when she'd imagined her future family.

"Dad and I wished for kiddos just like you and Andy. A boy and a girl. We would sit on the roof of your grandma's house and look at the stars and think up names for you."

"What did you want to name me?"

"Heidi."

"Yuck," I said.

Heidi. I could just picture myself bearing that name with my wooden leg, thick glasses, and buckteeth. No thanks.

"When you were born, your dad thought you were more of an Emily. We were excited about you," she said, sensing, I think, what these questions were about. I didn't fully believe her.

We were damaged, I thought, Andy and I. And no matter how loved and cared for you are, when you are damaged you are alone in that experience; this must have been the most painful thought for my parents, for surely they knew this.

Later, I would know that Mom and Dad understood the sense of isolation that Andy and I often felt because of our physical issues, but for different reasons. Mom's father committed suicide in a hot barn long before she could form memories of him, and her mother, after years of sickness from a heart ailment due to scarlet fever as a child—sicknesses Mom nursed her through—died the year Mom was married; she died while Mom tried to revive her using CPR. Dad never knew his father; he grew up in a town where everyone knew his family history, a place where his mother—young and beautiful but unmarried at the time of his birth—would never be forgiven for her misdeeds. My parents knew that pain was the great solo experience of the human heart, that it was as alienating as any physical surgery, as any amputation.

They must have hoped, sitting on the roof of my grandmother's house on a warm summer night, looking out over the cemetery where in less than a year she would be buried, that their trials, at least the health-related ones, would not be so severe in this next chapter of their lives, which they had chosen to begin together. Didn't all couples about to be married hope for a fresh start, a new beginning? I pictured Mom and Dad staring up at the night sky, counting the stars, making silly, romantic wishes as they swatted mosquitoes and listened to the cicadas hum, already naming children they could not yet fully imagine. I was sure that no parents in their right minds would ever have wished for me.

The feeling that I was a very real burden who was never made to feel like one or treated as such did not make me a sweeter child; rather, it made me a quick-tempered terror. The more attention I received as the poster child, the more attention I expected and demanded from everyone else and, in particular, from my family. Mom and Dad were afraid to say no to me. I sensed this and pulled out all the stops. The older I got, the worse it became. I was an expert at the silent treatment game. Door slamming and screaming fits were simply commonplace. I was sweet in my appearance as the poster child, of course, and I learned to always be good and nice and accommodating in public, but my anger flared at the slightest provocation whenever I was with my family. Andy complained to Mom and Dad that I was out of control and they should do something about it. I stopped speaking to him for weeks at a time; I called him "fatso" and pushed him around. I claimed to hate everything and everybody, but more than anything else, I began to hate myself.

Chapter Five

HANGING A STAR

In the winter of 1981, Dr. Elliot showed me a twenty-minute video about amputee skiers called *Two . . . Three . . . Fasten Your Ski*. The one-legged skiers raced down the slopes past throngs of cheering people. "I want to do that," I said.

"Good girl," Dr. Elliot replied.

Mom wasn't convinced it was a good idea. "Skiing sounds dangerous," she said.

"She'll love it," Dad said. And he was right.

I enrolled in the Winter Park Handicapped Ski Program in Colorado, a place known for its professional and successful education of disabled skiers. By the time I was twelve, we were driving to Colorado every two weeks during the winter so I could continue training.

Amputees are "three-track skiers"; they use one ski and two outriggers instead of poles. The artificial leg is left back in the ski lodge, usually in the changing room. Outriggers are two short skis that are secured to the end of a modified Canadian crutch—the metal cuff hits just over the elbow and hugs the upper arm. The skis can be flipped up by pulling on an attached string and then used as crutches. When the small skis are let down again, they skim the surface in front of the skier, creating balance and three points of contact with the mountain. The back of each outrigger has a serrated edge that can be dragged in the snow as a brake. Outriggers help maintain an amputee's balance and allow the skier to shift his or her weight from side to side more easily, providing greater control of speed and movement. The tripod is a remarkably steady shape.

In skiing, I found the sport in which my wishes for speed, agility, and grace were fulfilled. I was taught a distinctive skiing style: The foot was "educated" to steer the ski in a specific way; I learned to anticipate each turn and adjust my body, skis, and outriggers accordingly, producing a fluid, graceful motion. "Their skiing is fundamentally strong, aggressive, and dynamic," wrote the director of the program in his training manual. "We are proud of our amputees. They are beautiful skiers."

The modifications I had to make for my individual body seemed relatively minor on the slopes. Three-track skiers wear mittens instead of gloves, because we put constant pressure on our hands, which easily become cold. To improve circulation and avoid frostbite, I learned to beat my stump against the seat of the chairlift as it went up the mountain. But it was gravity that made able-bodied and disabled skiers nearly equal. Anyone with two legs was just as likely to fall as I was, and once I learned the art of falling, I no longer feared it. A person could *learn* to fall; it did not have to be an embarrassing accident indicative of a prosthetic malfunction, as it was in everyday life. When I felt my balance falter and the ski slip out of its correct alignment, I loosened my body and leaned into gravity, flinging my outriggers up and over my head. I didn't rip my pants or tights; I didn't scrape my right knee or my hands as I did wearing my leg; instead I fell gracefully, letting go of my balance and my fear—letting go of everything.

We never had to rent or buy outriggers or skis, although later I would have my own. Instead, when an amputee grew out of her gear, she donated it to the back room. "The back"—as we called it—was a sea of single boots and mismatched skis. It was a physical manifestation of an alternative history, proof that the lives of others like me had not gone unnoticed and that the people I often imagined matched up with artificial limbs at Schmidt's office actually existed. They not only lived and breathed, they skied, and here was the physical proof. I had company in my unique body. I was not alone.

It was exhilarating to feel free and whole without the leg on. I felt beautiful and strong as I had as a swimmer, only on the slopes I went so fast that I rarely noticed people staring at me. At the end of the day, exhausted and elated, I unpinned the end of my waterproof bib overalls and unwrapped my cold stump from its layers: two Ace bandages topped with two of Dad's wool socks. I warmed up, wolfed down an irresponsible amount of chocolate, and fell into the sweet blackness of perfect, uninterrupted sleep long before we reached the hotel room.

I woke up the next morning ready to go. I could not get enough of the speed, the cold, the soreness in my muscles that made me feel invincible. I got better and better, and I loved a challenge: moguls, steep slopes, icy runs, narrow runs, and finally, the winter I turned thirteen, expert runs. At the end of the day, my body felt like one taut, able muscle. I was seriously pleased with myself.

It was through the Handicapped Ski Program that I first met people with different kinds of physical and mental disabilities. In the central room where skiers and instructors gathered at the base of the mountain, the atmosphere was lively and diverse, convivial and active—so unlike the hospital wards or waiting rooms where all of us had spent time.

I learned much from my fellow skiers about bodies and what they could do. The deaf skiers taught me how to sign a few words: "ski" and "run" and "fast," all the important words for what we were learning. Men and women who used wheelchairs in their daily lives used mono-skis or bi-skis on the mountain: special chairs mounted on one or two skis. The user leaned left and right, using short outriggers or poles that were held in his or her hands or mounted to the side of the chair. People with more limited motion used the sit-ski that looked like a sled. I liked the brightly colored ones in yellow, green, and blue. Blind people learned to ski with a buddy skiing behind them, calling out instructions for turns and movements—embodying the meaning of trust. People with cerebral palsy, spina bifida, and Down's syndrome learned how to ski; everyone could ski; each did it a little differently, adapting the sport to the unique shapes and abilities of his or her individual body.

I felt deep respect for the people I met and for myself as well: We had all adapted, we had all made do with what we were given. I was accepted by this group easily and immediately; I was part of them. The names of the runs—Enchanted Forest, Jabberwocky, Cheshire Cat, and March Hare—were not lost on me. It felt very much like Wonderland, although everyone was a differently embodied version of Alice.

The bathroom where amputees changed out of—and usually left—their limbs for the duration of their lessons had a peculiar smell that I will always associate with transformation. It was a mix of sweaty socks, bleach, and that peculiarly fresh, bright smell of winter—sweat, snow, and sunshine—that stays locked in your hair and hat and mittens. I entered the bathroom with one body and emerged with another that was not deformed: It was a skier's body, an able body. Nobody stared at my stump when I hopped out the door. Everybody looked me in the face.

My instructors called me "Supergirl," because I went so hard and fast that I nearly dropped at the end of my lessons, especially on runs that bottomed out to flat terrain. It is difficult for a three-track skier to travel on flat stretches without momentum, because he or she must use both outriggers to push forward the entire body weight; this is more complicated and strenuous than shifting side to side using skis and poles for leverage as able-bodied skiers do. Snowmobiles were offered on such runs, but I insisted on taking myself the whole way in. I felt the burn in my arms and the beat of my heart, and knew that I was working hard. I held tight to my nickname, because it fulfilled the desire to be extraordinary that I had developed as the poster child; to be, quite literally, super. It fed my self-image as a fantastic overachiever that had emerged when I was crowned a temporary star by the March of Dimes.

It was on the school playground that the pride I felt in my body began to dissipate, when I realized how it was viewed by some in the able-bodied world.

I had learned to play tetherball when my physical movements were restricted by a cast or crutches. Even after I was in my leg, I still gravitated to the yellow leather ball suspended from its long, thick string and secured at the top of a high pole. I loved the slap of the ball, steady and rhythmic, against my palm.

One day at recess, as the ball swung away from me, I saw a girl in my class, Rita, limping along nearby in an exaggerated way. She was bent over and trailing her hands along the ground like a monkey. She hobbled and then looked over her shoulder at me. I slapped the ball back to my partner. After taking a few more labored, limping steps, Rita stopped and looked at me again. I realized that it was me she meant to imitate. The ball returned, and I held it in my hands.

I clutched the ball to my chest and felt my heart pound against the smooth leather. *Do I look like that? Like an animal?* I remembered the man I had met in Schmidt's office, how strange his body and gait had looked to me; how my mouth had dropped open in surprise and another emotion I had not, at the time, fully understood. I thought of the amputees at Winter Park: What would Rita think of them?

The strength of my shame confused me then, because it felt like a physical force—it was overwhelming. I didn't know exactly how to name it or know it. But I felt the same hot, stirring motion in my chest that I felt in my stomach before vomiting. I thought, *I'm ugly; I'm a bad person,* even though I knew it was wrong to think such things. But monkeys belonged in cages. People came to look at them through steel bars; they prodded them, teased them. I knew that people stared at me, especially during the summer when I wore shorts; I knew they gawked. I felt, in that moment on the playground, not so different from an animal after all. *Is that what people really think about me?* I wondered. I held that moment inside of me as if it were a fragile bowl, a moment covered in glass.

Rita kept limping ahead and looking back at me, sneering. I kept playing, watching the ball carefully with my eyes. There was my hand, the slap, the limp, the look. I looked at her. I thought: *Enemy.*

For weeks, I didn't play tetherball but instead sat on a bench reading and sulking, too afraid to be humiliated again. *Is that what I look like?* I wondered again. Certainly not. But then why had I known Rita was imitating me? It was not the way I saw or imagined myself at all. Did she see me not as a disabled athlete or as the famous poster child, which was the way I had begun to see myself, but as a grotesque object of fascination, like the people with physical anomalies who used to tour in carnivals? *The bearded lady. The four-hundred-pound man. The legless girl.* And if Rita saw me that way, how many more people did, too? I might be a skiing dynamo, but maybe that made no difference in the world of normal people. Mom told me repeatedly that I was just like everyone else, but now it was clear that to some I was not.

The situation with Rita made me feel hollow and transparent. I felt her ridicule had banished me to a world of freaks to be looked at only with disgust; she had rendered me useless on account of a visible flaw. A different, horrible reality had been presented to me, with myself and my strange body at the center of it. She had exposed me. Sometimes when I thought of Rita imitating me, I could hardly breathe. I had to do something to prove her wrong.

While Mom was making dinner one night, I walked the lines in the kitchen linoleum, carefully setting one foot directly in front of the other.

"What are you doing?" she asked. "Be careful walking by the stove, it's hot."

"Watch," I said. "Watch me walk." She did, holding a plate of lasagna in her two oven-mittened hands.

"Does it look good? Does it look right?" I asked.

"Of course it does," Mom said. "It looks fine. You know you have a good gait."

I had always been told this—*You walk so well, you get around so well*—but it was a huge relief to hear it again. I found Dad hammering something in the garage and asked him to watch me walk up and down the driveway. "Looks great," he said, and returned to his project.

I continued to practice my gait—this asset—whenever possible. At school, I would practically sweat with concentration on routine trips to the bathroom, to gym class, to choir, following a straight line on the floor while in my head reciting, *Right swing left, right swing left,* watching the others walk in front of me, staring at their feet, trying to match their movements and rhythm.

During recess, I continued to avoid the tetherball. As I obsessively surveyed the playground, searching for Rita, the girls on the double bars sometimes called me over to play with them. I sat on the back bar and slipped and locked both my feet under the parallel bar just in front of it, although I first double-checked the leg's waist strap, running my hands over the silver buckle—quickly, just once—to be sure it was fastened securely as the girls were busy scrambling up next to me, easy with their bodies as young children are. I always had myself precisely organized. Together we leaned back, five or six girls at a time, our feet hooked, until we were looking up into the sky and the world flipped over. On the count of three, we sat up quickly, chanting in iambic pentameter: "Open up the barn doors, kick out the hay. We're the girls from the U.S.A. Sittin' on the hay rack, sippin' root beer, turn on the radio and what do you hear? You hear Elvis Presley singin' a cheer." In subsequent verses, Elvis was replaced with Michael Jackson, Dolly Parton, the Rolling Stones. During these delicious, dizzying moments, I was just one of the girls.

I might have a disability, but I knew that I was smarter than Rita, and I felt it was crucial to emphasize this important attribute. I raised my hand for every question asked in science, math, and English, determined to beat her. Rita sat and scribbled in her notebook, and I became convinced that each of my correct answers was a failure for her. This was how I perceived the dynamics between us, although she had never imitated me again after that one incident and I had no idea if she was aware that we were competing. I watched her carefully. I knew what clothes she usually wore together and in what order; I knew where she hung her coat and who her friends were; I knew what kind of car her mother drove.

I thought it was important to know the competition, know the enemy.

A few weeks later, a line of single strings dangled from the ceiling of our classroom. We were hanging stars with our reading goals on them in order to "reach for the stars"—as our teacher said—and finish our books before the end of the year.

Rita was standing behind me as I waited to hang my star, and my neck was already burning before she whispered in my ear, "You can't do that, Emily, because you're crippled."

The way she said the word made me feel as though the air had collapsed around my face and become strange and ugly. It made me feel as if I wore a crinkly, cripple hat, the only one of my kind, and I would be forever singled out. Deformed. Unwanted. I felt like one of those people on television that others called in to help with their monetary pledges, a charity case. I pitied those people who sat in their wheelchairs, but I had never connected my plight with theirs. Pity: the dirtiest word. I was *not* like that, I thought. But Rita had hit me with the word "crippled" and somehow defined me, evoking a small world of undesirables. By making me feel so different, so wrong, she'd made me disappear, she'd forced me lower, forced me down. She'd done it again.

The late afternoon sun streaming through the classroom windows was hot on my back, and that heat spread quickly through my whole body. Shame again, that vomit feeling, that hot ball of corrosive anger in the belly. Up on that chair I went and hung my star, crippled or not. I thought about skiing down my favorite slopes, about my sleek and able body; I thought about what one of my instructors had encouraged me to do when I faced a challenging run: "Growl at the mountain!" she'd shout as I moved into a difficult turn on an icy patch of snow. "Get angry! Growl!"

I jumped off the chair and landed on both my feet. I felt the wooden lip of the prosthesis jam up into my butt and crotch, and I knew there would be bruises. It didn't matter. What mattered was that I won the game I had created in my mind. I looked Rita straight in the face, stuck out my chest, and said, "See? Did it." I could ski and jump and run, and I wanted her to know it. Then I pushed her as hard as I could. Rita fell back and landed on her butt. Her eyes registered anger, but also surprise and, behind that, a kind of satisfaction. I felt, strangely, that I had lost this battle in our unspoken war, even though I'd done exactly what I had intended to do. My face was burning. I would have pushed or kicked her again, and harder this time, but the teacher intervened. When she asked me why I had attacked Rita, I would not tell her what had been said; I refused to repeat the words out loud.

I had to sit in the corner for the rest of the afternoon, but I sat there happily, lit from inside with a righteous, powerful rage. This deep anger, the depth of which I was just dipping my foot into, like testing the force of a stream of fast-flowing water with one toe, comforted me somehow. It focused me and inspired me to achieve, to prove myself. I watched Rita for the rest of the day and told myself, *You are just like her, you are better than her.* I could do it, and I had proven that I was not a cripple. I had proven that this word did not apply to me, but I did not forget it entirely.

One morning that year when I had the flu, I was lying in bed, listening to the sound of the aspen leaves clapping together in the trees outside my window. I watched the round shadows of the leaves move over the posters on my closet: Madonna's made-up face; a fawn at Yellowstone; a drawing of two identical *Garfield* cartoon characters where one is saying to the other, "Be your own best friend."

I tried out the word, speaking it aloud: "Cripple." The shadows moved slowly back and forth. They seemed lazy and relaxed; the leaves rustled together and moved apart. Nothing happened. No God-like voice boomed out of the sky to correct me. Mom was upstairs and couldn't hear me. "Cripple," I said, louder this time. "Crippled." I never spoke those words out loud again. I didn't need to, because they would never again leave my mind. Worse, they already felt true.

What I had learned as a skier was a complicated freedom. While disabled athletics had taught me to view my body as capable and strong, part of my pride stemmed from the way others regarded me, the way I exhibited for others my superior strength and extraordinary resolve. Rita had shown me that no matter what I did, no matter how able or powerful I was in certain situations, I still *looked* wrong. This was my first taste of the competition that would haunt me. I decided, at that moment, that it would always be about looks. Nothing else mattered. It was about your body, your face, the way you walked, the way you looked, and, most important, the way others looked at you. I worried that I would never measure up; I would never be able to compete, but I would make myself crazy trying.

After the incident with Rita, my attitude toward other amputees changed. While most three-track skiers at Winter Park left their legs off when they went into the cafeteria for lunch, using their flipped-up outriggers to move around, I changed back into my leg. I began to separate myself from the group of athletes that had welcomed me so easily, judging them the way I felt Rita had judged me—as different, deficient, even freakish—and I no longer wanted to be a part of them. I was all about solidarity on the hill, but when we were back in the lodge and in the presence of other able-bodied people, I lost my loyalty. I wanted to again be normal, or as close to normal as it was possible for me to get.

Chapter Six

THE MUSTARD SEED

Growing up, I lived in a world where God was good. I was taught to believe this, and I did.

I loved the ritualistic elements of worship services, especially the sing-and-response psalms: Those perfect echoes of longing were like magical spells being cast in the dark, quiet sanctuary. I liked singing slow, meditative hymns as people silently lined up in the aisle to take Communion. I watched Mom pray and tried to imagine her thoughts. Sometimes she opened one eye and glared at me. "I'm praying," she would whisper, "so stop staring." When I was very small, I tried to stick crayons up her nose to break her concentration. I didn't like her energies to be focused elsewhere—I wanted her full attention all the time. She was the orbit I wanted to move around, because with her I did not feel different, partly because we talked about my disability only in terms of logistics and in a positive way. I felt normal and safe around Mom. Meanwhile, her daily life was a flurry of files, appointments, insurance premiums, and conversations with doctors. I hopped through it all, moving around on a metal brace, in various casts, and then with an artificial leg, always overactive and demanding.

At church I felt loved. When I was in the hospital, all of the older ladies from the quilting circles and prayer groups sent me cards with little girls and bunnies and flowers on them. They wrote in their shaky handwriting: "Get well soon! Love, Edith; Love, Dorothy; Love, Velma, Alma, and Ruth." When I arrived home, there would be a pile of gifts and cards waiting for me, some from people I hardly knew.

Not only did the members of the congregation dote on me, but I was always chosen for the most glamorous roles in the church musicals. I was a shepherd, an angel, and a sheep during different years, but after I reached a certain age, I played Mary, the pure, openhearted virgin and the model of a good—even perfect—woman. I cherished this role like none other. My thick glasses, wooden leg, and buckteeth seemed to disappear when I put on the blue robe and the white cotton headdress, picked up the plastic doll, and became the focus of everybody's admiration on the most important night in the Christian religion. The birth of Jesus. The mother of God. Was there any more powerful or sacred role to play? I sang lullabies with a chorus of shepherds and angels and rocked a fake baby Jesus to sleep. There was never a suggestion that God wasn't for everyone—He was. And at Christmastime I was His emissary, limping onto the stage with a baby in my arms—the savior of the wounded, the sick, and the sinful. My virtue became my beauty. People told me time and time again, particularly after these performances: "We're always praying for you," "You're in our prayers," and sometimes, although not as often, "God loves you best of all."

People have been praying for me my entire life: at the moment of my birth and throughout all of my surgeries. Yet I have always had an uneasy relationship with prayer. If you didn't get the answer you asked for, something people were always alluding to ("God always answers prayers, just not in the way we wish Him to or in the way we expect"), then how could you know it was really the answer—from God—and not just something random and inexplicable that happened to you? I didn't like the mystery of prayer itself or the ambiguity of the possible answers. The idea that "bad things happened" was no comfort to me—did it comfort anyone?—and was something I felt I already knew.

Still, I learned my prayers, and as I grew older I prayed for what

I most wanted, even though the idea was to recite the precise words from the chosen prayer and then lift up one's concerns, allowing God to take care of the rest. *Create in me a clean heart, O God, and renew a right spirit within me; cast me not away from your presence; and take not your holy spirit from me.* I hated my body. I prayed for a new one. Hadn't any of those faithful people prayed for me to be healed? How did I know if their petitions had been answered? How could they tell? Was it a light in my eyes? A spring in my limping step? I was praying for God to make me whole. I couldn't imagine that anyone might be praying for something entirely different. It was in church where I felt most wholly loved. It made sense to go there for the bodily transformation I desired.

Fourth grade was my last year of instruction in the act of prayer and the proper petitioning of God. I had memorized the appropriate creeds, prayers, and basic theological terms. I was only a few days away from the real body and blood. I was gearing up for something huge. I wanted to be healed on that first Communion. I figured I had dealt with this leg business long enough and it was time for my reward.

The day did not go exactly as I'd planned. As I stepped out of the car to head into church, I heard Brian Tanner screaming at me from the top of the church stairs. He was surrounded by boys I knew and would soon be kneeling next to with my tongue out to take the Communion wafer from my dad's hand.

"Peg leg, Peg leg! Emily has a wooden leg!" Brian sang at the top of his lungs. His friends gathered around him, laughing and pointing. I stood still for just a moment, deciding what to do.

"Piece of shit!" I yelled. Mom, who had been chatting with someone nearby, ran up to me, grabbed me by the arm, and swooped me into the church. Through the window of the main door, I could see the side of Mrs. Tanner's face; her painted lips were pursed in anger.

I couldn't bother with Brian. I had more important things to do. Mom stopped me at the bottom of the narthex stairs and straightened my dress. "Now," she said. "You be good. Honestly." I didn't care that I had embarrassed her. I had my eye on the prize. I heard the organ begin the opening hymn, and Dad walked by, singing, in a swirl of white robes.

"Brian's mean," I said in my defense.

"Well, he's still not a piece of blank." Mom looked at me. I opened my mouth.

"Don't fill in that blank," she warned. "That is not a word we use. You'll apologize to Brian later. Honestly!"

"What about what he said? What about him saying sorry to me?"

"Oh, he will," she said, and grabbed my hand as we went up the stairs and into the sanctuary.

In both Matthew and Mark, there are stories about the power of a small bit of true faith—the parable of the mustard seed. *For truly I tell you, if you have faith the size of a mustard seed, you will say to this mountain, "Move from here to there," and it will move; and nothing will be impossible for you.* Before my first Communion, I was given a necklace with a tiny, cream-colored seed inside a glass ball that hung from a short gold chain. In Mark, the mustard seed, the smallest on the earth, would grow up to be the biggest of all, putting forth large branches *so that the birds of the air can make nests in its shade.* This kernel of faith was strong enough to work miracles. Mine was whole, yellow, and perfect. It was just waiting to burst free of the glass and sprout into something huge. The idea of it made me giddy.

I believed that God expressed truth through the stories in the Bible and that each of them carried a lesson about life. This parable made me think that if someone believed in something enough, with his or her whole heart and soul, miracles could happen: Seeds would sprout, nests would be made, birds would fly from branch to magical branch.

Every time I read this biblical passage in the weeks leading up to my first Communion, I was filled with hope. My mission was this: If I prayed hard enough, if I believed He could do it, I thought God would give me another body. I stretched out on my bed and prayed. I closed my eyes. Silently, I recited the first part of the Lord's Prayer—*Our Father, who art in heaven, hallowed be thy name*—but

I filled in the rest of this newly memorized prayer with my own wishes. Nothing happened. I wasn't strong enough, I assumed. I just didn't have it in me. It was the Communion that would seal the deal; eating the body and blood of Jesus—even though, as Lutherans, we were taught that it was not the *real* body and blood—was the ticket, the missing ingredient in my magical transformation.

Brian was kneeling next to me at the Communion rail. We watched Dad bless someone farther down the row. The boy's pink tongue shot out and took the Communion wafer that was set in the middle of Dad's huge hand like a tiny white raft. I practiced my devotional gaze: I lifted my eyes and tried to make them glassy and unfocused so that God would know I was serious and worthy of His attention.

"Hey," Brian whispered, nudging me.

"Shut up," I whispered back. I concentrated on moving that mountain. *Move from here to there. Move this leg, give me a new one.* I thought of a word I liked: "aloft." I imagined my wooden leg floating up and away into space and a flesh-and-blood limb taking its place on my body. *Move it aloft.* God could do anything, I thought. It would be that easy. Dad got closer and blessed Brian. I shifted on my knees slightly, and then the wafer was on my tongue, dissolving, and Dad's hand was heavy on my head for the blessing. *Now, now, now,* I thought, but when I stood up, I still needed to use the railing. The artificial leg was still attached to me; my body was still my own. I didn't look at Brian, and he said nothing more to me. My faith had failed me; it was clearly not pure or strong enough.

I was numb when I went up to take my gift of a Bible and then march out with the rest of the communicants. I picked at a piece of our celebratory cake in the fellowship hall. Dad winked at me from across the room. I lifted my hand off my paper plate just a little. He turned his head to an older lady who had approached him. Mom was huddled in the far corner with Brian's mother, their two coiffed heads leaning in to confer. They both had one hand on their hip, and their faces looked serious. Mom's hand touched Mrs. Tanner's arm and stayed there.

I left the fellowship hall and went to the bathroom. I stepped into a stall and shut and locked the door. The air was bitterly cold and slightly stale and smelled of dirty water caught in a drain. Now, I thought—with heat and hate building up inside me—was the time to pray. I prayed that Brian would combust and blow up into many pieces. Then I prayed to be forgiven for my violent thoughts. Finally, I approached my real purpose one more time. I steadied myself on the toilet seat. I cleared my throat and closed my eyes. I prayed to God to make me whole. I'd give Him one more chance. Maybe difficult prayers could be heard only after the Communion was actually received. Maybe God was waiting for the wafer to be completely digested. I swallowed hard several times. *A new leg, a real one, a new one. Flesh and blood, flesh and blood,* I chanted. I clamped one hand around the mustard-seed necklace and another on my right thigh. *I believe, I believe, I believe,* I said over and over again in my mind. The murmur of voices in the fellowship hall dissipated and finally disappeared. *Do it!* I begged. *Do it now!* I could hear Dad closing and locking doors, and then he was calling for me. I heard the clip of his dress shoes echoing over the tile floors.

I held my breath, looked down, and lifted my skirt. Everything was still the same. The left leg was wooden, hinged, and shining beneath the white tights. I felt tears prick my eyes. I thought, *Liar.* "Liar," I said out loud, just as the door opened.

"What? Hey, are you in there?" Dad's voice echoed inside the bathroom. "What are you doing? Mom's been looking for you."

"I'm fine," I said, trying to keep my voice level.

"Are you ready to go? How long have you been in here?"

"Not long. Just a few minutes."

"I'll wait in my office for you. Hurry up."

"Just a second," I said.

Dad paused. "Brian didn't mean what he said. He told me so himself."

"I meant what I said."

"Okay," he said, and sighed. "We'll talk about it later. And I've got your Bible. You left it by the cake."

"Great."

The door whooshed shut. I stood up and flushed the toilet unnecessarily. I walked out with my head up as if I needed to preserve some dignity from what had happened in the bathroom stall, although I had obviously been alone. I vowed to never pray again. I took the necklace off that night and shook it as hard as I could. The mustard seed broke into tiny pieces inside the glass. There had been no magic in that seed or in the story after all.

The next Sunday I saw Brian, led by his mother, walking in my direction. I tried to escape, but Mom caught my arm. "No. Brian has something to say to you."

"I don't care," I said.

"Just listen to him," she said.

"Mom!" I protested.

"Shush," she whispered, and turned to greet Mrs. Tanner.

Brian stood looking at the floor. Mrs. Tanner's grip on his arm looked as firm as my mother's on mine.

We stood in the hallway that was lined with black-and-white photographs of the church founders, mounted behind glass. Brian looked at the floor and kicked at it with one foot. I turned my face away, but I could still see his profile in the reflective glass cases. "Go on, Brian," Mrs. Tanner said. Her jewelry gleamed in that narrow space full of reflections. Delicate beads of hair spray balanced on her hair.

Brian handed me a picture that he'd drawn of me, using a bright red marker for my hair. He'd also drawn me with two perfect legs and wearing an evening gown the likes of which I'd only ever seen on Barbie. Around my feet he'd drawn huge purple tulips and yellow daisies.

"I'm sorry I called you that," he said. "I think you're great." But in the picture I didn't have glasses or a wooden leg or big, unwieldy buckteeth. I was a perfect little girl. He'd even drawn me with blue eyes, which I was desperate to have. I thought Brian and God were mocking me.

Mom looked at me. "What do you think?" Her eyes looked sad. I knew what I was supposed to do; I'd been taught to be polite.

"Thanks," I mumbled.

"I didn't mean it," Brian said to the floor. Mrs. Tanner nudged him. "Honest," he said, looking up at me. "I'm sorry."

I looked at the image of myself in the drawing: perfect, whole, beautiful. I wished he'd never given it to me.

"Anyway, you were right," I said. "I do have a wooden leg." In that moment, it felt compulsory to say this. Before the shame of the statement registered in me I felt a strange power, like a shock wave, moving through my whole body.

They all looked at me. "Yes, you do," Mom said. "And you are great."

"Uh, sorry," Brian said, although he sounded unsure about what he was apologizing for. All I'd done was told the truth.

Mom squeezed my shoulder. "What do you say, honey? Brian said he was sorry."

"It's okay," I told him. "Uh, yeah, it's all right."

Mom held out my hand and grabbed Brian's hand as if we were appliances and she was plugging us in. We shook hands.

"There now," she said as Brian and his mother walked away. When Mom touched me, I shook her off and walked away.

Dad used to take me to the nursery and let me play, alone, while he counseled people. I'd peek out the door and watch another disturbed soul come up the stairs of the narthex and shake the snow off their boots before stepping into his office. This was the place I went now, for solace. I wanted to get lost in the sea of babies who always needed my help and didn't care how my body looked, as long as I changed their dirty diapers and played with them.

Growing up, I was considered special and different because I was the pastor's child. In this, Andy and I were finally equal, as the attention had nothing to do with my leg or being the poster child. At church, both of us received identical treatment. We got along best while we were shaking hands in the receiving line, trussed up in our Sunday best, the two cute pastor's kids, doing their best to act like adults. We stood up straight, shook hands with each person as they moved through the line, and said, "Merry Christmas," or, "Happy Easter," followed by a few seconds of idle holiday conversation.

I especially liked joining Dad in the receiving line at the end of the service during these two holidays, when the church was guaranteed to be packed with strangers. As they left the sanctuary, people bent down to say hello to me, people who had come for this one service and would probably never come again. I loved these visitors because I could easily fool them. My act worked perfectly. They would go home remembering me as the smiling, redheaded minister's daughter who would grow up to be beautiful and smart (or this was what I imagined). All of those people, literally hundreds of them on Christmas Eve and Easter morning, would be duped. None of them would know my secret, and I considered this a serious triumph. I could talk to any of those people in line, even longer than Dad or Mom could.

I had special, beautiful dresses for holidays: for Christmas, dresses with black velvet bodices, green-and-red-plaid silk skirts, and black patent-leather shoes; for Easter, pale yellow dresses with layers of white lace cascading down the front, a white straw hat with small plastic daisies nestled in the crown, and a white patent-leather purse in which to carry my offering. My long hair was always decorated with bows and ribbons that matched my dress. From the way I stood, nobody knew I had an artificial leg, and I relished this easy deception. It was intoxicating to pretend to be something you were not if you knew you could never be the way you truly wanted to be. I looked forward to those hand-shaking sessions; I felt they proved that I was strong enough to do the impossible, with or without God's help.

Chapter Seven

MEET YOUR MAKER

Instead of a line drawn on the kitchen wall that shows my growth over the years, I have more than half a dozen wooden legs that not only document the inches grown since my foot was amputated at four years old, but also reflect the progressive developments in prosthetic parts and equipment. At first, most feet were made exclusively for men; then prosthetic companies began to make more slender and aesthetic-looking feet for women with delicate toes and less ropy, more feminine veins. Eventually, in my twenties, I received a foot with an adjustable heel height and wore my first pair of heels at the age of twenty-six. For a while when it was first released on the market, I wore a man's Seattle foot, complete with bulgy, life-like veins and thick, wide toes.

Artificial limbs have changed enormously from the iron legs of medieval times and the crude peg legs of the eighteenth century; in the nineteenth century, wooden legs with metal joints were common and featured flexible leather sockets before the important advent of acrylics and silicone. Most were fastened to the wearer's body with leather lacings and sturdy cloth belts, not unlike the canvas waist strap on my early limbs.

Each of the legs stacked in my closet has a set of metal hinges on either side of the socket (on the first two, the hinges are on the outside; later, they are covered with wood) and a waist strap as the method of suspension. Each has layers of added length at the ankle—like flesh-colored bricks that have been glued together—which indicate how much I grew each year and in what increments. The shank of each leg is made of wood; the socket is painted to resemble wood but is made of molded plastic—a material perfected to meet the prosthetic needs of new amputees returning from World War II.

Limb technology has been continuously advanced by two historical factors: the industrialization of America (which led to accidents in mills or factories) and the needs of limbless soldiers returning from wars. In many cases, these prostheses were fitted to adult bodies that would change little. A person might wear the same leg from the time he acquired his disability until the end of his life. But for amputee children, "one limb for a lifetime" is clearly not sufficient; their unpredictable growth spurts pose a unique functional and financial dilemma. This was certainly the case with me.

In 1984, at the end of my fourth-grade year, I grew out of the prosthesis I had just been fitted with in the fall. The socket was too tight and made my stump throb with pain. I developed pressure sores that itched so badly, I would scratch them until they bled, trying to get to the source of the discomfort, which felt as deep and hidden as the bone. The leg was too short. When I walked, I felt as if I were stepping into a hole with my left foot. At the end of each day, my lower back ached and I was dead tired from the energy it took to move.

My parents hadn't yet paid off the leg I was wearing and didn't have the thousands of dollars for a new one. I had grown too fast.

"Aren't legs supposed to last longer?" Dad asked. He had taken an extra job as a bus driver to cover my prosthetic expenses, which were only partially covered by his insurance. Each morning he got up at five A.M. and worked a school bus route in Laramie before going to work. Sometimes he honked and waved as his bus passed me on the short walk to school. This embarrassed me. I didn't want anyone to know that he drove a bus because of me. It seemed like a menial job, even though many of the kids I went to school with lived on ranches and came from working-class families; there weren't that many rich kids in Laramie.

"It's a growth spurt," Mom said. "What can we do?"

As soon as school was out, Dad and I drove to Denver to see if Schmidt could make my leg fit until the money for a new one was found.

In the center of Schmidt's office, Dad and I stood on the prosthetic "runway"—the familiar stretch of dirty linoleum lined with two balancing bars. That day it was about one hundred degrees in the room. Dust particles made lit columns in the thick air. Everything in the office, from the brown floor tiles to the ceiling-to-floor windows to the cheap, smelly couches to the outdated magazines in the waiting room, was covered with a thin layer of the pale brown dust, fine as snow, which spun off the special blade as it made adjustments to wooden legs in the back room. Each time Schmidt took the leg to the "saw room" in the back of the office, Dad and I sat in plastic chairs on the runway, listening to the fuzzy whine of the leg saw spinning its magic.

I used to hop around in the back room where the limbs were made. I listened to the country music playing on the radio and to Schmidt's exasperated swearing over my leg's current problem. Sometimes he and I had talked about school or the weather as I leaned, legless and in my underwear, against the table with my elbows in the saw dirt—the remnants from people's plastic sockets and wooden calves. These chats would routinely be interrupted by his exclamations of "Shit!" or "Goddammit son of a bitch!" I fell silent while he continued cursing under his breath and grinding out the prosthesis with differently shaped sanding cones to accommodate weight gain or other changes in my body. When the moment passed, he'd ask me something like "So, what's your favorite subject at school?" in a cheery voice—this was my cue to renew the conversation.

The air was so thick with dust and dirt, you could practically chew it. The saws and routers didn't scare me. I knew these instruments could cut into the wood-flesh of legs, into the plastic sockets, but there was never any blood, never any gore. Schmidt was like a sculptor, manipulating body parts beneath his hands. I was fascinated by the clinical, artistic nature of this process, for

I knew that it differed greatly from other activities involving flesh and bone.

Each year during hunting season, people in our congregation gave us deer meat. Although Mom didn't like the taste, she felt guilty throwing it out, so the square sections wrapped in white paper ended up in the garage freezer together with ice-cream bars and flavored ices.

I had seen several deerskins hanging in parishioners' homes, and I asked one of the hunters how he skinned the animal and retrieved the meat. How did those lifeless chunks—frozen solid in our freezer—become separated from the soft skin hanging on the wall? "It's a messy business," he told me. The pieces of flesh had to be cleaned from the hide, bit by bit—the shoulder, ribs, loins, and legs—and these bits were called fleshings. When I looked it up in the dictionary, I found that it also meant "flesh-colored stockings" and was listed just under the definition for flesh and blood. I would think of fleshings again, that strange word, when I received my first hydraulic prosthesis and routinely ordered packs of expensive flesh-colored nylons to cover the leg.

Everything Schmidt did to the body parts that amputees entrusted to him was sketched out beforehand on small grids with light, careful drawings and meticulous notes: maps of the body that served as the prosthetist's guide. Everything Schmidt did to my artificial leg was bloodless and clean, although as I watched him I often thought of those skinned hides hanging on the walls of ranchers' homes or spread out like rugs on the floor.

Near the main worktable in the back room, the casts of people's stumps stood around like strange papier-mâché objects. They were long and short, fat and skinny, and they lay on the table, on the floor, and stacked up on shelves against the wall. Legs that were ready to be returned to their owners following repair were stored in clear plastic bags and lined up against one wall. Attached to the top of each was a little tag that read "Allen" or "Briggs" or "Rapp" to identify the source and owner of the bloodless body part inside. The bags looked like collected elements from a crime scene, visible to all for scrutiny. Later, when the prosthesis was tucked inside blue, opaque bags, I called them "body bags"—another crime scene image—and when I opened them, a strange antiseptic smell shot out.

During this trip, I was too tired and frustrated to chat with Schmidt while he worked, so Dad and I sat on the runway, waiting. All around us, wooden prosthetic limbs and rubber feet hung from the ceiling on frayed cotton straps. They looked like misplaced limbs severed neatly from their bodies. Estranged and neglected, they were objects without purpose or use, waiting to be inhabited again or claimed by the person who would pull them off the strap and give them a reason to exist.

I liked to imagine the people who belonged with those lonely objects. It made me feel less vulnerable and less alone as I sat there, separated from my own leg, waiting in a dirty, dust-filled room. I knew that those other legless people were out there somewhere, hopping around with one pant leg that filled with air as they moved—kids and old men and mothers and teenagers, people who got up in the morning and put on their leg straight away—people like me.

I felt amputees everywhere when I was at Schmidt's, like a community of people with similar bodies who lived only here and entirely in the abstract. It felt like the most natural thing in the world to see these parts of others' bodies hanging from the sky. Dad and I sat in silence, watching the limbs sway in the slight breeze from the single ceiling fan.

"He'll figure it out," Dad said, more to himself than to me.

Schmidt returned to the runway and slid a slim plank of wood beneath my artificial foot. He placed his hands on my pelvic bones to be sure my hips were even. When I grew, the foot was twisted off (it was attached with a thick screw) and a piece of wood was secured to the ankle. This would help for a while, but after so much length was added, the leg became unstable and it looked strange, too. The additions were never exactly the same color as the rest of the prosthesis or each other, and they were never lined up precisely, creating bumps and creases at the ankle. These reminded me of the ceramic animals with uneven hooves and lumpy ears that I created in art class and which Mom displayed in the living room.

For the next hour, I tried to walk, but the socket still felt too tight—despite the many times Schmidt ground it out—and when he removed the leg and touched my stump to check for signs of friction and heat, the skin was bright red and hot to the touch. "Shit damn," he mumbled. Sweat was draining from his bald head as he went to the back room again and again. He tried wooden planks of different thicknesses at the ankle. He toed the foot in and out. He ground out the socket again and again. He attached a thicker waist strap that covered more of my hips and would hopefully alleviate some of the leg's drag. He smoked an entire pack of Lucky Strikes, filling the room with smoke. Dad and I were sweating, too, and my right knee was bruised and dirty from falling down.

"We'll get it," Schmidt said. "But you must learn to balance." I took a step and fell again. Now the socket was too loose and felt insecure around my stump, but it was still terribly heavy. The new strap felt like a harness. It was upsetting to walk in a limb that had once fit so well and now felt foreign. What had once felt like part of my body now felt like an instrument of torture. Each step was more like a stumble.

"I can't do it," I said. "It's not right. It hurts."

"You can't fix it?" Dad asked Schmidt, his hand on my arm.

"I can fix it for now, until we get the new one ready."

"It's hurting her," Dad said. "Can't you fix that?"

The frustration and sadness in Dad's voice made me cringe. That morning, he'd been helping me put on my left shoe, which required a shoehorn and some serious pushing, and had finally given up. "Dammit!" he'd said, and he'd thrown the clunky shoe across the room. At that time, limb companies made artificial feet for men and sometimes for children, but not specifically for women or girls. I had a Seattle foot, which I had wanted because it had anatomically correct toes instead of just a smooth, toeless surface, but it was much wider than my right foot. Not until the early

1990s would I have an artificial foot that was small enough to match my own size seven foot. My parents became accustomed to buying two pairs of shoes to accommodate the difference in the size of my feet, and sometimes even the larger shoe was a struggle to fit over the Seattle foot. We frequented shoe stores that would give us a discount on two pairs. Particularly beloved store managers often threw in a pair for free.

Dad had looked at me and apologized. He'd sat on the floor, breathing hard and wiping his eyes. "Sorry, I'm sorry," he'd said. I'd picked up the shoe on the other side of the room and then sat next to him on the living room floor, ashamed. It was my fault that he was so tired, and now he had gotten angry.

"I can do it," I said now, stepping out onto the runway. "I'll do it."

"Don't walk on it if it hurts," Dad said.

"I can do it," I said. "It's fine."

"Try again," Schmidt said. I looked at Dad. He gave me the thumbs-up. I let go of the bars.

That day, I learned to walk with the extra height added to the ankle, but I knew it wasn't going to work for very long. "Well, I'm glad that's worked out," Dad said as we drove away from Schmidt's office. The relief in his voice was palpable, and I said nothing.

Despite Schmidt's efforts, by the end of the summer before fifth grade, the troubles with the leg had worsened and intensified. I was limping more, and at night I'd show Mom the sores and calluses that were developing. On my right big toe was a callus so big and unfeeling, it could be cut off with a kitchen knife almost every two weeks. I got blisters on the bottom of my stump that swelled and popped, leaking a clear, nasty liquid.

The leg felt nearly twice as heavy as the others. It was like a painting that has been altered too many times, making the canvas heavy and thick with layers of corrective paint. The alignment always felt off, and my gait was awkward. No matter how much Schmidt altered the foot, no matter how many times he adjusted the hinges for correct alignment, walking didn't feel natural. When the knee swung through, it made a louder than usual cracking sound and I felt pressure and vibrations through my stump and hip. Schmidt simply could not get it right, although he certainly tried. Dad and I were at his office nearly every other day that summer.

"That's not right," Mom said after what would be the last session with Schmidt. "You *still* look like you're stepping into a hole with the left foot. It's ridiculous. We're going to Elliot."

We assumed that Dr. Elliot had recommended Schmidt because he was the most reputable prosthetist available in the Denver area. To our surprise, when Mom asked him if there were others we might try, he handed her a slip of paper with a new name, number, and address.

"Larry Gibbons is a great guy," he said. Mom looked at the name and then at Dr. Elliot.

"Has he been at the orthopedic clinics before?" A group of prosthetists gathered each week at the Children's Hospital.

"Sure," he said, standing. "Is there anything else?"

"Wow," Mom said. The relief in her voice was infectious.

"That's it," I said brightly. *Problem solved!* I thought.

As we were leaving the hospital, Mom said, "I could just string Dr. Elliot up from his toes for not telling us about this new guy sooner." She smiled as she said this, sounding as giddy as I felt.

For all of my elation at the prospect of finally being able to walk comfortably again, I felt guilty and uneasy about leaving Schmidt. He had done so much for me; he had even convinced my parents that I would be successful in the dance class I had been desperate to join. He called me Ms. Ballerina Bo Bina and made a leg that enabled me to twirl and spin and leap; I still could not move as beautifully and straight-backed as the other students in my class, but I could fling myself across the floor in routines choreographed to tunes from the *Fame* sound track. I felt a deep loyalty to Schmidt. Our relationship was odd—transactional yet tender. Because he had made a part of my body, the care of his hands was with me; his mark was on me. He'd taken the leg to the back room again and again, trying to get it right. At the end of our relationship, I saw desperation in his old, wrinkled face.

What would happen to Schmidt? Would all his patients desert him as I had? I imagined him sitting in the back room in his filthy, plaster-flecked apron surrounded by legs and tools and full ashtrays, listening to the lonely drone of his melodramatic music and the dull roar of slurred conversation made by the midafternoon drunks next door: As the neighborhood had slowly deteriorated, the hamburger joint became a noisy dive bar. You could hear clinking glasses and arguments on the other side of the saw room wall where the repaired legs were lined up. Would Schmidt join those rowdy drunks? Would he chain-smoke himself to death in one of the ugly office chairs? For months, whenever I thought of his bushy eyebrows, his smelly, hardworking hands, his bald head covered in brown age spots, I felt like crying.

I told nobody about my fears or sadness. Instead, I expressed excitement at leaving Schmidt. Only secretly did I feel disloyal. We had shared something. He had been the maker of my first leg, the creator of a part of the body that I would have, in slightly different shapes and forms, for the rest of my life. I was also grateful to him, a fact I admitted to nobody, because I felt it bound me to him in a way that made me nervous. He had not only provided me with a means of moving, but the intimacy of the act was unique. Schmidt had enabled me in a significant way. His handiwork was part of my every footfall, my every move. It was strange to imagine someone else touching me in those same places again.

I developed a similar attachment to anyone who touched my body or saw it in its most vulnerable, legless state: friends and in particular, as I got older, lovers. Once I had revealed my deformity to them, exposing myself in a physical way, I was afraid to let them go. Much later, this thinking would become paramount and destructive in my intimate relationships with men.

But for now, at age ten, what I knew for sure was that I would have a new prosthetist, a new maker. There would be no more trips to Schmidt's office. How, I wondered, would this new man be different?

At first, Larry Gibbons seemed like a dream come true. I couldn't stand one more day of being forced to interrupt my activities to unbuckle the waist strap, slip out of the too heavy socket, peel off the stinking, sometimes bloody stump sock, and minister to the sores. I had begun to feel that my disability was slowly taking over my life. I just wanted to *walk,* to *run.* I didn't want to be bogged down with these cumbersome details and time-consuming inconveniences. Larry made a prosthesis that fit well. I never asked him how he made it, I was only relieved to begin sixth grade with a new leg that worked and felt right, that indefinable feeling when it feels less like an external tool and more like a fundamental, even natural part of your body.

I never asked my parents how they paid for this leg. I assumed they would find the money for what I needed, and they did. They never complained, and I never thanked them. I forgot all about Schmidt after a while. Larry was my new prosthetist, and without any further doubts or questioning, I put my absolute trust in him.

Larry saw clients in a run-down brick building behind a used-car lot in downtown Denver. The painted sign hanging above the lot read, "Lemons: 2 Rent or 2 Own," and featured a lemon traveling on wheels and wearing a toothy, painted-on grin; a cloud of exhaust rose from its back end. When the wind was blowing, which it frequently was, the sign swung back and forth from a metal chain. In the winter, the lemon's face was often covered in ice.

As we made our way down the small driveway that led to the parking lot at Larry's, the car salesmen stood near their office, which faced the door of Larry's building, and watched us. I felt their eyes on me as I stepped out of the car. At this point, Dad and I would become extremely chatty with each other, trying to defuse the tension we both felt but would never name. We watched the salesmen group up together at the edge of their lot, staring and smoking. I waved at them and smiled, knowing somehow that it was important to acknowledge them in their cheap suits with their cigarettes pinched between their fingers. Perhaps they were entertained by the amputees driving through on their way for a tune-up. I may have been the only girl they saw passing by on the way to Larry's. Gawking appeared to be the only activity they ever did, as we never saw any customers waiting to buy one of the sad-looking cars: huge, dented Buicks, old Fords, a few beat-up Camaros in strange shades of yellow and green.

As we drove past the "lot o' lemons," Dad always hummed to himself. Sometimes he lifted his index finger off the wheel in a subdued salute; this was a method of greeting farmers on gravel roads that he'd learned as a boy in Illinois. Requiring little effort, it was an expression of obligatory friendliness. In light of the way I felt about the "car-men," as we referred to them, the insincerity I detected in his gesture pleased me.

I never saw another female amputee in Larry's waiting room. The majority of his patients were friendly older men—mostly war veterans—who smoked cigarettes in the waiting room and flirted with Tanya, the office receptionist, who wore bright coral lipstick and had tightly permed blond hair held away from her face with small hair combs.

Thin sheets on shower rods served as examination room partitions. Every once in a while, a patient opened the wrong curtain and found me sitting on a bench in my underwear. This did not bother me. I usually waved and said hello as, visibly flustered and embarrassed, he closed the curtain and walked away to another room.

The veterans I encountered in Larry's stifling, dirty rooms had lost a leg or an arm in combat or from combat-related injuries in Vietnam or World War II. Some of the men could recall the moment of loss in precise detail. Their stories were full of war.

I envied the veterans in a strange way. They were intimately familiar with the sources of their own pain: land mines, shrapnel, or bullets. Nameable, knowable agents of destruction. They had medals and uniforms that explained the shape of their bodies. It was the fault of war, not an accident of nature. Plus, they were heroes. They had survived. They trusted me with the gory details of the truth; they told the story of their limb loss as well as they remembered it.

Eagerly I listened, fascinated by the way many of the men could recall the exact moment the leg was taken from them. They remembered a slant of light through trees or a particular gust of soft wind; someone shouting in the distance; sometimes such a stunning, obliterating noise that it rendered the world temporarily silent. In return, I told them stories about school and skiing and whatever else was on my mind that day. I was never made to feel anything but equal to them and valued.

Still, I felt that my story paled in comparison. It didn't seem dramatic or memorable, but more than anything else, it was vague. I remembered the surgeries, but I certainly wasn't awake when the foot was disarticulated, that fancy word. I had clear memories of pain and of being in the hospital, but the moment of the loss itself wasn't etched clearly into my memory as the veterans' stories were—the "story of the lost leg" was not a clear tale or a distinct narrative; instead, it was a reality I lived on a day-to-day basis. Could it be that I didn't remember the pain of the operations but just confused it with the pain the wooden leg sometimes caused me now? If that were true, what did it mean about the knowledge of my own body? And if I didn't have all of the critical information, how would the body ever truly feel as if it belonged to me?

I pushed aside these lurking questions as I wondered at these men who had walked out of war and survived—not entirely intact, but alive nonetheless. They didn't want to constantly talk about the pain of having a fake leg; they didn't want pity, and neither did I. It seemed to me that they just wanted to live—not as extraordinary or magnificent, but as men. They wanted to feel whole and normal and powerful as they once had. To me, they were regal and honorable: kinglike.

I felt united with them as they flipped nervously through thin magazines in uncomfortable, unpadded chairs, chain-smoking and waiting for Larry to summon them wordlessly with a nod of his chin or a wave of his hand to one of the crappy examination rooms. Once there they would be asked to disrobe and then be scrutinized, measured, and informed about the limits and shapes of their own bodies in a tiny cubicle surrounded by a sheet with a half inch of black dirt along the bottom edge. Half the time I wanted to go with them, as if they needed protection from Larry's monotone voice and his damp, measuring fingers.

Imagining those men wounded and exposed, with the details of their trauma palpably apparent to them each day they woke up and put their legs on, made my chest ache. It wasn't fair that people's bodies could be so easily and permanently destroyed. At the same time, I convinced myself that I was nothing like the vets. As much as I wanted to feel a part of them when it suited me, I used the veterans as a way to gauge my own luck. *At least that didn't happen to me,* I'd think, which was precisely what some people, no doubt, felt about me. It made me feel superior and allowed me to pity them without implicating myself in these thoughts.

I took up the vets' time with my constant chatter and continuous demands for their attention. I stood in the middle of the room on one leg and hopped around, singing until someone joined me in song, or I asked one of the vets to time me as I hop-raced around the room; they never refused me. I often referred to them as my "leg friends."

Still wearing their legs, the guys chased me, exclaiming, "You're just too fast on that one good leg!" I giggled and hopped in circles around them until my right foot was black with dirt from the floor.

One of the veterans, Hal, was a particular favorite of mine. With virtually no stump at all, he was the most one-legged person I had ever seen and one of the few who, when I asked him to, didn't seem embarrassed about taking his leg off in the waiting room, in full view of Tanya and the other patients. His stump resembled a square flap of skin attached to his body.

"Kind of like a bed skirt," he said.

"Or a curtain for a little window," I chimed in.

"Like a little dog door," he said, chuckling. "Now you, you've got yourself a bat there; a good solid piece."

Together, we checked out my stump. It was long and steady and bore my entire body weight without much trouble. It looked crafted and strangely complete. It had an even, clean-looking surface. The scars were like light etchings pointing down to the rounded heel and the small ankle bone; the even stitches reminded me of the delicate veins of leaves that ran from the stem to the tip, crisp but soft looking.

"It's like a hammer," I said, moving the stump up and down. "A gun." I grasped an imaginary trigger.

"A gun!" he said. "What's a pretty girl like you gonna do with a gun?"

I blushed. This was an obvious lie requiring a substantial stretch of the imagination. My huge glasses got thicker and heavier every year. I wore headgear with my braces at night and woke up with a face full of dried slobber. I was hopelessly scrawny and pale and never got a tan, just millions of light brown freckles. My long red hair was, to my great dismay, stick straight.

Hal had a broad chest and a scar near his eye where a bullet had grazed him and left an indent the size of my fist. He had muscular, hairy arms, and his fingers were so fat, I watched carefully as he removed his limb, surprised that he could maneuver the straps and buckles with his enormous, awkward-looking hands. Even more unsettling was to imagine him shooting a gun with those hands, something I knew he had done.

"How'd you lose it?" I asked when I first met him. It was so nice to be in a room where I could ask this question of other people and not always be the one answering it. At the grocery store, at school, or when I met someone for the first time, I was often asked: "What happened to you?" "Are you limping?" "What's the matter?" "Did you hurt yourself?" "What's wrong with you?" At Larry's, for once I was the curious one.

"Explosion," Hal answered. "Vietnam." I nodded, picturing it.

The first time the guys mentioned this strange country to me, I asked Dad to show me where it was on the globe in his study—it was halfway around the world.

"You?" Hal asked.

"Birth defect," I said. He nodded. I shrugged and continued. "Nobody knows why."

"Ah," he said. "Lucky girl. It's good you don't remember. This body is what you've always known." If I had lost my leg in a motorcycle accident or in a war, I guess I wouldn't have been so lucky, or at the very least I would have had a more compelling story. More and more, I was beginning to understand that I was not lucky, but I never told the guys that.

"At least I didn't lose my eye," Hal liked to say, as if this were compensation for losing a limb and gaining a crater in his head. "Now I can see when people are looking at me funny." We laughed about this, but nobody laughed about Vince, Larry's son, who was his father's apprentice and heir to the prosthetic business throne.

"Honestly," Hal once said, "he just doesn't seem right." He tapped his temple with an index finger. "You know what I mean?"

I nodded. I certainly did.

Vince was physically attractive, with curly blond hair and blue eyes rimmed with thick lashes. His well-developed biceps curved out of his short-sleeved work shirts, and he moved with remarkable grace. But his presence did not match his physical appearance and this was disturbing. During all the years I knew Vince while he was Larry's apprentice, he did not speak but simply listened to what his father said, nodding his head slowly and writing on a clipboard. Occasionally, he'd bend down and make adjustments to the leg while Larry instructed him. His palms were always sweaty; his hands often shook. Dad and I called him "Silent Vince." There was something about the way he touched me—respectfully and cautiously, but with a hesitancy that suggested it was difficult to maintain this restraint—that differed from Schmidt's or Larry's touch. If I thought too much about Vince's silence, his dirty white hands, the pressure of his fingers against the top of the prosthesis, near places I had never touched in an intentional way—places only doctors' hands had been—I felt sick to my stomach. I felt dirty.

Whenever Vince was in the room, Tanya stopped filing her nails or reading her magazines for a few moments and looked at the back of his head with disgust or with longing, it was difficult to tell. When he left the room, she let out a little "shht," or a "well," as if she were reeling from an imagined slight or was making a judgment about him to the person sitting next to her, who was often me. In the sixth grade, when I became more interested in things like makeup and clothes, I became more interested in Tanya.

"Let's make ourselves pretty," she said now. "You want your nails filed, hon?"

"Sure," I said. I liked it when Tanya included me in her beauty rituals. She sometimes brushed and braided my hair or carefully applied bright-colored eye shadow or lipstick. She called it "face decoration," not makeup: this was always my argument when Mom insisted that I wash it off. Because his work schedule was more flexible, Dad usually brought me to my appointments. He would often run errands, leaving me free to hang out with Tanya, who with her powerful smell of Giorgio perfume and Aqua Net hair spray, her high heels and cleavage-revealing blouses, was so unlike my mother that she fascinated me. There were three things Tanya did habitually: paint or file her long press-on nails; flip through *Reader's Digest;* and make quick, three-second phone calls (first she removed one of her big plastic earrings—just like female characters did in soap operas—and then reattached it when she hung up).

Mom liked Tanya—"She really is friendly and efficient," she once said. But Tanya was also the kind of woman I was warned about: how *not* to look. She was too made-up, too brash. Mom thought she was "trying too hard to look nice." I wanted to be beautiful like my mother, who was beautiful in a very obvious, traditional way: flawless skin; fine, well-organized facial features; an hourglass figure; soft, stylish hair. Although she had many other gifts—a fierce intelligence, a gift for practical, levelheaded thinking, a generous spirit—I realized that it was her beauty that got her what she wanted most of the time. Still, I thought Tanya looked great.

Tanya lined up several bottles of nail polish in front of me. "Choose a color," she said. I pointed to the red bottle—the brightest one.

"Good choice," she said.

As Tanya was filing away, she looked at me, put down her file, and lifted my chin in her hands until we were eye to eye. Her blue eyeliner looked as if it were leaking out of her green eyes, and this combination of colors looked slightly monstrous. Her hands smelled like peach lotion and cigarette smoke.

"You're so pretty, my lady," she said sweetly. Tanya loved to call me "my lady" or "doll baby."

It was exactly what I wanted to hear. I thought, *Could it be true?*

"Yeah, right," I said, blushing.

Gently, she lifted my big glasses from my face and smoothed back my hair. "See?" she said. "Now you're pretty." My heart sank, but I smiled back and thanked her for the compliment, all the while wondering: *What about when I wear my glasses? What about my limp? What about my braces?*

As puberty loomed and issues of appearance became paramount, Andy's male friends were the gauge of how successful I would be in the all-important competition of being "liked." In this, my leg seemed an insurmountable obstacle, as one's likability—as far as I could tell—seemed directly linked to one's prettiness. The braces and thick glasses were bad enough, but how could I be pretty with a clunky wooden leg? I wanted to be the girl Andy's friends had a crush on. Instead, I felt like the little sister whose leg you were trying to steal glances at—what was *wrong* with it—while eating pizza in front of the television. *That girl—Andy's sister. Who? You know, the one with the fake leg.* I heard this imagined exchange in my head, in all of my vanity, self-consciousness, and paranoia.

At the skating rink, where Andy and I often went on Saturday afternoons, I steered clear of boys in general and chatted with my girlfriends, who stayed off the rink for the agonizing slow skate that always happened just after "Whip It," when you swung with another person in a tight circle, your arms crossed and your hands clasped tightly with your partner's. "Whip It" was great. Slow skate was not. There was no way I was going to stand around and wait for someone to choose me while I watched perfectly formed couples move slowly around the rink as the colored lights crossed over their shoulders, knees, and skates, their gangling or chubby prepubescent limbs made suddenly graceful and slim as they moved in the dim light. It mattered little, because all of my friends hated boys as much as I did.

One day, the girls I would normally chat with during slow skate had suddenly left the benches, drawn by sudden crushes on boys and the desire to stare at them dreamily as they lined up on the other side of the rink in an awkward, disdainful-looking row.

I had no choice but to skate out with my friends or risk being alone and labeled a nerd. We stood there, all of us, straight-backed and trembling against the wooden fence that circled the rink. A boy would skate up, stop himself slowly by breaking on one toe, and wordlessly hold out a hand to his chosen partner. They were like birds landing on a wire, making a soft whooshing sound as they flew away. One by one, the girls were peeled away from the fence. It was too much to say a word, and the ritual of the partner's skate eliminated entirely the strained exchange of niceties. I stared down at my skates and picked at my fingernail polish, letting it fall to the rink in light pink flakes.

Finally, all the girls were gone, and I stood alone. I felt tears forming, and I stopped them. From across the rink I saw Andy moving toward me through the rotating blue, yellow, and red arcs of the disco light. My body froze; I gripped the fence so tightly, I felt a splinter slip into my palm. He stopped in front of me, and I waited for the pack of other boys to follow up behind. I narrowed my eyes at him. I did not believe he would be so cruel.

He held out his hand. "Wanna skate?" he asked.

It didn't matter that it was Andy, who had become an awkward stranger to me in his teenage years. What mattered was that it was the first and only time I would ever skate with those couples, my hand sweating in my brother's. We did not look at each other but simply glided around the rink; it surprised me how well we moved together. I had learned to skate as a Camp Fire Girl and was actually quite good at it. The skates made me fast, which I liked; the wheels helped the left leg swing through smoothly and gracefully. I kept my back straight, tightened my stomach muscles, and very rarely lost my balance.

Andy matched the speed of his skates to mine. As we skated by his friends, I listened for jeers and snorts of laughter, but there were none. I glanced at the boys' faces once—quickly—before looking away. I felt triumphant in some small way as my brother and I moved in a slow, embarrassed, and—for me—grateful circle under the soft, colorful lights.

Chapter Eight

PHANTOM PLAYER

As the student manager of the seventh-grade girls volleyball, basketball, and track teams at Laramie Junior High, I got up at four A.M. during the summer and stayed late after school during the academic year to throw balls at practices and take care of the gear and the uniforms. I kept score at all of the games, and in the spring I timed races and relays. I sang along with the cheerleaders at games "LJH is the best, c'mon, people, yell it!"—and traveled with the team on huge buses to meets and tournaments in Cheyenne, Casper, and Rawlins. I cried when we lost and celebrated when we won, dashing onto the court at the final buzzer and often being lifted in the arms of the girls as if I'd scored the decisive winning point. I hung out in the locker room and was invited to all the parties. I wasn't one of the team physically, but I was beloved the way a mascot would be.

The summer before junior high began, I had decided against a new surgery that would have resevered the bone of my stump, making it shorter and allowing my natural and artificial knees to line up correctly. Although it might have created more aesthetic prosthetic operations, it still seemed too risky. I remembered Hal's flaplike stump and how difficult it was for him to walk well.

I had also exhausted my search for the perfect leg. On one of my trips to Winter Park, Mom had discovered a leg in the changing rooms that did not have a waist strap but instead featured a suction socket. She made a light sketch of the leg and then asked around for its owner—a young woman from Texas. After that, this leg was referred to as "the Texas leg" and seemed to hold out the possibility of something different and better, as if a new leg might change my life entirely. The leg would hang magically from my body. The area around my waist would be perfectly smooth; no strap would dig painfully into my hips.

"I want a suction socket," I told Vince, who, after years of apprenticeship but no formal schooling or training, had finally taken over his father's practice. "That's what I want," I said, showing him Mom's sketch. He barely looked at it.

"Huh," he said. "Not sure I can do that."

"Try it," I said. "Please."

Although the leg Vince finally presented to me didn't look like the Texas leg, I was excited to give it a try. A thin flap of "skin" covered the suction apparatus—a plug—at the front and end of my stump. I was hopeful about the flesh-colored nylon sock over the thigh area; it looked a lot like real flesh.

When I took my first step in the leg, the socket made a distinct wet and sloppy noise—exactly like a fart. I took a few more noisy, labored steps. Vince laughed.

"What about that noise?" I asked, feeling desperate. "It's awful. Am I walking on it the wrong way?"

"Hey, you can just say, 'Excuse me, I had a big lunch.' " He chuckled and grinned. "The vets just point their finger when their legs make a noise." I looked at him, speechless. I was glad I'd asked Dad to wait for me in the "lobby."

My face burned. I adored the vets, but I was not a man or a war veteran. I was a girl on the verge of becoming a woman. I had recently requested that Dr. Elliot *not* bring his gaggle of medical interns to watch me walk around in a thin gown that was entirely open at the back. When I told him this, he looked at me as if I'd asked him for a million dollars. I was fully aware that I was of interest to the interns because of the ways in which doctors had worked on and altered my body. But I wasn't a car or an experiment, and I didn't want to be regarded as such. Eventually, Dr. Elliot understood and complied. "You're all grown up now," he said. Vince clearly was not going to acknowledge this. What was I to him, then, as a patient? Perpetually a little girl? A half-man, an almost-man, an almost-woman, an almost-*person*?

In addition to its disturbing noises, the leg was terribly heavy, and its lip came up too high and dug into my crotch. My stump didn't reach the bottom of the socket but felt suspended just above; the top part of the socket was too tight, as if hands were gripping me. "There's no other model?" I asked finally. "I thought it would be different." I felt humiliated.

"It's just impossible," Vince said, getting huffy. "The way your stump is shaped makes it impossible." I'd heard this before. Because I have my natural heel at the end of my stump, I also have my ankle bone; this creates challenges for crafting a well-fitting socket. To this day, the silicone sockets for my hydraulic prosthesis cost $1,000 each because they must be custom-made rather than injected molded silicone, a more durable and more affordable material. This puts the average price of each prosthesis at $25,000; my current leg is worth more than any car I have ever owned or even driven.

In my newfound role as student manager, anyone with a problem came to me first, whether it be the need for a new uniform (weight gain or loss), a request for counseling (a crush gone awry), or a gear issue (this or that basketball felt flat). I had my own desk in each coach's office that rotated each season and a file for each girl that held her health history, emergency contact information, and uniform size, as well as her statistics—baskets made, points scored, races won—which I tallied after each season before awards were distributed. I was the gatekeeper of secrets and gear. As my friend Sidney said, "You're totally one of us, even though you can't play on the team." Being a phantom player was good enough for me; being the manager was the next best thing to being a real athlete. I told everyone that I was an expert skier—which I was—and this achievement in one area of disabled sports somehow made me feel like an honorary athlete in any able-bodied sport of my choice.

At night or in the afternoon when I came home from practice, I did my own physical work modeled after the girls' exercises: jump rope, wall sits, running drills, jumping jacks, and sit-ups. I worked out in the basement in a kind of fury. I got sweaty and tired, but I could never do all the things the others could do or as well, but I carried on, fueled by an irrational, even delusional hope.

Although I was passing well as normal and had stopped actively searching for a better prosthesis, I continued to nurture a secret belief in transformation. All it would take, I assumed, would be the right leg and the right man who could make it. There was a suction socket out there somewhere that a girl not so unlike me was wearing and living in. There was a beautiful prosthesis that would someday belong to me. Like Cinderella's magical slipper, this leg would make everything fairy-tale perfect. Surely Vince was not the end of the road. I had to hope for something, because how could I possibly conceal myself forever wearing an outdated limb that gave me away with its every squeak, crack, and leak? I was convinced that I would someday wear a leg that made me new, different, and better. Normal. I was absolutely counting on it.

I held to this notion of transformation because I felt there had to be something that would level the playing field, that would restore to me—and the vets and other amputees I knew—the bodies we had lost. I had been taught that if you tried hard enough, you could improve your lot. My wishes for advanced prosthetics were intended to restore the balance in what I thought should be a rightly ordered world characterized by God's grace, fairness, and happy endings. Jesus died horribly, but the world was saved. Humans were sinners, but all you had to do was ask for forgiveness and it was granted, and then you were freed, as we said every Sunday, "from the bondage of sin." I was taught that God wanted humans to be capable and happy so that they could exercise free will and contribute to the world. If you had the misfortune to get your leg blown off during a war or lose your foot as a child, it made theological as well as practical sense that there should be an equally remarkable event to compensate for it. I believed that we deserved some reparation for our pain, some partial redemption for our wounded bodies.

The year I was in the seventh grade, Vince moved his office to an industrial town near Denver where smokestacks belched black smoke and the bumpy, potholed roads were clogged with diesel trucks. There were no high-rise buildings or any of the happy hustle and bustle associated with cities. Although the gaze of the used-car guys had been disconcerting, at least there had been people around. Vince's new office felt completely disconnected from the larger world. The only buildings visible through the windows were warehouses, physical plants, and oil refineries.

"I hate this," I said. "It's only trucks and road and smoke. Gross."

Mom had the day off and was driving us to my first appointment at the new office.

"Look," she said. "Horses." She pointed at a trailer passing us in the left lane. Bits of the horses' brown bodies were visible as they stomped and shifted; their tails stuck out of the trailer slats and waved in the air like soft flags. "They're not trucks and smoke."

"They're probably taking them somewhere to make glue out of them," I said.

"Oh, c'mon," she said. We didn't say anything more about the neighborhood.

I didn't see Hal in the new group of patients, and Tanya had apparently been fired or sought different employment. I missed them both. The new receptionist was quiet and unfriendly, with a fondness for tight, brightly colored skirt suits. The tables in the waiting room were littered with half-filled coffee cups, some with cigarette butts floating in the black, pungent liquid. Two dead ferns drooped from rusted hooks in each corner of the waiting room. A little bell attached to the front door made a sad, tinny jingle to mark a patient's arrival.

When I was small, I had imagined my feet were quickly and easily produced by happy little elves who punched them out of a clever machine. I pictured a strong, handsome man sitting on a table as a prosthetist carefully created a cast of his foot that would later be used to make a fake one for amputees like me. I envisioned feet on pedestals or under glass, as if they were famous pieces of art or ancient artifacts on display at a museum.

At Vince's, I saw the whole leg-making business for what it was: dirty and sordid. The process was reductive and strange. I felt as if my leg—this indispensable part of me—were being built as cheaply and heartlessly by Vince as a factory might make ugly plastic dolls or flimsy lawn chairs.

Vince still seemed determined to speak as little as possible. I explained to him what I needed. "The hinge is squeaky," I said, standing in a small partitioned room, my right foot bare on the chalky floor. I picked up the leg to show him, impressing him, I knew, with my ability to maintain rock-solid balance on the right leg. Although he made me feel uncomfortable, I also wanted to please him. I was indiscriminate in my search for others' affirmation.

"I need a new foot, too." It looked as if an animal had been gnawing on the heel. "It's like something's rotting," I said, and felt angry. What had I done to deserve such a disgusting fate as this? It was worse than thick glasses or braces and headgear and retainers. It was worse than anything I might have gotten stuck with. I wanted all signs of my body's idiosyncrasies and deficiencies to be promptly hidden if they could not be permanently removed. At the same time, I knew that no matter how well the leg worked or how clean the hinges or new the foot, I could never have what I wanted, which was the leg I'd prayed for years ago at my first Communion: one made of soft, pliable flesh and strong bones, with real blood running through its veins. Whatever Vince did, no matter how hard he worked and no matter how ardently I hoped, it would never be enough. I hated him for that.

"The length needs to be checked, too," Mom said, standing behind me. "I think her hips are dipping down to the left too much. You should watch her walk to be sure."

I glared at her. She was constantly watching me walk. Sometimes

I'd turn a corner and see her leaning out of a doorway, holding an iron or a shirt on a hanger or a mixing bowl, staring at me with a worried, discerning look, trying to decide when or if I needed to make an appointment with Vince. Every night when I stood up to take my dinner plates into the kitchen, I knew she was watching me.

"Stop it!" I'd scream at her, releasing all of my rage on the most convenient and undeserving target. "Stop looking at me!" Whereas I had once commanded her attention, it now annoyed me when she monitored my gait; it threatened my elaborate and carefully constructed plan of passing as normal. But even as I resented her preoccupation with my leg, I also relied on it. As long as Mom was thinking about it, I could do my best to erase the fact of the leg from my mind. So she was the one who had noticed the chewed-up-looking foot.

Vince nodded and left the room. "We'll see how he does," Mom said.

"It's totally gross in here," I complained. "He doesn't even have any other patients. The plants are dead. Maybe all the patients are dead. Everything stinks. Everything is *devastated*."

"Well," she said, "he's the only prosthetist you've got."

We heard the router winding up and starting to spin. Its scratching and whirring blended noisily with the rumble of traffic outside the thin office walls.

Even as I longed for a phenomenal new prosthetist to burst into my life like a handsome male suitor in a romance novel (and I devoured these in secret at the public library, always flipping first to the lurid sex scenes), I developed a split life.

With my friends I was chatty, energetic, easygoing, and renowned for telling an entertaining story and a good joke. But my interior world was far different. When I got my first B, I berated myself for hours, somehow connecting my inferior grade—and to me, inferior was anything less than an A—to my leg. If the teacher didn't choose my English assignment to read aloud to the class or if I wasn't the first person with the answer in history or science class, I found a way to blame it on my disability. *It makes me slow, it makes me weird, it makes me stupid,* I'd say to myself, and vow to do better the next time.

In the lunchroom, I took my time getting my food so that one of the picnic tables would be almost filled up on either side and I could easily slip the fake leg through or let it hang off the bench. I didn't want to look awkward trying to maneuver my body between others. If I couldn't find a seat that met my criteria, I pretended I wasn't hungry and didn't eat, or I ate a sandwich quickly in a locked bathroom stall with both feet up and pressed against the door. If there was a sport I couldn't do in gym class—flag football, for instance—I would fake a headache. I never said, "I can't do that." While I lay on the nurse's cot, trying to generate some convincing groans, I'd say to myself, *You loser. You gimp. You cripple.* But when I sat up again, I was all sweetness and light and positive energy. "I feel much better!" I'd say, and leap off to my next class.

Despite my extreme self-consciousness, my status as student manager and my flirtatious "public" self yielded me a slew of suitors. I'd had Jimmy after me in the fall, with his tight Wranglers, blond buzz-cut, and toned biceps from working the animals on his father's ranch. He'd put his mouth on my ear at a dance in the cafeteria.

In the spring there was Joe, who had written me a letter in English asking, "Do you like me, check yes or no," and then two empty stars to check. I was elated. A boy *liked* me, wooden leg and all. Perhaps my life would not turn out so badly. Soon Joe and I were expertly avoiding each other in the school hallways, a sure sign that we were "going out." I listened to Tiffany songs, daydreaming about him. He wrote me a letter clearly stating that he respected me way too much to ever stick his tongue down my throat. I was relieved. I couldn't imagine kissing a boy, although I longed to.

The bulk of my experience with or conversations about boys occurred in the world of female intimacy, where I was comfortable and where my wit and exuberance were admired. My friends and

I listened to Air Supply and REO Speedwagon and fantasized about kissing Tom Cruise. We called the local DJ and asked him to play a love song for Lance or Aaron from "Lou Lou" or "Buffy." I gave hours of love advice, although apart from my one experience with Jimmy on the dance floor, I had never been within yards of a boy I liked for more than the length of a slow song, and this limited motion was always strictly monitored by the chaperones and teachers standing in an awkward circle around the kids in their charge. I had a whole gaggle of girlfriends who were loyal to me and confided in me. I felt like the leader of my miniroost of insecure teens.

After so much struggle and agony over my own physical appearance, I should have been that much more compassionate toward others who struggled with similar issues. The reverse was true. I had numerous flaws, but in what I thought was a clear sign of my superiority, I had managed to hide them all. I looked down on people who had acne, a stutter, buckteeth, or thick glasses. What was wrong with them? I thought: *Go to a doctor, get a speech therapist, get contacts and braces—for God's sake, just* fix it *as I did. Try harder. Fake it.* I had no idea that the financial burdens of these procedures were too great for most of my classmates' families. I was completely and willfully ignorant of the sacrifices my parents had made—most of them way outside their means—that gave me the privilege to ridicule others. I was merciless and cruel. I gossiped as much as anyone else. I felt powerful and popular.

I got my chance to use my power over Christmas in the eighth grade, just after I dumped Joe and before my family moved to Nebraska. In prealgebra class, the boy who sat behind me, Dean, suffered from an extreme case of acne. Not only did he already have deep scars embedded in his cheeks that made it look as though he slept on gravel every night, but some of the pimples covering his chin and forehead were large enough to cast a shadow when he turned his face to the side; other blemishes leaked white puss or blood. He frequently mopped his face with the handkerchief he kept in his back pocket.

I sat in front of Dean and made a huge scene of flipping my long hair around and leaning back to talk to him and smile. Because he sat behind me, Dean was my partner. I was hopeless at math, but he was patient and kind with me. Any other less tolerant partner would have made me pull my weight more. I spent a lot of time chattering away about unrelated subjects and making eye contact with my girlfriends across the room, trying to communicate wordlessly with expressions while Dean solved all the equations. When he looked at me, I could tell he liked what he saw: long, tightly permed hair; gravity-defying bangs shellacked by Perma-Soft hair spray into a stiff wave suspended above my forehead; blue eye shadow and frosted pink lipstick that were both hastily touched up in the bathroom between each class period and wiped off before I went home. Dean had a low, pleasant voice, and I realized, as we sat together for nearly forty minutes every day practicing problems, that he was smart and funny. I liked his *personality.* What a concept.

One day, I found a note inside my math book. It was from Dean. I had been sent flowers once from a boy at church, but this was my very first bona fide love note.

Not only did I tell people about the letter, but I read it aloud in the hallway. At first intoxicated with this attention, as I read it and people laughed, I realized how much thought Dean had put into his expression of affection for me and the way in which I was abusing it for a few moments of cheap laughter at his expense. I hadn't even taken the time to enjoy its sentiments for myself. Once I recognized what it was, I impulsively gathered a crowd and read aloud the words that were intended only for me. In doing so, I had ruined the gesture as well as its impact on me. More important, I had deeply hurt someone.

People teased Dean all day, all *year.* He never spoke to me again in class—we worked in silence—but other people said plenty to him. I never apologized and almost failed prealgebra. But my cruelty gave me status, and pretty soon the most popular guy in school, Tristen, had started "liking" me, a fact he communicated by wandering to my locker between classes to stare at me without saying a word, a perfect smile lighting up his face. After he touched my hand briefly at a party before I moved to Nebraska, I forgot all about Dean; Joe, too. But every time I thought of Dean, I was ashamed of how I'd treated him. Now I was on the other side of some invisible line. I wasn't happy there, either.

The fun of showing off my body to my girlfriends at slumber parties rapidly disappeared when they discovered all that private, intimate pairings with boys could lead to. When a boy touched them a certain way or kissed them deeply for the first time, I believed that the girls who had once admired me began to see me the way I assumed that boys did, the way I did, and that was in comparison with the photographs in fashion magazines.

My friends and I flipped through the pages of *Seventeen* and *YM,* our flanneled limbs piled on top of one another. We watched *Dirty Dancing* over and over again, squealing madly when Patrick Swayze holds Jennifer Grey's face and practically sings into her mouth, looking into her eyes the entire time, and repeatedly rewinding and watching again the scene when they wake up together in the morning, their necks and shoulders bare, just barely suggesting nakedness in places below the waist. He chose her, I thought, because she was beautiful. Using my pillow, I pretended to kiss Lee Majors (my first celebrity crush), and my friend pretended to kiss his sidekick, and then we switched pillows. I imagined that sleeping on a pillow was like sleeping on a man's chest. I desperately wanted to be chosen.

At these gatherings, after everyone else had fallen asleep, I'd almost always have insomnia, having chattered away for hours and eaten too much chocolate. I was also kept awake by fears for my future that, although very present, also felt distant and indistinct, like thunder that can be heard everywhere around you even as the exact location of it remains unknown; all you can see are occasional bright flashes of lightning in the windows.

Sleepless, I was seduced by those beautiful glossy magazines. I pored over them. I saw myself in those poses and locales (the beach, the library, the forest), wearing that skirt or that dress or those shorts or jeans, and always those perfectly normal and lovely legs. What had made me special as a child I knew I'd now give anything to trade for what my friends effortlessly possessed: normal bodies, two legs, and—I thought—the possibility of a life with a man and a job and babies, the only future that I could imagine.

The bulk of my fear stemmed from one particular incident that had led me to believe that this desirable life would forever elude me. One Friday night, I found myself baby-sitting Sophie, a four-year-old girl. I was chasing her around the corner when I felt something catch in my ankle followed by a soft cracking noise—as if I'd stepped on a pinecone or a fallen tree branch—and then the foot was spinning around as easily as a merry-go-round on its axis. I knew the foot could move when forced: Vince toed it in or out with his bare hands and the strength of his arms; the year before I'd been in a car accident, and the force of impact had turned the foot all the way around, as if the left leg were trying to walk away from the crash in the other direction.

Sophie scurried out of sight, and I bent down. The foot swiveled in circles at will as I tried to steady it. When I realized that the damage was too severe to fix, I limped back to the couch in the living room and announced that it was time for television. I looked at my watch: only an hour until bedtime. I would have to trust that she could brush her teeth and sort out her pajamas without my assistance.

As we watched television, Sophie threw her toys all over the family room and I made no move to stop her. I laughed and tickled her and pretended that it was completely normal for a baby-sitter to let the child in her care trash the house.

After she was asleep, I tried to figure out what was going on with the foot, but I was afraid to take off the prosthesis in case Sophie wandered out and saw me legless, and I didn't want to leave the couch and worsen the damage. The minutes ticked by. Shortly before her parents were due back, Sophie had a nightmare and I had to go to her. I walked slowly down the hall, carefully dragging my barely attached foot behind me.

When Sophie's parents arrived home, I had to explain to them what had happened. I spoke to the floor, too embarrassed to look them in the face. Apparently, they had not even known that I had an artificial leg. Now, here I was, literally falling apart in their family room. They paid me—far too much—and I walked to the door, trying to look composed and nonchalant while I dragged the loose, turning foot behind me. I prayed that it would not fall all the way off, taking with it my remaining dignity.

Sophie's mother went to check on her, and her father, who was probably in his late twenties and a graduate student at the university, watched me struggle for a few moments and then offered to carry me. I nodded, accepting his offer.

He lifted me in his arms; it was the closest I'd ever been to a man who wasn't a member of my family. His chest felt solid—not soft—against my shoulders. It was not at all how I had imagined a strange man's chest would be. He smelled like aftershave and strong cologne—a clean, slightly acerbic smell that made me blush. When he shifted my weight in his arms, his button-down shirt was pushed to the right and I saw a little patch of hair on his shoulder. I was amazed, having never imagined such a thing about a man. I wondered if he had hair on the other shoulder as well. I felt the pressure of his hands against the back of my legs and the warmth of his body through my shirt. My left foot dangled like a booger from a nose, pulling on the ankle, as if it would tumble to the floor at any moment. His warm arms were strong and straining under my legs and back.

The image of a man carrying a woman in his arms was one I'd been taught to think romantic, but this was not how I felt now. I had imagined being swept away by a man who desired and loved me, like Debra Winger in *An Officer and a Gentleman*. Now this stranger was carrying me like a wounded bird, a broken doll, and I felt ugly and strange and horrible. Part of me was missing, and the compensation provided by an artificial stand-in that made me at least temporarily physically whole seemed disastrously insufficient. The presence of a leg's replacement only called attention to its glaring absence. An artificial limb merely intensified my awareness of the part that had been lost and no longer existed; the part that had to be reconstructed under a technician's hands. I had never internalized this truth until that moment, held and carried in the arms of a man whose first name I can't even remember.

After Sophie's father left me in the living room at home, I cried for hours, in full view of my family, and I could not tell anyone why. I felt isolated and strangely violated. I felt desire for the man who had held me, although it was inappropriate, and I thought it would be impossible for him—or, more important, for any man—to desire me in the same way because of my body. If I winced every time I looked at the scars and stitches of my stump or saw my limping reflection in a mirror or store window, how much more grotesque would I seem to a boy or a man who did not know the history of my body but was assessing it on appearance alone? The stage of romance seemed one on which I simply did not belong, one on which there would never be a part for me to play. Instead, I would forever be behind the curtain, mollified and invisible. Useless. Disgusting. Shameful. *Ugly.*

My parents were mortified. Dad was angry that the leg had done this, as if it had suddenly adopted a mind of its own and decided to betray me at the worst possible moment. He promised to call Vince first thing in the morning. The mention of Vince only made me cry harder. "Don't despair," Dad said, and then looked guilty, as if this had been the wrong thing to say. But it was absolutely accurate. This helpless, bottomless feeling: It was despair. That a feeling this hideous had a one-word description gave me some comfort.

"It can't be that bad," Andy said in a not unkind voice.

"Shut up!" I wailed, and Dad shot him a warning look.

Mom kept her arm around me, saying, "Oh, honey, don't cry."

But crying seemed the only sensible response. "It's not your fault," she said. It didn't matter whose fault it was. I was deeply, deeply embarrassed, as if a piece of humanity had been scratched off of me—or had it been denied me? And I was angry, so angry that I had to let some of it out or I felt I would not be able to breathe; the rest of it I kept bricked up inside.

For years, I tried to remember the warm and steady pressure of that man's chest against my arm and my shoulder and how it felt when his chin bumped against the top of my head. I held to that moment, afraid that he might be the last man who would ever touch me.

As a child, I committed countless biblical verses to memory. I spoke them aloud, feeling the ancient words roll and bounce in my mouth. As I learned them, adding a construction paper link to each verse I memorized until they circled my room like a ring of dull lights, they were simple word reels I unwound in moments of distress, as known to me as the patterns of my own breath, and equally calming. In my mind, I saw the words with the small chapter and verse mark between them. So I knew the line well enough from Ecclesiastes: *What is crooked cannot be made straight.*

Before this incident, I had only felt disabled during my routine checkups at the hospital, when I felt that I had stumbled into another girl's life, and she was not lucky or intelligent or "super" as I was, but had a body with a corresponding chart documenting precisely what was wrong and what had been done to try to correct these deficiencies.

I knew my medical records were thick and heavy—a massive accordion file of write-ups and prognoses. Numerous X-rays with slick, curling edges. Itemized bills and carefully recorded dates of contact with the insurance company. Pictures. Nurses' notes from specific surgeries documenting when IVs were inserted, when wounds were checked, when bowels moved. Notes Dr. Elliot had scribbled to himself that nobody else could decipher.

Each time I went in for an X-ray, I had to remind the technician to tape a lead shield over my lower abdomen so that the radiation wouldn't harm my reproductive organs. This was a task Dad delegated to me when I was thirteen, after he explained how important it was. "They'll forget unless you remind them," he warned me.

Once, when I had requested the lead, I said, "For when I have babies," just making conversation. The technician—a woman—said to me, "Oh, sweetie, I don't think you'll be having any babies." Another male technician laughed. I insisted on the lead anyway, telling myself that they were just kidding around with me.

When the X-rays came back, I saw my bottom half, from the belly button down, asymmetrical and lit up on the board. There was the dark gap in the screen—the space a normal leg would have filled; there was the shadow of a heart over my uterus and ovaries as if it had been drawn there as a joke, dark and arbitrary as graffiti. Sometimes the heart would be askew, the edges of the tape that held it to my lower belly visible as railroad tracks on the X-ray board. There it was: my body lit from the inside out and exposed for the mess, for the complicated accident, for the *trouble,* that it truly was.

In this moment, with my body exposed in front of not a doctor or an X-ray technician or a family member, but a stranger, the loss of my leg and its implications for the rest of my life fully registered for the first time. I would never be made right or restored to true wholeness—not ever. A missing leg suddenly made all the difference in the world, poster child or expert skier or student manager or pretty girl or not. It was the deciding—perhaps eliminating—factor.

I missed Hal terribly. I understood him now better than I ever had. Although I had not lost my leg at war, I knew now how it felt to think of a life full of possibilities—any that your imagination might conjure up—and then have those notions destroyed. I knew now what it felt like to wake up to a body that changed your future and your options. And what could you do about it? Nothing.

Now I understood why the vets had told me their stories in careful, whispered tones—the only way to partially redeem the loss was to remember it, although even this retelling brought with it its own wretchedness. My loss was never more clear to me than on that day I was carried home in a strange man's arms. Complete and irretrievable loss was just that: permanent.

The body has a remarkable ability to displace pain. First it's in the abstract, then it's in your skin as a feeling, before it moves into your mind as a story, but sooner or later the pain ends up in your heart. And that's where it stays. Words spoken aloud in your moonlit bed—crippled, deformed, unlovable—find their own darkness and then come back for you.

Chapter Nine

FASHION PLATE

Melissa's red Mustang was parked in the lot at the Gas N' Shop. I sat in the backseat of the car. Through the windshield, I saw my two friends—Melissa and Ashley—inside the store, buying candy and sodas. I looked at my two legs—the right one real, the left one artificial—in the rearview mirror. Melissa tapped on the glass window of the store and waved at me. I lifted my hand and forced a smile as my eyes found my legs once again in the mirror.

Bared in a black miniskirt, my white leg was very white and tinged with blue from the neon sign and the fluorescent parking lot lights. The wooden leg glistened; it was almost as reflective as the smooth side of a spoon. I tried to pull the black, slinky skirt farther down to hide my legs, but it slid between my hands and slithered up far above my knees, leaving the glossy metal hinges of my prosthesis exposed.

I had agreed to wear this skirt because it was the summer of 1990: the summer I agreed to do things I didn't want to do and laughed at jokes that weren't funny. I had just turned sixteen, and what I wanted more than anything else in life was to be beautiful. I didn't care about being smart, successful, or good. In fact, I believed that beauty was the prerequisite for achieving any of these other qualities.

I was wearing a miniskirt because I thought, somehow, that if I dressed like these girls, I would become like them—sleek and pretty, with lithe, tanned legs. Popular. Self-confident. Desired. I thought I could simply will myself into this type of being, into a different, magical life.

I had lied to my mother. I told her that my friends and I were going shopping, then to the movies, and then back to Melissa's to celebrate her entry into the adult world: She could now legally drive, having just passed her driver's license test that morning. In reality, Melissa and I hung out in her room gossiping all day, and now she was driving our group to a small town to the east, where there was a college fraternity kegger in a cornfield.

Earlier that day, Melissa had stolen a six-pack of Schlitz beer from her parents' pantry. "Nobody can stop us from going," she said, "and I don't want to go empty-handed. This is a night for *drinking.* What if the keg is drained when we get there?"

I didn't know what a keg was, but I said as emphatically as possible, "That would suck."

Melissa smiled. "Totally. Anyway, they buy this shitty beer when they have really big parties, and they only drink it after everyone is super drunk." I loved Melissa's disrespect for the rules. Her bright, confident voice made every idea sound delicious and worth doing.

"Let's get schlitzed," she said, giggling.

"Let's," I said, giggling, too, although I wasn't completely sure what she meant.

Through the store's big windows, I watched Melissa walk down the candy aisle with a smooth dancer's glide. Her head tipped back slightly in laughter as she watched Ashley, in the opposite aisle, shaking her blond, perm-perfect curls in an animated way that meant she was telling a joke.

I stared down at my legs again, then up at their reflection in the rearview mirror, grimacing, becoming more and more agitated. Down and up, down and up. My right leg was white-on-white aspen white. As a redhead, I could not aspire even to the gray brown winter color of girls' legs in Nebraska before the summer, when, bikini clad, they lounged on lawns and sloped roofs, tanning their legs and the rest of their bodies to a rich, oily brown color. They called this quintessential summer activity "laying out," as if they were arranging themselves on a surface to be examined or offered up for sale.

I looked out the window at the moon and wished to be in Laramie. I missed the ease of those days and the comfort I took in the fact that everybody knew the story of my disability. I had never known that such a thing could be a comfort until I no longer had it. I never had to worry about wearing short skirts or shorts in Wyoming, either, because even in the summer, the temperature rarely topped eighty degrees. This was my second summer in Nebraska. I hated it.

My family had moved from Wyoming to Nebraska in the middle of my eighth-grade year. During that first summer, the heat and humidity had been intolerable. My leg was unbearably hot, but I refused to wear shorts, preferring instead to sweat profusely in long pants or jeans. I watched soap operas and ate my dinner at four-thirty in the afternoon, bored. I discovered aerobics and calorie counting; it provided structure and meaning to my days, a controlled rhythm. I often cried myself to sleep at night. Once, Dad sat on the other side of my locked bedroom door and cried, too. I was quite melodramatically inconsolable. I could not imagine not being lonely, not being strange.

Nobody was happy in Nebraska. Mom worked as the nurse at a factory, a job with horrible hours and even worse pay. Andy worked long shifts stacking watermelons and grapefruit in the produce section of a supermarket to compensate for his lack of a social life. Although Dad was happy with his new position as assistant to the synodical bishop, he was distressed that everyone else was miserable. After school started, I made a list of all the activities I was involved in—I played the flute in band, took private voice lessons, and was active in the church youth group—to see if this made me feel better. It didn't. Dad assured me that things *would* get better. "This too shall pass!" he exclaimed optimistically. I did not believe him. "Have some faith," he said, but I didn't. All I did was talk about Wyoming and how much I missed it, which only made everyone feel worse.

We lived on a street lined with two-story houses, just off a busy highway and near a Piggly Wiggly grocery store. That first summer, the three girls my age who lived on my street did not invite me to do things with them. I often heard them in the backyard of the house next door, giggling and laughing. So when the school year began and I was asked to join their car pool, I was initially grateful.

Christine was one of the girls who lived in the neighborhood; she also sang in the school choir with me. One day, after the first few weeks of school, she leaned over to me in the car. Her look was conspiratorial, and I stiffened with expectation. If she told me a secret, it meant we were friends, that things were changing and maybe Dad had been right. Christine whispered in my ear, "You know that nobody likes you, don't you?" I did. I had simply assumed. Her words only confirmed my fears. She smiled at me and then stared out the window as we drove the rest of the way to school.

Every morning became torture. Christine usually found a way to sit next to me, even when I tried to avoid it, knowing what was coming. As soon as the car pulled out of the driveway, she whispered in my ear, "What's your problem?" or, "You look weird." She always spoke softly and with such a smile on her face that the driver would never suspect anything from where he or she sat, chatting with the girl sitting up front, who was never me. Even my own father didn't catch on when it was his turn to drive the group to school, and I never told him. He would wink at me in the rearview mirror as if to say, "See? You're making friends." I always smiled back as if his look had told the truth about the situation; I was too ashamed to admit otherwise.

My reaction to Christine's cruelty was to do nothing. My days of fighting back against insults were over; I kept silent. I accepted her statements, while at the same time feeling absolutely determined to prove them wrong. By the time we reached school, I was practically trembling with terror and rage that I hid behind a shy smile. Although Christine was a part of the cool gang, Melissa was the leader. Although Christine wanted little to do with me, Melissa had taken a liking to me, and there was nothing Christine could do—at least within earshot of the other girls—without risking her own exile from the group.

Eventually I figured out that Christine was jealous of me. At first, I found this discovery unbelievable—who would possibly envy a girl with one leg?—even though it filled me with a sweet, secret pride. She had always been the star voice in the high school choir. Now that I had come along with my trained singing voice and increasing skill at hitting operatic high notes, I threatened her top-dog status. I knew this, and so did everybody else, although I would have gladly shared the spotlight with her. I would have traded any solo in any choral piece just to be her friend. Still, I knew jealousy well enough to hear it in her voice, but I knew it was nothing to fear. I was jealous of everyone; it was a sick, spinning feeling animated by a swelling desire: for that hair, for that body, for wholeness . . . The list went on, but I had never felt that I deserved it or had made myself perfect enough to be envied at all. I firmly believed that envy needed to be earned.

Christine and I both took voice lessons from Mrs. Barry, an energetic older woman who had once been a star soprano. Now her high notes were a bit weaker, her scales more strained. Shortly before a scheduled performance, she asked her students to perform arias from the small landing between the two floors of her home, which she referred to as "the balcony stage."

My particular talent was vocal diction. I could pronounce Italian, German, and Latin better than anyone and was always given the most complicated numbers. Although I habitually choked up at contests—Christine regularly received higher marks—when I was alone with Mrs. Barry, staring at the thinning hair on her head and her wildly gesturing hands, I could really let it rip.

I stood on the balcony stage that looked out over the tiny living room littered with records and sheet music, and I let my voice echo against those walls, moving out of my body. I listened to my voice and rejoiced in it. Vivaldi, Mozart, Puccini: I felt the notes leap and move into the air. I imagined those notes going through the wall, moving up all those streets that would never feel like home.

When nobody was around to give me a score or observe me with a critical eye, I expressed that aching quality of the arias moving through me. I felt the freedom of the voice singing the wretched body beautiful, hammering everything I felt was sad about my life into something whole. I saw the real me as that disembodied voice, soaring above my physical form, separate and free.

Even though I felt sick to my stomach every morning before school, I wouldn't admit to anyone that I was picked on. I knew Mom was unhappy in Nebraska; she'd left her dream job as a private school nurse so that Dad could take *his* dream job. I often came home to find her curled up on the couch eating handfuls of M&M's from a giant bag. She had always been a healthy, careful eater concerned with her figure. This sudden change in her behavior alarmed me, and I didn't want to be one more thing to worry her. Also, I assumed that if I could convince Christine to give me a chance, I could get her to like me. I could *make* it happen. In the meantime, I tried to imagine myself as a spirit, as just my voice, unattached from my body, floating above all the fear and anxiety I felt each morning when I stepped out of the house to go to school.

I looked down at my legs in the miniskirt and felt angry with myself. My outfit before this one had been perfectly fine. Good, even. Mom had helped me decide, as she always did, waiting patiently in the hallway as I emerged from my room wearing different combinations of jeans with mock-neck turtlenecks; long skirts with ruffled blouses; patterned leggings paired with baggy shirts in fuchsia or bright green.

We liked fashion, Mom and I, and we shopped together for the best deals that fell within the range of "our budget," which on my parents' salaries was not very flexible. Mom was prudent and generous. Resourceful. She started shopping for birthday presents a year ahead of time. She spent hours with me at the mall, taking willing part in my teenage preoccupation with clothes and brand names, calculating and recalculating so that I might have the items I wanted, so I'd look my best. I trusted her opinion about what was too trendy, what was flattering and classy. Each fall, I made a wish list and she helped me whittle it down by figuring out which pieces would go together and where the sales were. I learned that it was a challenge to look pulled together, to be pretty.

When we came home from a shopping trip, I tried on my new outfits to show Dad. He always said, "Nice, very nice," although he was arguably much more concerned with adding up the prices on the tags that he caught between his thumb and forefinger as I spun around than he was about whether or not I'd successfully duplicated the latest fashion magazine look for half the price.

"Wear something you'll feel good in, something you'll feel comfortable in. Feel like yourself," Mom had said earlier that day before Melissa picked me up. That's how the stretch pants and the shimmering blue top were eliminated. "It's all a little tight," she'd said. The green hat from a vintage store was out, too, because it was too small for my head and had to be secured with a large hat pin. "It's too much," she'd said. I agreed.

We finally decided on my stone-washed Guess jeans and a short-sleeved white top with lace around the neck and sleeves. Mom let me borrow a lipstick and checked to be sure I hadn't lined the insides of my eyes with black eyeliner, which was the fashion. "Gunk in your eyes looks tacky," she said, "and it's bad for your contacts." If I hadn't been so desperate to be liked, I might have wondered what I was doing with girls who caused such an agonizing debate over what to wear and how to look. At the time, I felt lucky to have friends at all. The memory of that long, lonely summer was fresh in my mind. I hated living in a town where people stared at me and my leg more intensely than they had anywhere else. How had Mom dealt with taking me out in public when I was little and in my brace? I wondered, but I never asked her. She and I rarely discussed how members of the community might view my disability. Instead, we were united in the goal of making my life and my appearance as normal as possible. Both of us wanted me to "pass" in able-bodied society; usually, we succeeded.

"You have to give people a chance," Mom had said that first summer.

"Nobody wants to hang out with me," I'd said. And that was true. My attempts to make friends had been unsuccessful. I felt bored and hot. At night, I did aerobic tapes in the back lawn, carefully recording estimated calories burned after each session. I read countless fashion magazines; I wrote long, sappy letters to my Wyoming friends and racked up the long-distance bill; I read voraciously and fantasized: about love, about the day when my life would make perfect sense, about a body that was different and perfect and the fabulous boyfriend it would enable me to attract.

Mom, pleased that I had found a task I seemed to enjoy and was committed to, often joined me in my exercise sessions.

"Anyway, I need to lose weight," she said as we started a series of squats. "This is something we can do together."

"Lose weight, you mean," I said as matter-of-factly as possible, testing out the idea with her.

"No." She laughed. "Not you, skinny-minny. We can exercise together. It can be a mother-daughter thing." We started doing jumping jacks. "The activity will be good for both of us. Maybe it will cheer you up."

"I doubt it," I replied.

To the songs of Prince, Rush, and Whitney Houston blasting out of my pink boom box, Mom and I jumped and stretched in the backyard, our movements hidden by the tall fence covered with thick vines and richly colored flowers. We sweated together, giggling and motivating each other.

Mom had no idea that I'd already started to keep food-intake journals. I discovered calorie counts in one of her nutrition books and calculated in secret, as if this information were as forbidden as pornography. She didn't know that I cut out pictures of models in magazines, tucked them into the sides of my mirror, disrobed, and then pointed out all the places where I came up short against an ideal of beauty that I simply did not question. I'd continue to do this for another ten years, berating myself as a motivational technique, sometimes on a daily basis. There was a gulf between my reflection and the faces and bodies staring up at me in prone poses of perfection. I was determined to bridge the gap between those two images; at the very least, I would give it my best shot. I resolved to keep this agenda a secret. That way, if I failed, I would have nobody to blame but myself. After I'd stood in front of the mirror and decided which parts of the body needed help or required work, I folded up the magazine clippings and tucked them into my underwear drawer.

But now, only one summer later, I was hanging out with the popular girls. I was wearing their *clothes,* which I realized was part of the problem. I was not like my new friends. As much as I mixed and matched my clothes to create options, there weren't that many artificial limb colors to choose from. My leg may have been "couture" in the sense that it was custom-fit for me, but it certainly wasn't fashionable. A prosthesis was not a teenage girl's accessory. I didn't get to try several of them on, consult a glossy catalog full of options, or choose which color looked best on me. As it was, the wood was at least two shades darker than my fair coloring.

My fingertips traced the metal on each side of the wooden socket. In the store, I saw Melissa and Ashley talking to a boy in front of a display of Doritos. I wanted to open the trunk and put on my jeans that were folded up in a plastic bag under the stolen beer. The girls exited the store and joined me in the car. I wished my skirt would stretch out a few inches or a few feet or, even better, that I would disappear.

My friends giggled and talked inside the car as it sped past the flat land. My upper body felt cold and clammy, even though the night was warm and the humid wind rushed through the open windows and made our flesh sticky. I was used to the all-season Wyoming wind that came in straight, strong gusts; wind like arrows that made precise contact with points on your body—cheeks, elbows, nose. The hot Nebraska wind got under your skin, making it sweat from the inside out. I had never been so sweaty before I moved to Nebraska.

I'd also never worn a miniskirt, not even a short skirt, not once in public, unless it was with thick tights, and that was in Wyoming—ages ago, it seemed, from this night when I was just sixteen and going to a kegger with two other underage girls.

Melissa told a joke, and I laughed when I heard Ashley laugh. I shifted on the seat, trying to figure out how I was going to get out of this one. Why hadn't I noticed how horrible my legs looked when I got dressed a few hours ago in Melissa's massive pink bedroom in her impressive house?

Maybe it was the house, I thought; maybe it was all those huge rooms and tall windows and gleaming counters and framed posters of places I'd never heard of: Belize, St. Martin's, Bonaire. That house was built to make you feel out of place, and maybe that's what had made me think it was a good idea to borrow this expensive skirt with the impressive brand. Spiegel. There had been a magazine with the same brand on Melissa's dining room table, sitting on top of a pile of thick bills. Her mother's eyes slid over the two of us as we walked in the door; her hands fluttered over the bills as she lit a cigarette.

"Hey, Mom," Melissa said quickly before bounding up the stairs. Her mother didn't say a word.

I said, "Thanks for having me over," and scampered up the stairs.

"Is your mom okay?" I asked, trying to adopt the calm and steady pastoral voice I often heard Dad use. She had looked sad and kind of deflated, as though her skin were loose enough to drop from her frame; then she'd be a half-smiling skeleton, smoking, with the breeze from the ceiling fan directing the smoke through the half-open window.

"She's fine," Melissa said, her voice slightly buried as she walked into her large walk-in closet. "She's sober, at least."

"Oh," I said, but since I'd never seen anybody drunk, I didn't have a clue how to clearly envision a sober person.

I didn't have a clue about a lot of things then: drunkenness, tanning methods, how to kiss boys, the benefits of "ultra *ultra* hold" hair spray, which Melissa told me was "rad" as she swept up my hair in a side ponytail, crimped it with a special iron, and then sprayed it until it was absolutely immobile and sticky enough to catch a bug. "This is going to be fun tonight," she said. "You'll see. We have tons of fun in the summer." I wanted to believe her.

I loved being alone with Melissa. She was glamorous in a sloppy, carefree way that I envied and admired. She seemed the epitome of all rich, beautiful girls who didn't plan their outfits but just picked up pieces from the floor and threw them on at the last minute, the look falling together naturally. Melissa didn't plan what to wear or what to buy. She just bought. It was an appealing idea. I wanted to be like her: unstudied yet confidently beautiful. Bright and gleaming.

Melissa's carefree elegance reminded me of the old fashion plates I used to play with at my grandmother's house in Illinois. The dolls were made of thin metal; they had magnetic shirts, trousers, scarves, skirts, shoes, and even hats that clung to their bodies. Once you decided on an outfit, the clothes snapped into place, with everything perfectly aligned. Mixing and matching was easy and effortless. Beauty was guaranteed.

A half-eaten box of chocolate-covered Oreos was spilled out on Melissa's Ralph Lauren comforter. She stuffed one into her mouth and began rooting around again in her immense closet, which was stuffed with piles of shoes and racks of expensive-looking clothes. "I'll let you borrow something," she said, tossing out an empty shoebox and some hangers.

I looked enviously at Melissa's long legs poking out from beneath her blue satin short robe: the two perfectly matched, well-designed calves; the soft impression at the back of each knee; the even, brown tan. I imagined her sitting on the bed, talking away on the phone with her lean legs stretched out in front of her, dialing the numbers with her toes. All of that perfectly constructed flesh taken for granted. And here I stood with my wooden leg and chubby white thigh. Melissa was the girl I aspired to be; the girl who could reach into that open box of cookies and eat one after the other while twirling the cord around her fingers and talking to her boyfriend. And she would not gain one pound because she was blessed with a rich family, a dark tan, a whole, beautiful body, and, of course, a high metabolism. She pinned up her hair in an arranged mess and looked naturally beautiful without a stitch of makeup.

I felt completely fabricated next to Melissa. Her designer skirts arrived in plastic and smelled like new fabric, while my prosthetic feet arrived in bubble wrap and smelled inexplicably like mushrooms. I coveted her possessions, her body, her life.

I envied her because there were so many things I had to assemble in the morning in order to leave the house. There was the cloth sock that rolled onto my stump before it fit into the artificial socket; there was the thick support underwear I wore to avoid sores near my crotch and cuts into my hip if the waist strap rubbed too hard. I buckled the strap below and to the left of my belly button and then adjusted the leg—twist left, twist right—before pulling on my pants or jeans. I used a shoehorn to put on my shoes. I slipped in my contacts and squeezed my eyes shut until the stinging stopped. I applied makeup because I didn't like my face. I was never seen in public without lipstick on. I was absolutely fanatical about brushing my hair, making it shine. I had my rituals.

So when Melissa offered to let me wear a new and expensive black knit miniskirt that was still wrapped in its catalog plastic, I felt seduced by what I saw as her wonderful, easy way of living. She was like a living fashion plate—everything she threw together looked perfect and wonderful. I, too, wanted to rip a new identity from a package and clothe myself effortlessly in it. I slipped on the skirt and stood in front of her full-length mirror.

"It looks nice," she said. "Do you like it?"

"Do you?" I asked, and she nodded.

"You have such a tiny waist," she said.

We'd skipped out of the house, jumped in the car, and headed out. Everything had been fine until the girls piled out of the car at the Gas N' Shop, leaving me alone with my bare legs.

Guns N' Roses' *Appetite for Destruction* album was in the tape deck, and as we approached our destination, Melissa and Ashley sang along at top volume and I joined them halfheartedly, taking frequent long, slow sips from the Slurpee. I squeezed the flesh around the knee of my right leg and then pressed it against the cold plastic cup. *I'm fat,* I told myself, *and strangely proportioned. My thigh is too big, and my calf is not muscular enough.* I felt so helpless in my difference that I was utterly disgusted by it. *You're pathetic,* I told myself. If I had only one leg, the least I could do was make it perfect. How hard could that be? I had trained as a skier and developed strong, lean muscles. I had gotten lazy; if I wanted to fit in, I needed to try harder. If I couldn't have two real legs, I would alter the rest of my body to suit my desires. *Back to the calorie books first thing tomorrow,* I thought. Back to doing my homework days ahead of time. Back to the long workouts that left me exhausted. Now what to do about the problem in this moment? *What to do about the leg?*

As we pulled off the interstate, the moon reflected off the tall cornstalks waving in the humid air, waiting to be harvested. The air smelled of burning flesh and singed hair, thanks to the new slaughterhouse that had been built on the outskirts of town the year before.

"Gross. *Peeee-ewwww,*" Melissa tittered, and the three of us held our noses until the smell faded.

We passed a carload of boys at a stop sign, and Melissa waved and giggled. We were sixteen years old and in a car on our own. Endless fun seemed possible just by driving on a flat stretch of highway to go sit in the dirt around a fire in a clearing near a cornfield. But it was not fun for me; I could not imagine that it would ever be fun.

I had looked in the mirror earlier that evening and seen what I wanted to see, as if borrowed clothes could transform me. I saw the two legs I had always imagined myself worthy of—and in my mind, it was certainly a question of worth—not the fake, creaky one I pulled on each morning. I saw the body I would have chosen for myself had it been possible for me to choose. As if a real flesh-and-blood leg could snap on as quickly and easily as an item of magnetic clothing and be changed at will. I felt sure I was about to be exposed for who and what I was, although I had no words at that moment to explain what this meant to me. What I knew for sure was that I felt entirely alone in this car with my new friends, headed for a crowd of yet more people.

My stomach felt spiked with acid. I hoped it would take us our whole lives to get to that party, but we were passing quickly through town, past trailer homes that looked as though they were sinking into the soggy ground. I felt sweat on my upper lip and neck.

"Ryan's going to be there," Melissa said. I blushed. Ryan had the locker next to mine. He had blue eyes and a crooked smile. I guess it was a crush, but I had never said two words to him. Whenever I saw him, I walked in the opposite direction. Sometimes I ran.

Melissa looked at me in the rearview mirror with her round, doll-like eyes. On my first day of high school, a day I had dreaded after the long, miserable, and friendless eighth-grade year, she had asked me if I wanted to play tennis with her after school. When I told her why I couldn't play, she said she thought my leg was really "neat-o" and "cool." Soon every kid at school knew what Melissa thought, and because she was popular and liked me, I was accepted. It had been a great relief, but now I wondered what I had gotten myself into.

These friends—Melissa and Ashley and others—asked mostly simple cause-and-effect questions: When did I lose my leg? Was it cancer? Did it hurt when it was cut off? Dressed in my pajamas and sitting on the floor, surrounded by empty pizza boxes and cans of soda, I told my story to their scrubbed faces, to the mound of warm, skinny bodies dressed in flannel and satin and piled up like puppies on the bed. I liked telling my story—I'd throw in a few jokes or embellish a few parts and feel delighted with the brief moments of concentrated attention. Laughter was the currency I accepted for the telling of my story. Make someone laugh about your faults, I had learned, and they almost always accepted you.

None of the girls wanted to hear about the logistics of prosthetics: where they were made, who made them, the pain of walking with an outdated wooden limb. They didn't want to hear the macabre facts of my life. And I did not want to tell them.

Another song came on: "Sweet Child O' Mine." The girls sang as the car sped past tall, skinny trees and rows of raggedy cornstalks.

This time I sang along, too, but inside I panicked. Everything but the leg felt borrowed. I looked out at the Nebraska sky—so pressed down and changeless, so unlike the sky in Wyoming that opened up like a big dome, with clouds at one end of the horizon and blue sky at the other. I knew I'd never be able to compete in the strange, secret world I was about to enter with these girls. I would never be able to play by the same rules. Maybe I would always be running from boys instead of sauntering up to them with naïve confidence tinged with nervousness as my friends did. I knew, as we sped through the abandoned gas stations and warehouses on the edges of town, that someday someone was going to want to see this leg, with a miniskirt, without any skirt, with the leg *off*. I felt a horrible, hollow feeling deep in my chest. It was as if someone had set a bell in the middle of my stomach and started ringing it. The ringing would never stop. The warm air rushed in through the open windows, and the whole car reverberated with my friends' singing voices, the notes spinning out into the hot night.

Melissa revved the engine and turned onto a gravel road that led to a clearing. She put her hand out the window and pretended to lasso the air to the tune of Ashley's hollers and shouts and Axel Rose's final, glorious guitar riff.

I thought again about my jeans in the backseat. They were my out. I watched Ashley's tanned, smooth, stick-thin legs move as she bounced in her seat. We were almost there, and I would be forced to get out of this car. I needed those jeans. Now.

There was a pile of sweaters in the backseat in the unlikely event that we got cold later on. Ashley had winked at me as we were putting the sweaters in the car. "Really, they're just so we have something to sit on when we make out with boys," she said. Over my legs I stretched the sweater that matched this skirt; it was also Melissa's, also from Spiegel, but it was softer than any sweater I had ever owned. "Cashmere," she'd said. Although it made me feel even more uncomfortably warm, the sweater felt unbelievably soft on my leg; the wonderful fabric moved quickly over the slick surface of my prosthesis.

Thick columns of smoke were visible in the distance. The bonfire at last! Melissa and Ashley squealed in their blissed-out way as we pulled onto a gravel road. The cornstalks crinkled like rustling paper. I heard snippets of laughter and words.

"There better be so much beer left in that fucking keg," Melissa said. "I only took that Schlitz so I wouldn't come here empty fucking handed."

"Fucking right," Ashley said. "Aren't you *excited,* Em?" she asked, reaching over the backseat to squeeze the top of my arm. She smelled like Exclamation perfume.

"Yeah," I said, my stomach roiling. "Uh-huh."

We took another right down a small dirt road, and there was the bonfire: a tall tower of sticks leaning into one another and burning.

People's shadows jumped in the intermittent flames of the fire, making their bodies look short one moment and tall the next. With the flames spitting and leaping behind them, their shapes changed rapidly and strangely. Their movements were animated and precise, almost tender in the flickering light, like the delicate movements of shadow puppets. Sometimes the figures looked headless or armless, and that's how I did what I did next. I didn't even have to try very hard. I imagined myself suddenly legless, forced to hop into that mass of whole bodies with the scarred-up end of the left leg, stinking and red from being shoved inside the socket all day during the heat of summer. Everyone would stare. Everyone would see. Everyone would know the horrible truth about me, about my body, because what was a person without the body? Even more important, what was a *girl* without her body? With the image of my legless self in my mind, exposed to everyone, including these girls—my only friends—I moved the sweater off my legs and threw up in my lap.

"*Oh,* my God!" Ashley screamed, turning around to look at me. "Gross *out*!"

Just when I thought I had ruined everything, Melissa took a quick turn and stopped the car near a row of corn. "Shut *up,* Ashley!" she said. "Not another word."

Openmouthed, Ashley looked at Melissa. Melissa stared at her. Ashley shut her mouth, stepped out of the car, and slid into the backseat with me. She looked up at Melissa and then scooped up the puke with Melissa's expensive sweater. I felt as though I had won some unnamed battle, that this round in the invisible fight was mine. Although it had seemed impossible, I had found a way to hide.

"Don't worry, Emmm," Melissa said, stretching those last sounds into both a purr and a warning for Ashley, who patted my arm sheepishly, her eyes on Melissa.

"Sorry," Ashley whispered. "Sorry I had a cow and freaked out."

"It's okay," I said, holding the soiled sweater in my lap—it was a warm, stinking ball.

"The jeans!" Melissa said, as if it had just occurred to her. I nodded. "Get them, Ashley," Melissa ordered, and then looked over her shoulder. "Don't worry," she said. "All clear."

Ashley quickly got out of the car, opened the trunk, grabbed the plastic bag, and handed me the jeans. Melissa sat beside me and rubbed my back. I thought I might start to cry—not with embarrassment, as they all assumed, but with relief. No way would I be forced to enter a party with the school's most popular girls while wearing a skirt covered in barf. Ashley stood watch facing the bonfire in case anyone strayed over and tried to see what was going on. I pulled the jeans on under the skirt and then carefully wiggled the soiled skirt over my legs and handed it to Melissa.

"Sorry about your clothes," I said, and I was, but I was also strangely, deliciously happy. "I'll wash them or replace them."

"Don't worry about it," she said. She put the sweater and the skirt in the bag and tossed it far into the field. "Now I know what barf bag really means." She laughed. "Plus," she said, "I have another sweater and skirt just like it. Duplicate Christmas presents."

I didn't know if she was lying or not, but at that moment I felt a sudden surge of hope mix with the hot air and the smell of dried corn and the stink of my blue Slurpee vomit. Maybe these girls really were my friends—maybe someday I could tell them the truth about the leg, talk about it with them. Just as quickly, I realized that this would never be possible. I would never be able to do it.

"Thanks," I said, getting out of the car.

Melissa fluffed my ponytail with her fingers. "C'mon," she said. "Let's go." We all left our Slurpee cups on the floor of the car, per Melissa's instructions. "We go in with only the Schlitz," she explained. "And hopefully we will not be forced to drink it."

Ashley handed me a stick of gum. "Good thing I have this, cutie," she said, and squeezed my arm, steering me toward the bonfire.

At the party, I sat in one place the whole time, holding a plastic cup full of beer that I pretended to drink; every once in a while I forced down a few small sips. I saw my first drunk person, stumbling as he walked, spitting into the fire. I met my first college fraternity guys, all of whom wore the same uniform: a Nebraska Cornhuskers ball cap, a Cornhuskers T-shirt, denim cutoff shorts, and flip-flops. Those boys looked huge and monstrous to me. They drank and drank without stopping; I'd never seen anything like it. With all the smoke from the campfire and the wet dirt kicked up by dancing, drunken feet, the slight odor of vomit coming from my leg was just a low smell lurking beneath the air's surface. I was probably the only one who noticed.

Melissa drank until she began slurring her words. Ashley flirted with Jonas, the most popular guy in our grade, crossing and uncrossing her legs as they sat together on the ground. I didn't talk to many people; I just smiled a lot and sipped the horrible keg beer. Ryan did bring a date, but I didn't care. I was happy looking normal in my jeans and sitting in the same spot on the ground, just watching the action from a distance. With the leg mercifully hidden, I was protected.

Later that night, Ashley drove us home. "Don't worry," she said. "I only had a few." Melissa was passed out in the backseat and needed to sleep some of it off, she said, before she walked through her front door for eleven o'clock curfew. "See ya," Ashley said as she dropped me off. She sped away before I was inside the house.

I opened the door quietly and went upstairs. My throat felt chalky from the sugary Slurpee and the "accident" in the car. I knew the fact that I had just made myself sick with thoughts about my own body was linked to cute boys and hiding or running from them, although the connection was unclear and would be for some time. I did know that I would never allow anyone to see my artificial leg up close or free of my body, not ever. I resolved that nobody—especially a boy—would see my real body, even if it meant wearing jeans during the summer and not wearing the latest fashions and never going on a date. I wasn't going to tell stories about the leg anymore or talk about it one bit.

I resolved—as I had so many times before—to be as normal as possible, only this time the resolution felt more desperate and urgent. I would go on a real diet, the punishing kind that made you sick with hunger. Mom had been on several of those restrictive plans before; I had a vivid memory of her pulling out a plastic bag filled with only five thin crackers and eating them slowly and carefully, one at a time, as she drove through the Dairy Queen drive-through window to get me a chocolate sundae. I would do that if I had to. I would work harder; nobody would be able to match my control, my discipline, my drive. If there was going to be pain in my life, I would be the one to inflict it.

I promised myself that I would make the one leg I had perfect; I would contain my body and control it. I would punish it for not being the way I desperately wanted it to be. I felt strangely empowered. If Schmidt, Larry, or Vince couldn't do it with prosthetics; if God—my first Creator—had refused to do it in response to my prayers, then I would remake the body myself. I would have vigilance over this process and make myself new. I knew such control and self-denial would be challenging, but in all my youthful ambition and narcissism, I believed there would be a payoff, eventually, if I gave myself over in full to what I saw as this necessary task. In joining the trend of girls' obsessions with their bodies and adopting pathologies around food, I was in fact making myself more normal than I'd ever been before.

I tiptoed into my parents' bedroom to announce that I was home safely. Mom shifted under the quilt.

"How was it?" she asked groggily.

"Fun," I lied. She nodded, looked at the clock on her nightstand, which read 11:15, and smiled at me before closing her eyes again. Dad was a loudly snoring mound beside her.

I changed into my pajamas, went to the bathroom, and wiped down the leg with a few drops of Mom's lemon-scented body splash, which masked most of the vomit smell. I dabbed some of the splash on the hinges because they felt sticky and smelled like wet, rusted metal. I gave the entire leg a final once-over with silky Avon bath powder.

I felt both protective and resentful of my leg that night. I felt that we had weathered some trial together, and through that experience it had become more than just an object, more than an expensive, human-made artificial device designed to make me appear whole. But even if my disability experience made me strong, as my parents told me; and courageous, as so many had claimed; and special, as the March of Dimes had led me to believe, how could I ever truly accept that it wouldn't be better to have a naturally whole, normal body and simply avoid all of this?

I propped the leg against my vanity table and crawled into bed. A bright moon hung in the window. The houses in the neighborhood were quiet, boxy shadows with a few windows full of light. A dog barked twice and then was quiet. In the distance, tires squealed around some unseen corner.

I felt restless as I lay there, conscious of wanting the leg back, even as I longed for it to disappear and play no more part in my life. It looked exposed, naked, and separated from me, just as I felt vulnerable without it, even in the privacy of my own room.

My reflection over the top of the leg looked old, and finally I rolled over to face the wall. For weeks, when I looked in the mirror I saw myself in that hot Nebraska field, limping along at the edges of a party. I saw myself holding a cup full of beer, wearing jeans, and smelling vaguely of my own vomit. That girl was trying to tell me something, but whatever she had to say, I didn't want to hear it.

Chapter Ten

GUARDIAN

"Emma, hand it here." Liz, my first-year roommate at St. Olaf College, stood near my loft bed, and I placed my artificial leg in her outstretched arms. Gently, she lowered it to the floor and leaned it against my desk. She tucked the waist strap into the socket. "There," she said, hoisting herself up into her bed on the other side of the room. "Sometimes I just can't stand to watch you throw it around."

I had developed a system for sleeping in the loft. Once I had climbed the ladder, I removed my leg and dangled it over the side of the bed by its waist strap, as if I were slowly lowering a fishing line into the water. I got it as close to the floor as possible before dropping it the rest of the way. The knee automatically buckled, and the leg crashed to the floor. Sometimes it hit the desk underneath the loft with a crack and a thump.

I felt self-conscious just before I did this for the first time, so lying in my bed, I told Liz a story that had always made people laugh. I hoped that humor would mitigate any nervousness she might experience as a fake leg careened off the side of her roommate's bed.

The story was this: When I was a junior in high school, I ran for thespian state board, the student governing body that planned events for high school theater clubs across Nebraska. Each candidate had to give a speech before the convention voted. My friend Nancy's boyfriend, Gabe, walked out with me onstage in front of the assembled group. We held hands. I wore a long black cotton skirt, a tie-dyed tube top, three or four tarnished crosses from a pawnshop around my neck, and green Converse sneakers. I said, "I'd give my left leg to be on the thespian board." With shaking hands, I unbuckled the waist strap through the skirt's thin fabric and let the prosthesis tumble to the ground. Gabe picked me up in his arms and whisked me off the stage as Nancy ran out to retrieve the leg, hoisting it up like a torch as she ran backstage. The crowd roared their approval, and I won the election.

But Liz didn't laugh. Instead, she sat up on her elbows and looked at me. "Man, that story makes me a little sad," she said.

"Why?" I asked, slightly annoyed. "It's funny."

"Yeah, but I don't know, the leg's a part of you. I like it."

"It's not exactly its own person," I said. *What do you know about it, anyway?* I thought. *You don't have to wear it.*

"Yeah, but it's part of *you*, and *you're* a person." She flopped down on her bed. "And you're *my* roommate," she said. "*And . . .*"

"And?" I asked, smiling now.

"And you're way too hard on yourself."

I didn't need to make Liz laugh in order for her to accept me—she already did.

I *was* hard on myself. Liz and I were kindred spirits from the start: We took college seriously; we didn't hate our parents; we were virgins; and neither of us had ever been drunk before we were drunk together, although Liz, like me, had had plenty of opportunities at her own high school keggers in small-town Wisconsin. We had nicknames for each other—"Emma" and "Lizzy"—and our conversations and interactions were tender, intimate, and supportive. We ate every meal together, wrote letters to each other over school breaks, and when we both got sick that first semester, we ate soup and saltines and reassured each other that missing a few classes would not precipitate a steady decline into flunking out of school. Liz kept me sane those first years in college; without her, I would have drowned myself under my own pressures to be perfect. She provided levity as well as a levelheaded analysis to situations that I reacted to with raw, unguarded emotions.

Our floor had group showers, and this caused me great anxiety. Worried that I might fall and hurt myself by hopping around on a wet floor, Mom had always insisted that I take baths. "What if you fall in the shower?" she asked. "Then what?" I had started taking showers in high school to spite her, to scare her, and when I arrived at St. Olaf, I was glad I had because there was no other option. Mom's words stayed with me, though. What if I fell and broke my neck in a group shower while a freshman in college?

I took spit baths late at night in the bathroom sinks for the first few days, but it was clearly not a good system. "I'm scared of the showers," I admitted to Liz as we lay in the dark in our bunks, listening to Bach on the stereo. She immediately suggested that we shower together. The next morning, wearing my waterproof shower shoes, I walked to one of the wall spigots, took off the leg, and handed it to Liz; silently, she leaned it against the wall where we hung our robes, ensuring that it would not get wet. Only after the leg was out of sight, Liz had returned, and we had turned on the shower taps did we begin to talk, as if the ritual of disassembly required respectful silence. She got out first, toweled off, and brought my leg to me just as my cousins had done years ago at the public pool. Our new ritual. Pretty soon, others were volunteering for this job. So with the women on my floor I felt—and was—safe.

The rest of campus felt wholly unsafe—a hormonal miasma of insecurity and competition. The coed, nonalcoholic "mixers" Liz and I attended were especially nerve-racking, as it was appearance in these circumstances that seemed to matter most, and I needed to prove that I was desirable; I had convinced myself that success in life hinged entirely on this fact. My only future vision for happiness involved marriage and children. I felt this was what was expected of me, and it was what I expected of myself as well.

Although I admitted this to nobody, I had come to college intent on finding a husband. I thought that by clinging to traditional values regarding relationships, I could be more confident of my acceptance into "normal" society. What was a disabled woman on her own going to do without someone to care for her? I had an image of a horrible future in which I was a crippled old woman, alone, being taunted by boys as I limped my way to the supermarket pulling a plaid grocery cart. Someone else would need to make me acceptable by wanting me and thus providing the proof that I could be desired, even in my deformed state.

As Liz and I were walking back to our room after these parties, which I spent hours trussing up for, I'd routinely ask her, "Do you think I was as pretty as all those other girls?"

"Yep," she replied. "You're you, right? Seriously, you're making me nuts."

"Yeah, you're right," I said. "Sorry. I'm sorry to be annoying." But I needed her reassurance.

"So, you would notice me if you were a guy, right?" I pressed.

"You're beautiful and wonderful," she said, knowing what I wanted to hear, but I detected the increased annoyance in her voice and stopped pestering her, at least for now. "Plus," she said, "none of those guys seemed that interesting."

"You're so right," I said, although I hadn't even noticed. I never thought I'd be in a position to choose. What mattered was that they were boys and that one of them might choose me.

While I waited to find my fairy-tale suitor, the rest of my energy in college went toward being as perfect as possible, just as it had in high school. Overachievement was the method by which I organized my life. I carefully recorded everything I ate (I had memorized calorie counts long ago) and worked out daily and excessively on the school's lone StairMaster that was planted in the entrance hall of the cavernous gymnasium. I read every page that was assigned to me and wrote my papers weeks ahead of time in order to revise them at least three times by hand before typing them up in the computer lab.

While many of my friends slept in on the weekends, I was usually in a study room by eight A.M., actually studying. I did not take naps. I did not skip class or ask for extensions on projects or papers. I watched television on Saturday nights for exactly one hour, making exceptions only for events like Bill Clinton's election and Tonya Harding's unsuccessful medal bid at the Olympics. My days were carefully constructed, as if deviating from these scripted activities one bit would mean total failure in all other areas. I went to bed most nights at ten o'clock, partly out of exhaustion and partly out of concern that if I stayed up any later, I would get hungry and start snacking.

Between my junior and senior years in high school, I dropped fifteen pounds in less than three weeks, going from 120 to 105, then 105 to 100 over the next few months, and then dipping even lower to 98 pounds by graduation; at 5' 7", I was disastrously underweight. When a doctor commented on my rapid weight loss at my yearly exam, I said, "Well, you know what they say about a hollow leg, only this time it's true." He found this so funny that he repeated my joke to the nurses as I left the office, my stomach rumbling.

My typical schedule, food included, at the age of seventeen: Wake up: one hundred sit-ups. Breakfast: dry toast and Diet Pepsi. History, PE, study hall, trigonometry. Lunch: salad with no dressing; one piece of fruit. English, theater, yearbook, free period in which I drove home and slept for an hour. Aerobics. Three hundred jumping jacks. Two hundred sit-ups. Dinner: one piece of broiled, skinless chicken. Homework. Bed. Meticulously I recorded the events of each day, calorie count first.

I have never received as many compliments about my appearance as I did when I stopped menstruating and became monstrously thin. "You look great!" "Look at your cheekbones!" "How did your ass get so small?" And this, the best one: "You have the perfect body." These testaments to what I saw as my superiority in willpower and self-denial were narcotic and strangely sustaining when little else in my life was: not academics, which were not challenging at all; not music, which I had once loved; not religion, which had once given me comfort.

I felt unencumbered, as if I were floating through life like a thin-skinned, delicate doll. I did the classic anorexic ritual of "body checks": compulsively wrapping my fingers around my wrist to be sure I hadn't gained weight; circling my stump with my hands; tugging at the waistband of my jeans to be sure they were as loose as they had been the day before. I took approximately twenty minutes to eat one tortilla chip. I proudly bore a new hole in my leg's waist strap with a screwdriver to accommodate my weight loss. I had reduced my life to a sequence of simple, specific needs that rotated around bird-size amounts of food and copious amounts of exercise. Weirdly, the expansion I felt as a skier was not dissimilar to the feeling I experienced while starving myself: In both situations, I felt sleek, compact, contained, and, strangest of all—at least in the second scenario, when I was barely able to drag myself through the day—able.

Mom took me to several doctors, but I was always just above the weight limit to be classified as anorexic or hospitalized. "She's very thin," they'd tell her, "but she's not anorexic."

"I told you," I'd say to Mom after these appointments. "I look good like this."

"No, you don't," she said, "and I have my eye on you, young lady."

So did Dad. "Write down the three square meals you ate today," he said every night after dinner, and I wrote out a list of lies, making up a healthy lunch and not mentioning that I'd tossed the heavily buttered toast he'd made me for breakfast in the trash.

He and Mom looked over what I'd written. "Good," Dad said. "Remember: three squares." Without an official diagnosis, there was little my parents could do. Mom broiled my measly, fat-free chicken breasts because I would eat them, although I ignored most starches and all desserts. Sometimes I splurged with a vegetable like summer squash or creamed corn that wasn't in my self-designed "program."

In college, as I tried to maintain an abstemious lifestyle, I placed some parts of the body under constant scrutiny—examining every dimple of fat on my right thigh and every small bit of flab under my impossibly skinny arms—but neglected the artificial leg or what was within it. When I showered or slipped into my prosthesis, I kept my eyes elsewhere; once the stump was freed for the night, it went straight under the covers. I couldn't control the fact of one leg, but when I refused to give it what it needed, my body responded the way any teenage girl's would: It got smaller, it stopped bleeding. In short, it obeyed me. I began to question this strategy of living only after I met Samantha, another disabled woman my age, also born with PFFD, whom I met through Lutheran church connections.

Samantha was involved in competitive disabled sports. She had half a dozen legs—one with a suction socket that appeared to be what Mom and I had once referred to as "the Texas leg"—and many others that looked strange and wonderful to me. I was amazed by her "gear," as she called it, and remembered the way I had mythologized the Texas leg, as if possessing it would change my life. I remembered pressuring Vince and challenging him when the leg didn't fit right. Now here it was—strap-free and leaning against the wall in my new friend's closet.

Samantha was beautiful and smart; she could run and windsurf and swim; she wore high heels using a special foot that adjusted to the shoe's heel height; she was from New York City, a place I had dreamed of going but had never been; her "walking" leg was not wooden but soft and flesh colored. Finally, none of her legs used the detestable waist strap that had plagued me for years and given me rashes, sores, and other headaches; it frayed and smelled bad and created weird bumps in my butt and hips when I walked. Next to Samantha, in my clunky wooden limb, I felt like a dilapidated robot.

Samantha's legs were built on advanced technology, not on outdated models that had been developed for war veterans decades before. She moved well and with confidence and was not afraid to wear shorts or skirts. "Who cares if people stare?" she said. I felt elated whenever I spent time with her; I was encouraged to know that there were other ways of living. Her concerns were not about being thin or "perfect." Instead, she wanted to be strong, sexy, and athletic. My new friend was practically a celebrity in my eyes.

I visited Samantha in New York City, and we went to parties on Long Island and to nightclubs in Manhattan. At her house, we hopped around without our fake legs and slipped them off while we watched videos—with her, it was no big deal. We smoked pot and talked about sex, although I fastidiously avoided saying the word out loud.

"Do you take off the leg?" I asked. "Like, during it?"

"Of course," she said. "Absolutely. It's just so much better without the leg on. You have no idea."

I certainly didn't. "Really?" I pressed. "You take the leg off in front of him? He sees you take it off?"

She shook her head. "No, usually while he was in the shower or in the other room, but I have had sex *in* the shower, and that's great."

Sex in the shower; sex with more than one man; sex with *any* man: It all seemed unimaginable to me.

Although I never admitted to Samantha how limited my sexual experience actually was, during these trips I had elaborate fantasies about how my "first time" would feel. But no matter how much I tried to keep them going, they always resolutely stopped at the waist. A man kisses you, puts his tongue in your mouth. Okay. I could get on board with that. A man slowly removes your shirt, removes your bra, touches your breasts, and caresses your neck and stomach. That was all fine, too. But just before those imagined hands touched the small buckle to the left of my belly button that belonged to the waist strap that attached the leg to my body, the fantasy dissipated quickly and was replaced by shame.

Samantha had taken one look at my leg and said, "No way! You *must* get something better! First, we'll get you a decent-looking one and then we can worry about sports legs for running and stuff. Plus, you've got to get a foot for heels, too." *Sports legs. High heels.* I nodded, stunned.

She wrote down precisely what kind of leg I should ask for, and I took this slip of paper to Dr. Elliot. Finally I had the specifics, and from a young, reliable, and active female source who was also a trusted and valued friend.

"This is what I want," I said, showing Dr. Elliot Samantha's instructions. "This. I need a man who can make this." My pulse raced. *Please,* I thought. *Please.*

"Okay, peanut," he said. "We can do that." I burst into tears. Finally, after years of hoping, it seemed that transformation would be that simple. The secret, festering hope I'd harbored that my life could change dramatically had not been unfounded after all.

Dr. Elliot referred me to Nick, a new prosthetist in Denver. He had worked with elite disabled athletes and had even been to the 1988 Paralympics in Seoul. I thought of the image I'd adored as a child: the prosthetist who runs out on the track to fix a part or a foot. Nick was this dream come to life. He was professional, knowledgeable, intelligent, and respectful. He understood and had access to all of the latest prosthetic technology and a willingness to convince insurance companies to pay for the specialized, high-priced equipment that is a reality of custom-fit prosthetics. He allowed patients to pay what they could each month without accruing interest on the outstanding balance. My parents' insurance company agreed to pay for 80 percent of the leg's cost, and Mom and Dad promised to come up with the rest.

At Nick's, the waiting room was clean and climate controlled; recent magazines were stacked in neat piles on glass tables. The receptionists were friendly and helpful. All the surfaces were white, and the walls were decorated with posters of amputees skiing, running, or climbing mountains. Waiting on the leather couches were bright-faced young people and even toddlers, as well as older men and women.

I was ready to ditch my wooden leg as quickly as possible. I wanted a state-of-the art prosthesis and an updated body that was beautiful and mobile and, of course, as *normal* as it could be. Yes, I admired Samantha's athleticism, but what I really wanted was to be pretty and real looking enough in order to pass more effectively. This seemed easier than accepting the body the way it was.

"I'll pot plants in the old legs or make them lamps," I joked with Dad as we were driving to Colorado Springs for my first fitting.

Skeptical, he replied, "Don't ditch all of them yet." I ignored him.

During my first fitting with Nick, he gently pressed where thigh and pelvis meet, making sure the lip of the prosthesis fell in the right spot. He touched lightly and only where he needed to, always careful not to touch *there*. It made me feel honored, his careful attention to how everything fit together, the way he knew how my body worked, the way he saw me: as capable and active.

"What kind of leg would you like?" It was the first time a prosthetist had ever asked me this.

I told Nick what I wanted, just to feel this new language moving in my mouth: a Flex-Foot with a cosmetic toe shell, a polycentric four-bar hydraulic knee, new silicone suspension sockets. He nodded, scribbled in a notebook, and presented me with other options I had not even considered. I walked out of the office with everything I'd asked for.

That year—1993, when I was nineteen—I was finally fitted with a prosthetic limb that featured a suction socket and a hydraulic knee unit. The exterior was made of a soft, pliable material and covered with a latex spray that matched my skin tone more closely than any wooden leg had ever done. My Flex-Foot was a carbon-fiber, energy-storing foot that allowed ease and power of movement. Later, Nick made me a leg for running and another with a nine-bar hydraulic unit—the rock-solid knee locked out and was perfect for activities like kickboxing.

The leg not only felt better, it looked better, too. My thighs were the same circumference instead of the artificial leg being much thinner than the real one. It did not have an unnatural, greasy shine that was impossible to mask, even in tights, but was instead covered with flesh-colored cosmetic socks. The things I had always done—walk, run, dance—became so much easier. My body felt literally new. Transformed at last, I put my wooden leg in the closet. I felt reborn.

The fall of my sophomore year, I walked onto campus bursting with confidence and prepared to experience a corresponding renaissance in my love life. With this new leg, I believed I could compete in the dating game just like everybody else. I couldn't wait.

I became a regular at parties at Carleton College—a neighboring "wet" campus where alcohol was freely allowed and abundant—and often went on my own. At one party I was standing around, idly watching the television, trying to see if I was catching anybody's eye. I saw a man with dark hair lean in to talk to his blond friend; they were both wearing jeans and sweaters and holding cans of Pabst Blue Ribbon. They looked at me, and I quickly looked away, becoming suddenly fascinated by the television program. Out of the corner of my eye, I saw the dark-haired guy approaching me, but I pretended not to notice.

"Hey," he said.

"Oh," I said, feigning surprise. "Hey."

"What's up?" he asked.

"Not much," I replied, my heart beating fast. We introduced ourselves and chatted about classes, about how nice the fall in Minnesota was, about what a great party this was. I was so nervous, I forgot his name seconds after he told me. Eventually we sat beside each other on the couch. When I crossed my legs, he asked, "Hey, why are you wearing hose on just one foot?" I took a quick sip of my sloe-gin fizz.

"Oh," I said. "My leg is artificial, that's why." I felt comfortable saying this, partly because I was already quite drunk and partly because it was clear that this man thought I was attractive. A male friend had once told me: "I know if I want to sleep with a woman within the first five seconds of meeting her." I felt that I had cleared the first hurdle, the one I had rarely gotten past in situations like these.

"That's not funny," he said, and gave me a dark look.

Flabbergasted, I laughed. "Really, it's true," I said.

"Seriously, it's really not funny. What the hell?"

I stared at him and realized that he truly did not believe me. What, he wanted proof? A jolt of anger made me pull up the left leg of my jeans, all the way to the gap between the socket and the shank that held the hydraulic, mechanical knee.

My would-be suitor lunged back. "Oh, shit, sorry," he said. I looked up and saw that several people were staring at us. They quickly looked away.

"Uh, I'll be right back," he said. "Need another drink?" I shook my head no, and as soon as he was out of sight, I stood up and stepped through the chatting crowd. I knew he would not be returning, and even if he did—where would we go from here? As I was about to walk down the stairs and out the door, I heard a conversation to my left in the hallway that led to the bathroom.

"I've got a bone to pick with you," said the man I'd been sitting with.

"What, dude? I'm totally wasted. What are you talking about?" I stood motionless at the top of the stairs.

"About that girl. She's got a wooden leg, man. What the hell? I thought you said you'd seen her before."

I didn't wait to hear any more. I walked home quickly through the sharp, fragrant air of a Minnesota fall.

"Hey, what's wrong?" Liz asked the next morning. She'd been out when I got in, watching movies in a friend's room. "You're never here in the morning." She looked at the clock. "Shit, it's almost eleven. You've usually written five pages by now." I'd been awake since dawn, trying to process the previous night as I listened to Liz's heavy breathing punctuated by the sounds of chattering birds. I shook my head.

"Emma?" she said, looking concerned now. "You look funny. What happened?"

"Nothing," I said, too ashamed to tell her. "I'm fine. Just tired."

"I don't believe you. How was the party?"

"Oh, fine."

"Just fine?"

"Well, there was a guy," I started. "He said . . ." But I couldn't finish. I could not repeat the words that had confirmed my greatest fears. I wanted to tell Liz; I wanted her to say, *He's wrong, he's a jerk, it will never happen again,* even though I wouldn't have believed her.

"Yeah?" she asked.

I shook my head. "Mmmm," I said. Liz squeezed my hand and didn't make me continue. I began to cry. She didn't say, "Don't do that" or "Stop crying," she just held my hand and never asked me to explain.

For a decade, I'd been pinning the advent of my new life on the acquisition of an improved prosthesis, but I knew now I would not be prancing around or going on romantic dates as I had imagined. Boys were not going to start ringing me up or chasing me down to blurt out expressions of admiration. I feared—even believed—that the encounter at the party had been an accurate glimpse of my future.

That night, I got completely wasted at another Carleton party with Liz and her new boyfriend, Jason, both of whom I ignored. Each time Liz tried to talk to me, I found something else to do or someone else to engage in conversation. She was clearly hurt and confused, but I didn't care. I spent much of the time with my head tipped back in a barber's chair for "Suicides," which involved two people (in this case, strangers) dumping a mystery concoction of hard liquor down my throat.

Back in our room later that night, we ordered a pizza and I ate four pieces in about five minutes. I ate normally only when I was drunk, my loss of control lifted by alcoholic euphoria.

After we cleared away the pizza boxes, I ran to the bathroom and was sick in the nearest stall. Liz came running in. "Let me in," she said, rapping on the locked door.

"Go away," I told her, and started to cry. "Go!" I shouted.

"Fucking let me in!" she screamed. "What's the matter with you?" On my knees, I hung my head over the toilet. I had eaten too much. I was a terrible person, a horrible friend. I was so jealous of Liz—acquiring a boyfriend had seemed so effortless for her!

She crawled under the stall and held my head as the last of the pizza and what she identified as schnapps came up. "Why are you doing this to me?" she asked.

"I'm the one puking."

"You know what I mean." She let go of me and sat against the bathroom door.

I pushed off from the toilet and faced her, wiping my mouth with my sleeve. "I'm sorry," I said. "I don't know what to do. Something's wrong with me. Does that make sense?"

Liz stood up and flushed the toilet. "Nothing makes sense right now," she said, and held out her hand to help pull me up. "And there's nothing wrong with you, either, so cut that shit out."

As we walked back to our room, Liz steadied me with one arm around my waist. "You know you're great and I love you," she said. "Right?" I nodded, but I still felt that I was the one at fault.

How was I going to pass as normal when my girlfriends were doing the ritual "walk of shame" back to their dorm rooms on cold Minnesota mornings after cuddling naked with a boy in his bed all night? Was I going to ask some dude to lift my leg off his bed the way Liz had gently done before I went to sleep that first year in college? Was I going to ask him to *remove* it when the first guy who'd seem interested in me had been disgusted by a mechanical knee? No way. The body in two pieces was an image of violence, not of sexuality; it was what detectives came to examine after some terrible crime. I thought of the legs that arrived from the prosthetist in "body bags." Disability evoked a zoolike curiosity that was hardly sexual. No matter how hard I tried to pass as an able-bodied woman, the act of removing a leg was not normal—it never would be. How was I ever going to enter this realm of intimacy and sex? My body would always give me away.

I felt desperate during that spring semester. St. Olaf felt like a cage full of happy couples from which I could not escape. I envied them but scowled at them behind their backs. I drowned myself in my studies, which I fully enjoyed, all the while feeling that I was a social failure, which made me care less about my academic success.

"Every good thing you have is already inside you," Dad told me when I slumped around during school breaks, mumbling about how I was worthless and would never find a man with my hideous body. "You don't have to work at it. You don't have to earn it. That's the meaning of grace, and it's for everyone."

Mom nodded her agreement. "A boyfriend is not going to

make your life perfect," she said. "You've got so much going for you. Concentrate on that."

"You're not the one walking around as a cripple," I told them.

"Neither are you," Dad replied.

"Don't use that word," Mom said.

"Whatever," I said. Dad's theory seemed naïve. It wasn't realistic; it wasn't enough. And Mom? She was kidding herself. "What do either of you know about it?" I'd say. "You try this crap for one day!" They'd look at me with sad eyes as I huffed out of the room.

I didn't want to be an outcast on the edge of society and the known world, the way the blind, crippled, and lame had lived in biblical times. I knew those stories well: the paralyzed man who is lowered to Jesus through the roof to be healed; the woman who is made well merely by touching Christ's clothes in a crowd, her salvation accomplished with a flick of the Messiah's wrist; the woman with the crippled spirit and bent back whom Jesus sets free from her mysterious ailment. I had tried to seek this healing myself, years ago, on the day of my first Communion.

I had learned from my college religion courses that disabled people in the ancient world had made their money begging, waiting for others to offer help and pity. They had no social currency, no standing in society. Instead, they were lessons. If you fell from grace, your punishment might include blindness or deformity, or you might inherit your ancestors' sins. The disabled body was a sign of sinfulness: a symbol of what was degenerate and unholy. I wanted to live and thrive, only what kind of life was I really having now, willingly trapped in outdated social mores and my own self-hatred? How could I make it a good one? How could I be a good person with all this rage inside me? I agonized over this.

The task of making choices that would lead to a good and right life versus an immoral or unsatisfying one—what I began to think of as a "crippled" life—drove me to declare a religion major that year. As an early reader of the Bible and a lover of its stories, I gravitated to these old—what we called "classical"—texts. Perhaps there were more elements of truth in those time-honored books, those ancient words, and maybe I would find some answers there. Eventually I did, although not the ones I had expected.

That summer, my feminist theology professor sent me *The Disabled God,* a book by the theologian Nancy Eiesland, who lives with a disability. At first I couldn't bear to read it, for I immediately recognized my own experiences reflected there. After a few pages, I thought, *Not now,* and would read several novels before I read two more paragraphs of the book, and then I'd put it away again. *Later,* I promised. But the book called to me in an irresistible way. There were lessons for my life in there, and I knew it.

I finally read the book from cover to cover on a pleasant summer afternoon in Colorado. I was sitting on the back patio with our border collie, Fred, at my feet; he was waiting for me to finish reading and throw his Frisbee. I had the day off from my summer job, and Mom and Dad were both at work. The sky deepened slowly to its sunset shades of brilliant red and orange and glimmering blue. The smell of dry sagebrush and lilacs hung in the air. I held the book in my hands. I had underlined almost every word of every paragraph and scribbled voraciously in the margins. I threw the book in the grass, sat on the patio, put my face in Fred's neck, and wept. He wagged his tail and licked my face. After a while, he'd had enough. He nudged the Frisbee with his nose, and I finally threw it, watching him chase it quickly and gracefully across the lawn.

I felt elated and terrified. In the book were detailed analyses of biblical texts and sociological studies explaining the emotional impact of feeling on the edge of the world or being viewed as a lesser person because of the shape and limits of your body. I read bleak statistics and stories of hope. Eiesland envisions God as disabled, as the body that is broken at each Eucharistic celebration. Her "bones and braces" embodiment challenges the notion that there is one normative standard for correct bodies and focuses instead on the "mixed blessing" of the unconventional—or crippled—body. "The disabled God makes possible a renewal of hope for people with disabilities and others who care. This symbol points not to a utopian vision of hope as the erasure of all human contingency, historically or eternally, for that would be to erase our bodies, our lives. Rather, it is a liberatory realism that maintains a clear recognition of the limits of our bodies and an acceptance of the truth of being human." These words made a "difficult but ordinary" life possible and permissible; a life that required no healing touch, no miraculous transformation, in order to be complete or worthwhile.

My reaction to the book was emotionally complex: I felt anger at my body for being disabled, for forcing me to experience shame and loss of control. I felt gratitude for Eiesland for having the courage to write this book, drawing from her own experiences and also intelligently reinterpreting old myths and stories I had internalized and used as beacons to guide my interior life and self-image. In the Gospel of Mark, the blind Bartimaeus sits at the roadside, begging and shouting at Jesus, "Son of David! Have mercy on me!" When Bartimaeus asks for the return of his sight, Jesus says, "Go. Your faith has healed you." I remembered my wish for healing at the Communion rail; how I had blamed the lack of a godlike response on my weak faith, my inability to pray with the right amount of strength and conviction. I knew the story of the man born blind in John—the man born deficient, as I was. When the people ask, "Why was he born like this?" Jesus tells them that it is not the fault of sin, but so that God's works might be revealed in him. In Jesus's reply I located a source of my desire to overachieve, to be the poster child for strength and determination, as if I could somehow be a revelation of God's works; as if my deeds could compensate for the deficiencies present at birth. In Matthew, great crowds brought "the lame, the blind, the crippled, the mute and many others, and laid them at his feet; and he healed them." I had daydreams about being carried in my father's arms to an old, dusty temple, one hand up to shield my face from the bright Jerusalem sun. I was laid at Jesus's feet; he touched me lightly and then I was lifted into the sky in front of the gathered crowd of believers as a healed girl, a whole girl. At an early age, I took from these stories an understanding that disability was something that needed to be fixed: by faith, by Jesus, or by God's mercy. And you had to ask for it, pray for it, and, above all, believe that such a transformation could occur. As I read Eiesland's reinterpretations, it was like discovering these stories for the first time, for in her book Jesus, the holiest one, is disabled: broken, wounded, and real. And he is God. The image of God as disabled—and worthy because of this and not in spite of it—freed me, in part, from the guilt of having a deformed body. It was a guilt that ran so deep, it took the words of this author to coax it out and make me aware of it.

As I read stories of what other people with disabilities had endured, I felt a different kind of guilt that was linked to privilege: I could walk and do aerobics, I could sing and see and move and work; I was getting a first-class education, my parents loved and provided for me, and our relationships had evolved into complex—if often volatile—friendships as I became an adult; I was encouraged and emotionally sustained by my professors and my friends. Sometimes I had the extraordinary feeling that the whole world was open to me the way I'd imagined it was when I was the poster child, only this book suggested that I might have to find a new way of imagining myself as an adult. Who could I possibly be if I wasn't Supergirl? These questions made me anxious, and I tucked them away. I had my whole life to worry about them, I thought. There was plenty of time to come up with a response to *The Disabled God*: an answer back. In any case, I had more exciting things to think about.

I was going to Dublin for my junior year as a visiting student at Trinity College. I had chosen Trinity because it was one of the few programs that would take me away for an entire year. I was desperate to travel on my own and experience life in a new place. I shared this reasoning with Mom and Dad, but the other motivation I kept secret: I hadn't had any luck finding a man at Olaf, but I might have better luck with Irish men.

In the weeks leading up to my departure for Ireland, I abandoned *The Disabled God,* deliberately getting lost in a flurry of preparations. At my farewell parties, friends and family commended me, once again, for being the super, fantastic woman about to be set loose to awe and amaze the world, as if I were some kind of goddess: "What an incredible young woman you are; how brave and adventurous!" I lapped up the attention and convinced myself that although Eiesland's book had been instructive, her words and theories did not apply to me. I thought I was different from those other disabled people, and this year abroad was an opportunity to prove it.

When I arrived in Dublin, I immediately realized I had packed all of the old fantasies that had defined my life in my baggage: A handsome man would fall in love with me and in so doing make my life perfect. I wanted to be possessed, remade. Just as many men had tried to fix my body with their hands, why couldn't a man fix my life with his love?

Having left home and traveled thousands of miles to a new country, I saw that I had never lost the need to be and feel defined by someone outside myself. It never occurred to me that I might be my own guardian. I expected someone to fill that role, which my parents had begun and which my surgeon and prosthetists had continued by keeping me mobile and active in the world, aligning and adjusting the body with their various tools and expertise. My one lurking fear was this: Now that sex was part of the package, would anyone want the job?

Chapter Eleven

DIRTY OLD TOWN

Luke walked into my bedroom carrying two steaming cups of instant coffee. Just before he shut the door with his bare foot, I saw my flatmate Elodie; she waved and blew me a pinky kiss—the signature gesture we had adopted in the seven months we'd been living together in our second-floor flat along Usher's Quay in Dublin. I heard her giggle; Claire, my other flatmate, shushed her. I couldn't be sure that they didn't have their ears pressed against the door, although it occurred to me that this did not seem like a very French thing to do. Elodie had told me how deeply privacy was prized in France. "You Americans are so free," she liked to say.

"Here you go," Luke said. Carefully, he sat on the edge of the bed and handed me the cup. He wrapped his arm around me, and I settled my bare back against his bare chest, sipping the coffee. Trucks rattled by on the quays below the open balcony windows. The curtains fluttered in the late morning breeze. Sunshine sparked off the Liffey River and made the room look and feel bright.

"How do you feel?" Luke asked, squeezing my shoulder.

I looked up at him and smiled. My body hurt in new places, and my stump itched terribly from being trapped inside the silicone socket all night long. "Brilliant," I said, and it was true.

After Luke showered and left the flat with promises to call later, Elodie and Claire tumbled in, eager for the details of how I'd lost my virginity. They brought a bottle of cheap champagne and three glasses with them to toast my successful deflowering. "When did you get this?" I asked, taking the bottle. "I wasn't sure it would happen!"

"Stop that," Elodie said, and put her fingers to my lips.

I opened the bottle, and Claire filled each of our glasses. "Drink your champagne," she said.

We made a toast. "Welcome to being a woman," said Elodie. I had put henna in her short dark hair a few days before, and the light in the room caught the reddish strands and made them glow. Between sips of champagne, I told them everything.

The girls knew that I had met Luke in the bakery section of Dunne's Stores in Blackrock, a southern suburb, where I had been living with them at an international student dorm. Soon after, the three of us moved out and rented a flat along the Liffey River that was impossibly cheap and made even cheaper by the fact that Elodie and I shared the bed in the bigger room, while Claire kept the tinier room to herself. The flat was new and had been hastily constructed. The furniture was horrible, the wallpaper was pink and already peeling, and the kitchen was ridiculously small. But from the small wrought-iron balcony off the main room, you could look out over the Liffey and the streets of the Northside. It was fantastic.

On the nights when Luke picked me up for dinner in his black BMW with its fragrant leather seats, I felt my knees go weak, as they had that first moment I'd spotted him holding a loaf of soda bread. At night, the city looked as if it had been lit on fire; it zipped and hummed with the pulse of noise, laughter, and music. Dublin was as far away from a small Minnesota town as you could imagine.

On our dates, Luke and I split one or two bottles of wine with dinner, and afterward we usually met up with Claire and Elodie at Merchant O'Shea's pub or the Brazen Head. Luke always ordered four pints just before last call at eleven o'clock—two for him and two for me—and on many nights I found myself bent over the stone walls lining the Liffey, puking into the dark, polluted water.

The constant and overzealous consumption of alcohol seemed as much a part of Irish student culture as anything else. Drinking was not the moral issue it had been at St. Olaf (where "good girls" avoided it) but instead felt like a social requirement.

The more Luke and I drank, the more comfortable I felt when we went back to his swanky duplex and he leaned over me on the couch, his eyes glittering. I was thrilled but tense. "Relax," he said on the night of our first make-out session, and I laughed. I was thinking about the one and only time I'd kissed a guy in college, in his car. He'd taken off his glasses, and I was so anxious that I'd nearly hyperventilated, steaming up all the windows. I remembered the boy's lips were tight and strange, possibly as inexperienced as mine. Luke's lips were soft and supple; they moved well. It was kissing as I had never known it. I felt both released from and nudged more deeply inside my body—a potent, addictive feeling.

I often slept over at Luke's on weekend nights, and although I'd wake up the next day with itching sores on my stump from having confined it inside the silicone socket all night, it was worth it. After he fell asleep, I would stare at Luke's soft skin and the curls at the nape of his neck. I'd touch his broad chest lightly with my fingertips and listen to his deep, even breathing. A naked man in bed with me: an experience I thought my disabled body had rendered off limits and impossible. Melodramatically, I wrote in my journal: "It's a fucking revelation, and it's about goddamn time."

I finally decided that I wanted to have sex with Luke. I invited him over for dinner and told my flatmates to go out. They happily obliged. "You go, girl," Elodie said, using her favorite American expression.

Luke and I downed some wine, then started our usual "heavy petting" on the couch, and I told him what I wanted to do, which I thought was totally obvious since I'd answered the door—my heart pounding—wearing the turquoise silk robe I'd purchased at the lingerie store where I worked during the summers. And nothing else. He asked me if I was sure, and I said yes, and that was the truth. I trusted Luke, and our care and respect for each other was genuine and mutual. But I wasn't in love with him. I had decided that this was a prerequisite for having sex with a man, because if I really loved him, true intimacy might be overwhelming, too risky; part of me still expected every man to reject me on the basis of my body. Although this initially surprised me—hadn't I been waiting for someone to cloak with my affections, no matter who it was?—the longer I thought about it, the more sense it made. If you were in love, rejection would be that much more painful.

Of course, I didn't tell my friends this. I told them I was horny and wanted to do it.

"And that was that," I said, sipping my champagne.

I told Elodie and Claire about the way Luke and I had kissed (duration, intensity, and technique), about the way we'd fondled each other, totally desperate to get it on. There were other elements of the story I did not share with my flatmates. I had learned early on that discussions about my artificial leg were out of the question.

The first night Elodie and I had shared a bed, she was acting strangely. "You all right?" I asked.

"I'm just . . . what if I freak out about seeing your leg? I mean, what if I think it's disgusting?" She looked at me, waiting for me to put her at ease, waiting for me to make it right.

Those words. *Disgusting. Gross.* I even knew the slang term in French: *dégueulasse.* "Freak out": that expression I'd taught her. I'd already disassembled myself quickly while she was in the bathroom and secured the leg in the space between the bed and the wall, tucking my stump under the covers so that she wouldn't have to see it, as if I needed to protect her from the gruesome sight of my body. Now I knew that this decision was the right one. It wasn't going to be the way it had been with Liz; I would need to adjust.

"What do you mean?" I asked. I was angry and hurt, but I smiled and kept my voice light.

"It's just that disabled people don't go out in France," she said.

Later, she apologized. "I'm sorry I said that," she said. "I'm sure it's not true." And then, "You're not Cindy Crawford, but you're pretty."

This was a compliment from Elodie, who was a terrific flirt and always had Irish boys begging to take her to pubs or to their cheap, unheated flats on North Circular Road; she had related these conquests to me in great detail.

I adored Elodie and Claire, but I understood the deal. My status as their friend was precipitated by what they thought was my quintessentially American enthusiasm, friendliness, and "good mood," as they called it. Talking about real issues of the body—with my different body—was not possible. That was fine with me. I was through talking about it; I was too busy living, and now I had crossed the final threshold to womanhood.

So when I told them about my "first night," as they referred to it, I didn't mention what I'd done with my leg or how I'd agonized over what to do with it. How would it work? If I left the leg on, would it hurt Luke, would the rubber that held the cosmetic hose on my thighs rub against his legs and give him a rash? Would I be able to easily manipulate the leg, or would the knee lock out at embarrassing moments and inhibit my movements? Not once did I seriously consider taking the leg off, even after I phoned Samantha and she told me that was exactly what I should do. "It feels so much better," she said.

I appreciated her advice, but to remove the leg in front of a man was unthinkable; the very thought of it sickened me. I had no sense of myself as a desirable, sexual woman as an amputee. The only activities I did habitually without the leg were skiing, showering, and sleeping—and even these were tinged with shame. The person I wanted others to see—the person I wanted to be—had two legs. The only way for me to have sex—this whole body experience—and remain psychologically safe was with the leg on. When it was attached, I felt like a complete person; when it was removed, I felt monstrous and deformed.

With Luke, I had insisted that the lights be off. I wanted my lower half completely covered by blankets, and I stayed partly covered by my robe from the waist up. I'd never been completely naked with a man before and, I thought, one thing at a time. He complied with my wishes.

Luke had never asked me about my artificial leg. We both pretended it didn't exist, that everything was normal. I assumed that, like many people, he didn't know what kinds of questions to ask or what would be rude. At some point, without any prompting from him, I rattled off my story, which was yet another modified version of my poster child speech: It was all bubbly platitudes, happy memories, and stories of learning to ski. I made it sound as if I'd been cutting a swath through my adoring public since the day I learned to walk. I had learned to tell that story multiple times, using the same inflection, the same nod of the head, the same laugh and toss of my long hair.

After Elodie and Claire left for the afternoon and I was getting ready to take a nap, I pulled back the curtain and looked out across the Liffey to the Bargain Town storefront. A man and a woman attempted to drag an orange sofa out the door; they kept laughing and losing their grip. The Guinness brewery just down the road filled the air with the yeasty smell of hops. I watched three skinny boys sitting on the bridge, fishing in the river with rudimentary poles and slapping their heels against the bridge's stones. Drifting off to sleep to the sounds of a man singing a tune as he walked down the quays and the rattle and honk of trucks driving past on the road below my window, I felt exhausted, relieved, and, more than anything else: lucky. I was deformed and damaged, yet I had been fortunate enough to find someone who would sleep with me. Even if I never had sex with anybody else ever again, at least I had done it once; at least I had been sexually attractive to someone. It never occurred to me that the expectations I had about people's perceptions of me might be myths and that other people might have issues with their bodies, too. I believed my deformity trumped everybody else's physical preoccupations. Narcissistically, I thought, *What could possibly be worse than a missing leg?* and organized my expectations around this assumption. That morning, I felt freed from what I had convinced myself would be a lifelong prison of virginity.

I had felt an overwhelming freedom and independence the moment I arrived in Dublin in the fall to be a visiting student at Trinity

College. I enrolled in history and theology courses, but I went to lecture when it suited me, which was usually about once a week. When I wasn't drinking with Luke or my flatmates, I read the books listed on the syllabus in pubs and cafés or in Phoenix Park, which was only a twenty-minute walk from my home. I wanted to abandon the person I was before I went abroad and start again, become someone new.

I had never been so cavalier about attendance, but I was learning so much more. There was only one major paper or exam at the end of the year in each course, sometimes a few short ones scattered in between, and I found the writing challenging and enjoyable. I read Joyce's *Dubliners* and *Ulysses;* I read heavy history books about Ireland; I read Seamus Heaney and Eavan Boland and any contemporary Irish author's book I could get my hands on. I was learning how to develop my own voice, without the fear of failure or the pressure of a grade.

I walked everywhere in Dublin: I had to get out and wander the streets, discover the neighborhoods, drink the beer, and meet the people. I began to know this new city intimately and to love it. I walked for hours. My leg worked perfectly. I rarely had sores. Nothing went numb. It was like a miracle. The rain was slow and soft. Night fell at four o'clock. All of this suited me. Under the quickly darkening sky, the colors of the city became more pronounced: the bright blues and greens of houses and storefronts, the rough gray stones of the ancient buildings and cathedrals. I walked through the streets at night without a stitch of fear.

Dublin glittered: with history, with people, with an uncomplicated glamour and mess. I felt as though I were absorbing the layers of its stories, its dirt, its nooks and crannies and idiosyncrasies. I watched workers inside the scaffolding outside Trinity as they peeled away layers of soot and grime that had collected over decades, the dirt from the polluted Liffey River having sunk deep into the limestone. Each day, more progress was made: A layer of dirt was removed to reveal a white and gleaming surface. I saw myself as linked to those buildings; I was obsessed with the workers' progress as they made the stones shine again. The more stories and history and life I absorbed, the more I traded the old for the new, the cleaner and happier I became.

I fell in love with a place and the person I felt I could be in that place. I could morph and change and even relax. After class, I drank Guinness and smoked cigarettes. For the first time in my life, I felt that I belonged somewhere. I broke old bad habits and adopted new ones.

My time in Dublin and other parts of Europe released me from the stringent lifestyle and schedule I had developed as a teenager and maintained through the first two years of college. After years of whittling the body down and assiduously controlling it, I was released from my self-made prison in a new culture where women didn't think twice about having dessert, where people didn't go home to study for hours. After the first week, when I had been practically alone in the library for three days running, I realized that nobody did this until exam time. At the end of term, I, too, was madly photocopying articles and chapters, desperately reading books I'd never opened, and writing the names of professors I'd seen twice in my life at the tops of exams while sitting in a dusty room under huge oil paintings of former Trinity graduates. I felt proudly irresponsible.

I'd always been such a "good girl": Now I navigated a private life that was unfathomable to my parents and sometimes even to me. I felt like Supergirl all over again, only this time because I was *not* overachieving. I had discovered a new kind of excess. Instead of focusing on schoolwork, I went to nightclubs and parties. Instead of saving my limited spending money for food and necessary expenses, I racked up credit card debt traveling to Galway, Cork, and Donegal; Paris, Amsterdam, and Vienna—anywhere I had never been before, and I often went alone. Instead of waiting to have sex until I was married—something I'd been taught was the right thing to do—I was having it regularly with a man I didn't love and didn't even call my boyfriend.

I fired off postcards to friends and family from the great places I visited and, later, entertained them with elaborate stories of my adventures. *Look what I can do!* those postcards and stories communicated, practically daring someone to call me broken or different in any way. But this mask of normalcy was like a deep, unhealed scar: If I peeled off this protective layer—the bright, wonderful, adventurous, and now sexy and well-traveled Supergirl—I thought the revealed wound would destroy me; that open wound would gush, become infected. I thought it would kill me.

When I returned to St. Olaf, I immediately began surfing the newly expanding Internet, consumed with which part of the world I might get to next. How about an internship with the Lutheran World Federation in Geneva? I sent away for the application. A stint in Africa with the Peace Corps? I investigated that for a whole week before changing my mind. Want to try a one-year teaching gig in Slovakia? I wrote up future teaching plans and imagined what life would be like in Eastern Europe before I abandoned this project as well. I wanted to be the most adventurous, the most fearless. I was ready to seize any opportunity at any place in the world. Although I didn't realize it then, solo travel and adventure had become a part of reinvention and, also, forgetting, as if folding myself into life in another country would help me discover or accept myself by allowing me to release my own identity completely. I naïvely thought that if I got lost in another life, I'd find the person I'd been searching for: myself.

On a chilly November afternoon, I entered the Marriott Hotel and saw Luke sitting on a couch in the lobby, reading the *Chicago Sun-Times*.

"Hey there," he said. He folded the newspaper, stood up, and gave me a hug and a kiss. He wore loose jeans and a crisp white shirt. His hair was shorter than I remembered it, the curls hidden by the new cut; his hands were soft and warm. He was beautiful.

"How about a beer?" he asked. I nodded, and we stepped into the hotel bar.

A few days before, Luke had called me in Northfield to tell me that he'd left Dublin for a corporate job in Chicago. When he invited me to the city, I hopped on the next bus from Minneapolis.

After a few pitchers of beer, we went up to his room and started fooling around. I had spent the entire bus journey telling myself that this time I would try sex with the leg off. In my theology courses, I'd been reading Paul Tillich, a theologian who defines sin as estrangement and separation. Tillich identified three kinds: from the self, from others, and from "the ground of being"—namely, God. Tillich's definition of sin as estrangement fit my predicament exactly—I was suffering in my separation from God because I was estranged from my created, deformed self. Although Tillich's philosophical understanding of "self" does not include the physical body, in a recent paper I had expanded the definition to include it. If sin was separation—from body or soul, from self as God's creation—I certainly felt guilty. With Luke I saw an opportunity to turn this around: I wanted to have sex with just my "real" body, as an amputee and not as a woman masquerading as able-bodied. If I did this, I thought it would make me feel more whole, more grounded.

Luke carefully dismantled my carefully planned outfit: the silver, button-down silk shirt, the black crepe pants, the designer negligee I'd splurged on during my last week as a lingerie store employee. When we were both naked and turned on, I said, "Just a second," and wrapping his shirt around my body, I walked to the bathroom.

I took off his shirt and looked at myself in the mirror under the too bright lights. I turned to the right side and then back to the front—not bad. My cheeks were flushed, and my eyes looked bright. With my heart hammering away, I took off my leg and set it to the side, but as soon as I peeled off the silicone socket and looked at myself in the mirror, I felt a catch—like a punch—in my stomach. *No way can I do this,* I thought. The stump was hideous; it was scarred and disgusting—even penis resembling. *If I saw this, what would I think?* There was Luke waiting for me in the other room with his lovely, softly muscled body, his warm scent, his wonderful back and chest. *How can I offer him this?* I quickly put the leg back on and splashed some water on my face. I looked at my reflection once more and forced a smile.

Looking at my one-legged form had killed all sexual desire in me, but I went through with our liaison anyway, thinking that I had already let it go this far. It was the postcoital moments I craved the most anyway: being close to Luke; feeling his arm around me; hearing his laughter vibrate in his chest; listening to his breath deepen and slow as he fell asleep.

For all of my self-talk about how sexy I was and how liberated I'd become during my year abroad, I didn't feel either when I left the hotel the next morning. I felt terribly confused and even strangely trapped. With Tillich's ideas in mind, I felt more like a sinner than ever before. As the bus rumbled back to Minneapolis, I wondered: *How can an act as intimate as sex detach me even more from my body and from myself? What happened with me in that hotel room? Why can't I be as free as Samantha? What the hell is wrong with me?* It occurred to me that continuing this behavior and refusing to sort out the dissonance between my projected self-image and how I truly felt was taking me down an even darker path from which it would be twice as difficult to turn back. But I bragged about the rendezvous to my friends, many of whom were engaged, as if I were leading a more romantic, thrilling life than they were. Secretly, I was jealous.

Soon after this, every paper I wrote became about the body, in particular mine. I found a way to weave disability into any subject at all, and delighted at doing so. Here I could use elements of my own experience to illuminate theories and philosophies. My theology professors particularly encouraged me to explore this line of thinking, and I began to vigorously investigate disability as a theological issue.

One afternoon, I was doing research for a sociology paper in the library, where I spent most of my time, when I came across a book called *With the Power of Each Breath: A Disabled Women's Anthology.* I matched the call number to a colorful paperback book at the end of a long row and slipped it from the shelf. As soon as I opened it, the book came alive in my hands. In it were disabled women speaking honestly about their experiences. The stories read like recorded acts of resistance. For the first time, I understood how deeply the disability experience informed my identity and the identities of women like me. The three themes repeated over and over again were the shame of being different, colored at times by anger; the silence of alienation and isolation, with an effort to break it; and the active longing for a more holistic vision of the self. I shut the book and stared at it. Whispered conversations floated up from the stacks, a stray giggle. I felt the rush of discovery and hope, like looking in a mirror that reveals a new and unexpected reflection. On a note card, I copied down a quote and taped it to the wall near my bed: "Able-bodied people tend to view us either as helpless things to be pitied or as Super Crips, gallantly fighting to overcome insurmountable odds. Such attitudes display a bizarre two-tiered mindset: it is horrible beyond words to be disabled, but disabled people with guts can, if they only try hard enough, make themselves almost 'normal.' The absurdity of such an all or nothing image is obvious. So, too, is the damage these images do to disabled people by robbing us of our reality." I read these words every morning—thought about them, mulled over them. I did not want to be denied my own reality—but what was it, exactly?

For my senior thesis, I decided to create a theology of wholeness. I would call it "Rescuing the Whole from the Parts: An Embodiment Theology of Disability." If estrangement from God and God's creation was the greatest and most devastating sin, and it was my thoughts that had taken me there, why couldn't they take me in the other direction? If I couldn't force myself into wholeness with my physical actions, I was hopeful I might find it on an intellectual level. I was determined to solve the problem of the body with the mind.

Every weekend, I scrabbled away at my computer. The walls of the dorm room were plastered with note cards full of gathered information and research from twentieth-century Christian theologians Paul Tillich, Sallie McFague, Letty Russell, and Rosemary Radford Ruether; quotes from Flannery O'Connor's story *Good Country People*; *The Disabled God;* and the anthology of women's voices. I delighted in this project, in dealing with the idea of disability in academic language. The disabled body as an object of research and an opportunity for intellectual inquiry seemed a safe way of approaching the issue. Or so I thought.

It was a cold Saturday in January one week before the thesis was due. The landscape and all the trees were covered in ice; the weaker trees bent to the ground in a nasty wind that howled and shook the single dorm window. I scattered the note cards one last time around the room and began slowly to piece together my ideas. I stayed up for two days, living on coffee, peanut M&M's, and saltine crackers. I could feel that I was digging to a larger truth, and as I wrote the last sentence of my newly created embodiment theology—"The path to becoming whole is lengthy, daily, and lifelong. I'm happy to be on my way"—I wept on top of the computer. I felt relief—it was finished—but I also felt a sense of terror. Was I really on my way? To where? Luke and I had planned more liaisons, and I rushed headlong into them. Not once had I succeeded in taking the leg off for sex—the image in the mirror stopped me every time. I still winced at my body every time I saw it in the mirror; I still picked apart elements of my appearance that could be changed or improved. Would this paper—these fifty-odd pages of theory—really help me reach the wholeness I desired? Did it have the power to restore me to the ground of being and to myself?

The attention and academic honors my work received muted any concerns I had about how what I'd written affected my life, but as pressure to make decisions about the next year mounted, I panicked. I felt I had to get away, see more, make myself new in a new place.

When I received a note about the Fulbright in my post office box, I was giddy with relief. Here was a scholarship that could transport me to a place so far away, I could hardly imagine it: Southeast Asia.

I believed that travel would heal me, make me whole. The day I boarded the plane for Seoul, I walked down the jetway thinking, *This will be the adventure that changes everything; this will be the one that makes things right.*

Chapter Twelve

FEAR OF DARKNESS

"Hana! Tul! Set! Net!" I stood in the middle of a brightly lit gymnasium, kicking my right leg into the air and counting to ten in Korean. *"Tasot! Yosot! Ilgop! Yodol! Ahop! Yol!"* It was three in the morning, and the overhead lights buzzed and occasionally flickered and snapped in the massive, empty room. Starting my count again, I did the sequence of forward steps and arm movements I'd learned during my month of weekly tae kwon do lessons in the city of ChunCheon, where I'd also received my Fulbright teacher and language training. For two hours every other day, I had kicked into the air hundreds of times and punched imaginary opponents in a purposefully sealed, saunalike room on the top floor of a commercial building. During the test for my yellow belt, my artificial leg had suddenly given out and I fell. The tae kwon do instructor gave me the belt anyway. I wore it now, tied securely around my waist.

"Ahop! Yol!" My shouts echoed down the hallway that led back to my small room with a single bed and a television that I left on all night, after the screen had gone to static. I imagined my voice rattling around in the huge shower area at the end of the hallway. Designed for groups of kids during the daytime, I had the enormous room to myself in the early mornings, at night, and during the weekends.

My life as a public high school English teacher in Seoul began in this gymnasium with an all-school assembly. The floor in front of the stage was divided evenly in half and packed with rows of uniformed girls on each side. I marched through the middle of the group with Ms. Kim, who I gathered was some kind of administrator, although I wasn't entirely sure. Seconds after I met her in the hallway outside the gym, she grabbed my hand and led me through the group of girls.

I stepped up onstage and was invited by the principal, Mr. Cho, to stand at a podium and say something into the microphone. I looked out at the sea of girls; their faces were lifted in anticipation. I smiled, said, "Hello," and waved. The crowd erupted into shouts and wild applause. Mr. Cho shook my hand; Ms. Kim took my arm, and we walked back the way we had come.

Now, in the predawn hours, I kicked and punched and jumped, turning in a new direction every few minutes so that I could keep my eye on the locked entrance door of the building as well as on all of the entrances and exits to the gym. I was waiting for the first hints of sun to appear through the tall, dark windows, behind which the shadows of trees were motionless in the night air. There were only a few more hours until daylight, when I knew I would be able to sleep, only then I would have to be moving through the hallways efficiently and with a purpose, preparing to teach my English classes.

After I finished the series of moves I had learned, I lay down on a blanket I'd spread on the floor—like a little raft in the middle of the gym—and stared up into the fluorescent lights. This was where I sometimes caught a few hours of sleep, before the alarm clock I set next to me went off. I lay on the floor in my tae kwon do outfit made of stiff cotton gone limp with sweat and waited.

After the six-week training in ChunCheon, I was assigned to a girls high school in a middle-class *gu,* or neighborhood, in Seoul, to teach five conversational English classes of thirty students each. The girls, all between fifteen and seventeen years old, stood and bowed to me when I entered the classroom each morning. In the beginning, every word I said prompted them to giggle, holding their hands in front of their mouths. They wore pink-and-black uniforms and had identical bob haircuts with straight, carefully clipped bangs. Each morning, the length of their hair was measured to be sure it matched the school's set standard.

It was not just the school administration that enforced conformity of appearance; the students imposed these standards on themselves. Sameness was paramount, and deviation from these norms could make a girl's life unbearable. Girls whose shirtsleeves were a little longer than the others' were teased relentlessly; those who were slightly chubby, in a country where most girls are slim, were ostracized. I saw one student with acne pummeled with fruit at recess, ridiculed for a condition beyond her control. With these realities in mind, I began the school year.

My initial lessons were basic English phrases. "What is your name?" "Where are you from?" "Where is the bathroom?" The faces of the students in the front row bloomed with excitement when they knew the answer; they waved their hands frantically, begging to be noticed. I had to wake girls in the back row and confiscate Walkmen, eyeliner, a pack of Brad Pitt playing cards. I returned these items at the end of class, although I was informed by Ms. Kim, who was in fact the assistant principal, that I could either throw them out the open windows or keep them for myself. "That's how I got this," she said, holding up a Sony Discman.

Teaching was difficult, physical work. We moved desks around to imitate city streets and navigated through them. We memorized the words to a Céline Dion song and sang it like a choir, the girls' mouths and tongues bending around the words. I tried to be energetic, encouraging, and kind, as all my favorite teachers had been.

Usually the girls ran out of the room as soon as the lesson was finished. They had only five minutes between classes to visit their lockers, eat *kim'chi* (spicy cabbage fermented in clay pots in the ground) from the sealed containers they brought to school, gossip, and peruse the latest tabloid magazines that were stuffed into the trash cans at the end of the day.

One afternoon, Sue (each girl chose an English name for the class), my brightest and hardest-working student, hung back after class. She had a wide face, small, round glasses, and a terrific smile that she never hid from me. "Hello, *sung sang nim*," she said, giving a quick bow. Then she glanced around, leaned her face close to mine, and whispered, "Let's be friends."

As I became better acquainted with the girls, I longed to explain my disability. I felt their eyes on me when I mounted the stairs to the teacher's platform in the classroom; I sensed their stares trailing after me when I walked down the halls.

I wanted to explain, but I didn't have the language skills. How could I tell them that I went to the bathroom between classes, locked myself inside a stall, waited to be sure the other stalls were empty, and then wiped the sweaty socket dry to keep my leg from sliding off my stump?

My students' curiosity was never offensive or even overtly expressed, but their code of sameness made me anxious. I was afraid that if they discovered my glaring difference, if they saw the leg, they would be horrified. I imagined a group of them coming upon me unexpectedly in the bathroom and running away screaming.

I was certainly a novelty in the teachers' room, a place I despised and feared. It was perpetually hot in this open-plan room, even when the windows were thrown open wide. Although I wore a suit jacket over my sleeveless dresses in the classroom, I took off the jacket at my desk, which was marooned in the middle of the room. One day, a teacher approached me and said, "Your clothes are wrong." I looked around. Everyone wore long sleeves, even in the heat. I slipped back into my sweaty jacket, blushing.

Once, when I was leaving the room and had to return to my desk because I had forgotten a class ledger, I found every teacher staring directly at my feet. Chairs scraped against the tile floors as people pivoted to get a better view. They continued to watch every footfall forward as I moved across the room. Suddenly, I saw myself through their eyes: I saw my left hip shift to accommodate the swing of the prosthesis with each step forward; I heard the slight creak or click in the hydraulics as the knee bent; I noticed the way my artificial foot meets the floor, stiffly, on the edge of the heel, betraying its inflexibility. I was used to being an object of fascination, but it had never felt so intense, never so pointed. I could not break the tension in the room or close the space between myself and these able-bodied people. Language was useless. Humor? Impossible. I never forgot anything in the teachers' room again.

The days of teaching were a healthy challenge, but the nights were miserable and long. I hardly slept. Until I could be placed with a host family, I was expected to live in a small, white-walled room with a single bed at the end of a long corridor next to the school gymnasium, where the students had greeted me some weeks before. I had always been afraid of the dark and knew that every night would be torturous for me.

Each afternoon, the students and teachers left and I began to panic as the sky darkened. The days were never long enough. There were no security guards or permanent night staff at the school, only the steady drip of the mass showers at the end of the hall, the occasional sound of leaves rattling together in the courtyard, and hundreds of empty rooms. Fear made my head spin, kept me up in a constant state of anxiety, and sent me on repeated trips to the bathroom to be sure nobody was hiding in the shower stalls. I left my television and every available light on all night. I tried drugging myself with Benadryl, but I still woke up terrified throughout the night.

I survived the first week with little sleep. During my lunch break, I hurried to my basement room, where I slept deeply for thirty minutes, thankful for the loud activity upstairs and the warm sun shining through the windows.

In an effort to distract myself from constant worry and panic, I added the tae kwon do ritual to my evenings and early mornings. I thought exhausting exercise might help me sleep. After finishing my punches and kicks, my sit-ups and push-ups, I went back to my little single bed or lay down on my blanket in the middle of the floor and tried to sleep. Sometimes this system worked, but usually it did not.

At the end of my first two weeks in the basement, I had the

recurring dream I hadn't had since my final orthopedic operation in 1982, when I was eight years old. The dream was always the same: Animals floated by in a pool of thick blood in the following order: cats, unicorns, dogs. All of them had the wrong limbs in the wrong places: Cats had hooves where their eyes should have been; unicorns had dogs' legs for horns; the dogs had no limbs at all. The animals groaned and cried out; they begged and whined for help, but when I reached out for them, they recoiled. I could never see myself and didn't know which body parts were mismatched or missing on me.

The dream, which I started having when I was six or seven, used to wake the whole house. Mom would run downstairs to my room when she heard something fall or the piano keys sound. It must have sounded like a break-in, but it was me, sleep-hopping without my leg, floating along with the animals, trying to get away, shrieking and swatting at everything in my path—lamps, tables, toys, the telephone.

In Korea, when I woke up in my little room or in my makeshift camp on the gymnasium floor, I was so scared that I could hardly breathe. I stared at the black-and-white television static, trying to slow my breathing and remain calm, or I looked up at the huge gymnasium lights as they flickered and hummed. I told myself there was nothing to fear. My body told me otherwise.

Mom used to calm me down after the dream by sitting next to me on the bed, singing hymns or telling funny stories. I would fall asleep with the hall light shining directly on my face. I did the same in Korea—I stared into the single lightbulb on the ceiling or the gym's bright overhead lights—only I felt completely, horribly alone. I fought until sleep took me, or I struggled up and went through the tae kwon do routine again. I often slept with my leg on, truly afraid that I would have to run from some imagined intruder, and I paid for this phobia by nursing sores during the weekend. I often stayed in bed on Saturday, drinking only Coke, eating nothing, and attending the sores on my stump while watching reruns of *Baywatch* dubbed in Korean.

Tae kwon do lessons had been an effective way to relieve stress during language training and the long, hot days of waiting for school assignments. I took lessons with some other Fulbrighters, and this was how I learned to count in Korean. At night, as I practiced my moves in the gym, I thought that whatever danger might come for me would at least understand that I was a force to be reckoned with.

After a month of almost no sleep, I was exhausted and irritable. During my classes, I was muddled and short of breath. I lost my appetite and my interest in teaching. After school, instead of going to the neighborhood market or working on my lesson plans, I sat in my room and watched mindless television for hours. I wandered around the gymnasium hallways in the hours before dawn, looking at sports trophies and old photographs of the school's athletic teams. Sometimes I sat underneath these displays and sang the Italian arias I had memorized and performed in high school. They didn't sound as they once had when my voice was younger and more flexible, but I liked to hear the notes echoing against the walls. I sang the love songs our Korean teacher had taught us in ChunCheon, trying to make myself cry, thinking it might put me to sleep.

I called Mr. Adams, the Fulbright program administrator. I didn't tell him the details of my struggle, because he was the last person to whom I wanted to admit failure or fear. I had never forgotten his warnings that disabled people were shunned in Korean society. Instead, I reminded him that placement with a host family was a stipulation of my fellowship, which mandated a "cultural immersion" experience. I asked him if it was because of my disability that I could not be placed with a family. "No, it's not," he said. "I'm working it out." He told me to trust him.

Shortly after my conversation with Mr. Adams, I attended the Lutheran church in Seoul. I wept through the entire liturgy and each one of the hymns. During the service, I kept imagining my father at the front of his church. I saw his hands rise to give the benediction; I heard his voice sing the blessing. A soldier dressed in full uniform who was seated in front of me handed me a handkerchief and touched my hand gently, but apart from that, nobody paid any special attention to my weeping, and I was thankful for it.

At the coffee hour following the service, I met Heather, a young Canadian who was working at a *hogwan,* or "cramming school," where many of my students went after regular class.

Heather and I made plans to have drinks in Itaewon, the mostly English-speaking section of Seoul near the Yongsan Garrison, site of the U.S. Army headquarters. "Itaewon has great sports bars," Heather said. I hated sports bars, but I would have gone anywhere with her. I was lonely, and I thought maybe I could convince her to crash on the floor of my room later. If there was a living, breathing body in the room, I thought I'd feel safe and be able to sleep.

The streets of Itaewon were lined with stalls selling cheap Nike shoes, Armani knockoff suits, and Coach bags at half price. The sidewalks rippled with rainbow colors from the neon signs overhead. Most of the American men traveled in packs of five or six, and many of the groups were accompanied by several Korean women who were dressed in short skirts and skimpy tops. The men strutted down the sidewalks confidently; the women clicked along carefully in their high-heeled shoes.

The air was thick with aftershave and sexual tension—the soldiers who did not have dates were looking at us openly, sizing us up. "I love a guy in uniform," Heather said, skipping up the hill. Heather and I were both wearing jeans and tight tank tops. I had a sweater tied around my waist because buildings were overly air conditioned during the hot months. I felt uncomfortable in a way that was strangely energizing. The soldiers' lusty eyes made me nervous, but I also liked being looked at; I liked being the object of a man's attention.

At the Free Willy Bar, a mechanical neon whale moved up and down over the door. The interior was lit with red lights; the smoky air throbbed with techno music. While we ordered mai tais at the bar, two soldiers dressed in green fatigue pants and tight black T-shirts approached us. Heather immediately started chatting with one of them, batting her eyes and flinging her blond hair over her shoulders. I put on my sweater while the other guy told me how lonely he was. Then he reported that he was Mark from Alabama, had graduated from high school last year, and hated Korea.

"This place is fucking backward." He did a tequila shot at the bar and ordered a beer. "What are you doing here?"

"I'm a teacher," I said, and sipped my drink.

"Right." He looked at my breasts, which, thankfully, were mostly hidden now by the loose sweater.

"Most of the guys here like the Koreans," he said, and waved his hand in the direction of a corner table. Dressed in garter belts, skimpy underwear, and bras, three Korean girls who didn't look a day older than my students were draped over the laps of red-faced men in uniform, who were drunk and loud. "But I like your kind." He wrapped his huge fingers around my wrist. "I like you." So much for preliminaries.

"Excuse me," I said, removing my hand from his grip. I walked to the bathroom, looking for Heather. I found her wedged into a corner booth, necking with the other soldier, whose hand moved beneath her shirt. Two Korean girls, dressed in scanty leather outfits, gave me the once-over. I wanted to say something to these girls, but what? I could make no bridge to their world. I thought of the bar we had gone to as a group in ChunCheon, where young women in bras and panties danced in cages that moved up and down under strobe lights.

Back at the bar, Mark put his hands around my waist and pulled me between his legs, which looked as wide as tree trunks. "Hey," I said, trying to unwind his arm from around my back, "I need to go." I looked at my watch. "Yep. I'm supposed to be meeting someone."

He nuzzled my neck. His lips were warm and wet. "You don't want to stay here with me, Amy?"

"Emily."

"Right." He released me and took a long swig of beer. "Could I at least have your number?"

On a napkin, I wrote down the first seven numbers that came to me and handed it back to him. I turned around before I stepped out the door to see if he was watching me. He wasn't.

Outside, the street surged with a ring of soldiers and civilians three rows thick. The hot breath and loud voices of inebriated people made the air seem liquid, viscous. Someone threw a beer bottle in the middle of a writhing circle to shouts and encouraging cries. "What's going on?" I asked a woman dressed in green fatigues and black boots who was chugging a can of Obi lager a few feet from the outer ring of the crowd.

"It's a chicken fight!" she screamed at me. She grabbed my arm and cut a path for both of us to the center ring. There, encircled by screaming men, was an American soldier and a Korean man.

The soldier danced lightly on his feet like a boxer. His green pants were rolled up to his knees, and the muscles of his calves were flexed and defined. The thick ropes of his arm muscles moved when he stabbed a fat fist in the air. He said, "C'mon, c'mon," and threw a flurry of punches. He tilted his head from left to right, loosening up. He made eye contact with the crowd, nodding and yelling.

The Korean man moved when the soldier moved; his eyes never left the soldier's hands. A diagonal scar ran from his shoulder to the center of his pale, hairless chest. He wore jersey shorts, and his legs from feet to knees were black with dirt. One of his eyes was swollen shut, and he swiped at it every few seconds. His lean, steady body was calm and watchful, while the soldier's bounced and shook with aggression and excitement.

Both men were shirtless and sweating and covered with blood—their own? each other's? I didn't ask. Their bare feet kicked up dust as they circled each other; the black dirt settled on their skin, their hair.

The woman shouted something else and then looked at me, waiting for a response.

"What?" I screamed.

She put her mouth up to my ear. "They fight until the death. It's a betting fight. Do you want to bet?" She held out a stack of *won* wrapped with a rubber band. The noise felt huge; it seemed to absorb the air. When I looked around, all I could see were big fists pumping the air and stretched, screaming mouths. I barreled back through the crowd alone and walked as quickly as I could down the steep hill.

At the bottom of the hill, I tried to hail a taxi for fifteen minutes. I wanted out of the neighborhood as quickly as possible. I wanted to be lifted out of there, whisked away. The sounds from up the street swelled, and my stomach lurched. An eerie silence followed and was broken by a chorus of cheers splitting the air. I imagined the soldier's fists making contact with the small man's chest; I envisioned the Korean man scratching at the soldier's eyes as the big soldier sank his teeth into the Korean man's thin arm. I started walking, waving frantically at every taxi that passed me by. A fight until death? I was sweating heavily, but my heart was a cold stone rocking inside my chest.

I finally ran after a taxi until it stopped. I forced myself into the backseat with three other people, flashing a wad of money as proof that I would pay everyone's fare if they'd just let me share the taxi with them.

When I returned to my room, there was a message on the answering machine from Mr. Adams. I was to move in with a host family in two days. I took a hot shower and lay on my back for a long time, blinking up at the ceiling.

The next night, my last night of nocturnal exercise, I did my kicking and punching routine, stretched out on the floor, and wept with relief.

I had my own room in Mrs. Park's third-floor apartment on a steep side street about a ten-minute walk from the school. My host mother was a thin woman—all angles and cheekbones—who wore thick eye makeup and red blush in an almost perfect circle on each of her cheeks. Her husband, a short, thick man, never cracked a smile or appeared without a beer or a cigarette in one hand. Mrs. Park's daughter, whom I was told to call Jane, was a timid, round-faced seven-year-old who, although not exactly pleased about giving up her bedroom for a strange American teacher, was curious about me nonetheless. She followed me around the house for the first few days.

I expressed daily gratitude to my host family by eating multiple helpings of the food prepared for me: different kinds of *kim'chi*, small fried fish, sticky rice scooped up with dry, cut seaweed, *pul go gi* (marinated barbecued beef wrapped in lettuce leaves with garlic and hot sauce), *bi bim bap* (rice and vegetables topped with a fried egg), and sweet bean paste drizzled over ice. My family took me out for *makguksu* (buckwheat vermicelli noodles topped with slivered cucumbers, a hard-boiled egg, and hot red sauce that is served cool and mixed together before eaten) and sometimes for *ttakgalbi,* a meat dish I'd enjoyed in ChunCheon, a city rumored to have the best restaurants for this specialty.

Although I tried to explain to Mrs. Park that she was not responsible for my lunch and I could eat in the cafeteria with the other teachers, she still prepared ten peanut-butter sandwiches for me every day and left them in a tinfoil tower on the kitchen table. I could not eat them all, and I threw the leftovers in the garbage can at the far end of the gym, near the room where I used to live.

At my host family's, my sleep was often long and delicious, but I still had nightmares. When I had the recurring dream, I'd wake up and sit near my window, where I could look over Seoul's red rooftops, which stretched out in an endless checkerboard pattern, with a tangle of electrical wires—like a complicated and dangerous trapeze—strung between them. Tiny squares of light were illuminated all across the city. The lit cityscape, however chaotic, calmed and charmed me. How could I feel truly alone when I was surrounded by so much life?

At night I tucked my prosthesis underneath my bed, and each morning I woke up a half hour before anyone else, so that when Jane came to wake me I would be assembled.

One night at Mrs. Park's I awoke from a rare, untroubled sleep to the sound of a loud argument. A loud shout. The front door slammed shut, rattling the apartment walls slightly. Silence and shuffling feet. What was going on? I heard Jane and Mrs. Park talking, then silence. I was up all night, listening to Mrs. Park cry in the bedroom next door. Although I was sure she tried to muffle them, the sobs ripped through the wall. I wanted to go to her, but what could I tell her? What could I say?

That week, I recited the girls' first English test over the school's PA system. I knew they were nervous, so I spoke slowly, leaving an impossible amount of time between questions. Ms. Kim stood behind me, saying, "Go, they should know answer now."

Looking out the window, I watched a detention session: The girls ran up and down the grass field with their backpacks lifted above their heads while a teacher shouted out orders. A few did push-ups until they fell on their faces. Those along the fence stood with their book-filled bags hoisted, straight armed, in the air. They wept and wailed, but they did it. I thought of being alone in the basement and kicking into the air; those movements—like those I witnessed now—seemed to be exercises in futility as well as expressions of loneliness and a kind of triumphant despair.

I waited before I recited the next question. Ms. Kim could sweat it out a little bit.

Sleep remained an enormous difficulty. In my journal I wrote, "I am floating somewhere," and it was about to get worse.

I had my first panic attack in the classroom while I was writing "lice" and "rice" on the board, pointing to the words one at a time and exaggerating the correct pronunciation of both. Suddenly the chalky words began to blend. I saw pops and flashes at the corners of my vision. It was as if someone had reached inside my skull and set my brain spinning. I felt myself losing equilibrium at an alarming rate. I clutched the board for a few long moments. When I turned around, the girls in the front row were crying. I smiled and dismissed the class, but they watched me suspiciously, glancing back to see if I'd crumpled into a heap. A few days later, a new rumor was circulating: American *sung sang nim* is dying.

The panic attacks increased: two per day, then five, ten, fifteen, sometimes every ten minutes. I had them on the subway crossing the Han River—in the middle of rush hour, I'd claw through people to get out of the car and into different air. I stayed seated for most of my lessons and tried to keep smiling when the world started to spin. I had attacks in the middle of the night at my host family's; I woke up and wrote letters, read through my lesson plans, burned incense. Nothing seemed to help. I felt as though panic were peeling my skin back, leaving me completely exposed.

Rattled, I made an appointment to see Dr. Pavlovich, the English-speaking doctor. His office was surrounded by palm trees that reminded me of the army base. There, once you walked past the beggars and homeless children—all of them skinny and hungry, and many of them limbless—and stepped through the gates, you were greeted with a gleaming building that featured expensive shops, a TGI Friday's, and a man-made waterfall. Around it were clusters of quaint houses with well-tended flower beds and tiny swing sets perched in the yards. The hospital appeared equally sleek and tidy.

After listening to my heart rate and my litany of complaints, the doctor explained that I was exhibiting all the symptoms of post-traumatic stress disorder. I was relieved to know that I was not about to have a heart attack every ten minutes. Post-traumatic stress disorder sounded as serious as a cold; it wasn't cancer, or heart disease, or anything like that. If it wasn't going to kill me, then of course I could deal with it.

"Tachycardia *is* unhealthy," he said. "Your heart is beating too fast too much of the time. Are you under any inordinate stress beyond what you're telling me?"

I shook my head. "No, I'm fine." I said nothing about my troubles sleeping, about my self-consciousness in the teachers' room or the incident at my host family's.

"Nothing at your placement, nothing at school?"

"I'm handling it," I said. The words felt hollow, even to me.

"No," he said, writing out a prescription for Xanax, "you're really not."

Dr. Pavlovich told me that it might be impossible for me to keep teaching if the attacks persisted. He said I needed downtime and counseling. He asked me if I had considered leaving Korea or taking a leave of absence. I told him absolutely not. I wanted to tell him to fuck off.

"You never had counseling after your amputation?" he asked.

I shook my head. "No. I had my last operation *years* ago."

"You need counseling."

"I'm fine," I said. "I can deal with it." I felt defiant and offended. *How dare this man tell me what I can handle and what I cannot? He has no idea what I've been through,* I thought self-righteously. *He has no idea what I can manage.*

As soon as I was outside the hospital doors, my strength faded and I wanted to turn around. I wanted to run past the rock garden in front of the hospital and tell the truth. "I'm terrified!" I imagined myself saying. "I'm losing my mind!" I did slow my pace as I walked past the security guard, but I kept walking, past beggars and blowing trash and the dirty alleyways to the subway station.

Back at Mrs. Park's that night, I floated in that murky, tranquilized state just before artificially induced sleep. I heard laughter on the street below, dialogue from the Korean television sitcoms Jane was watching in the living room, and the clink of dishes being washed in the kitchen sink. I squeezed the lumpy scars on my stump. What secrets were sealed behind those smooth white stripes that divided the skin into strange geometrical patterns? Why would the body plague me now? Those surgeries were behind me, the pain long ago absorbed and forgotten. I felt betrayed by my body and by the stories of its disfigurement that I did not want to revisit and recall. But the memories lurking and spinning in my bones were coming to me in nightmares. Growing and multiplying like a mysterious infection, they were leaking into my blood until I was saturated with fear. *What do you want?* I thought, kneading the scars and cursing my body. *What more do you want from me?*

At that moment I felt, for the first time in my life, purely disabled, in the most blatant sense of the word: limited, ineffective, weakened. It was the most debilitating revelation of my life.

In October, I traveled with Mrs. Park and Jane to the family's village to celebrate Chuseok, the autumn holiday of harvest that is an occasion for giving thanks to one's ancestors for health and prosperity and to the earth for bounty. I was told that Chuseok is the Korean equivalent of the American holiday of Thanksgiving. We traveled north on roads clogged with traffic, remaining completely car-locked for hours at a time. We bought dried squid that tasted like car exhaust and grease from a vendor who, on foot, weaved among the idling cars.

Once at Mrs. Park's family home, we sat on the floor of the two-bedroom house and ate with Mrs. Park's mother, whom everyone called Oma. She stabbed her food with chopsticks held loosely in one hand and swiped at the flies circling our plates with the other hand. We ate *dok, kimbap,* fruit, and three different types of *kim'chi.* One was so spicy that I couldn't stop sweating. Jane laughed as I drank glass after glass of water.

At some point, the talk became very animated. I suspected they were discussing my host father, who had not set foot in the house since the night of the argument. Oma's wrinkled arms shook as she gestured. She talked as she chewed, the bits of food like moving black pegs inside her toothless mouth. Mrs. Park stared into her hands, eating nothing.

Jane and I slept on rolled-up mats on the floor. I took my leg off inside the sleeping bag after I knew she was asleep. I carefully peeled away the socket's Velcro strap, waiting for ten seconds between each rip to be sure the noise wouldn't wake her. Then I pulled my stump out of the leg and unrolled the sock and then the socket, tucking both inside the empty leg. I slept with my arm secured in the space underneath the artificial knee, its hydraulics cool against my wrist. I rationed out my Xanax, snapping the pills in half and taking them only at night.

On the morning of Chuseok, the house swelled with people for *jarye,* the memorial ceremony that takes place in the home. A table was laid with fruits and nuts, rice cakes, meat, fish, vegetables, and white wine. Mrs. Park's brother and his sons sat in the brocaded armchairs in the low light of the main room; they smoked cigarettes, chewed tobacco, and spat into silver bowls that Jane brought to the kitchen and rinsed clean.

I sat on floor cushions in the kitchen with the women, who were making *song pyan,* crescent-shaped white and green rice cakes filled with a sweetened seed mixture. The women rolled and worked the cakes into perfect half-moons as they chatted to one another. I concentrated on making mine just like theirs, but the women's practiced creations sat next to my lumpy, lopsided attempts; it was clearly an acquired skill. The women's soft voices rose like thin ribbons in the air to mix with the cigarette smoke and laughter floating up from the men's side of the room.

That afternoon, we visited the family graves for *seong myo,* the ceremony to honor the spirits of ancestors who retain power to influence what happens to family members in the living world: a celebration of kinship and bloodline. The graves were on top of a steep hill. It had rained recently, and the mud was smelly and deep. One of Mrs. Park's younger nephews, wearing Levi's and Converse sneakers, grabbed my hand and practically pulled me up the side of the hill.

At the ancestral graves, which were set in a clearing of tall bamboo trees, another feast was spread. Oma lit incense, and the whole family bowed; one by one, each person threw a small cup of rice wine on the grave.

Oma shook my arm, inviting me into the family ritual. I thought of the Korean man's smooth, sweat-soaked skin. I looked at my host mother's pale, drawn face. I looked at the calm and reverent faces of my host family. A thin stream of jet exhaust drew a line across the sky. I felt a sob blooming in my throat and let loose in my brain a prayer so powerful, I expected the air around us to stir. I tossed the rice wine. Everybody clapped.

On the way back to Seoul that afternoon, we visited a temple. It was another steep hike, but this time up paved roads packed with people. As we climbed, Mrs. Park bought me "sweat cloths" at every roadside stand. She offered water and long breaks as we worked our way up the hill. We saw women sidestepping their way down the steep path in their strappy high-heeled sandals, clinging to the arms of men. Mrs. Park watched me limp along at a slow pace in my sturdy hiking boots and took my hand.

That night, I had a panic attack so severe that I had to go outside where I could be sick. The humid air smelled of goat shit and wet dirt. I ran the garden hose and rinsed my mouth and hands. Back in the room, I allowed my last dose of Xanax to melt on my tongue.

The panic attacks continued, and over the next weeks I spent a good chunk of my wages on taxis to the hospital. I sat slumped in the backseat, looking out at the huge, sprawling city of Seoul that had begun to frighten me in its enormity: the crowded streets, the thick car exhaust, the bright neon lights. Every kind of stimulation felt like too much. When I finally got to the hospital, the doctor often refused to see me; he couldn't see many of his critical patients four times a week. On the phone, he told me what I already knew but would not admit: that I could not continue to live like this. He told me to go home.

One night after I spoke with the doctor, I had three panic attacks and was sick in the trash can underneath the desk in my bedroom. The next night, I woke up after having the recurring dream to find my right leg dangling out the open window—if I had tipped in the wrong direction, I might have toppled three floors to the concrete path below. I didn't remember opening the window.

In the morning, I called my parents and told them what had been going on. Shocked and concerned, they begged me to take the doctor's advice and give up the scholarship, leave Korea. "Listen to what your body is telling you," Mom said. "You have nothing to prove."

I arrived at Mr. Adams's office in central Seoul unannounced. I was on the verge of tears, because I had never in my life quit anything. Never. Not as a skier, when I went so hard and fast that I would literally drop at the end of each run. Not as a student, when I pushed myself to study for hours on end. Not as a person with a disability, when I did everything to overcome the circumstances of my birth. I was the superachiever; the poster child for what a person could accomplish with guts and determination. But now I could not force myself to function; the night before had been my wake-up call, and I was finally paying attention.

I walked past the protesting secretary, opened the door to Mr. Adams's office, and said, "I'm leaving. I can't stay here." I felt sweat gathering in my scalp. "I'm resigning," I said. It had been almost four months since the day of my arrival. "Today."

"You'll work it out," he said, turning in his chair to file something in a cabinet drawer. "Nobody quits the Fulbright."

Hearing that word made my whole body shake. *I am not a quitter,* I thought. I wanted, for a moment, to retract my statement. But I could not. The decision to quit was the right one. Something was shifting inside me—something that perhaps had been waiting to do so for many years, but I would have to address it now, and quickly. I understood this without fully wanting to admit it.

Without saying more, I walked down the stairs and out the door of the building. I walked past a small *dabang* (tearoom) with a tree-lined courtyard and stone pathways. Sunlight poured through the trees, and leafy shadows rippled like water across the stones. I stood still for a moment and watched the watery shadows spill over the bricks, over my feet, over a young couple holding hands on an afternoon stroll. I saw a travel agency on the corner.

I crossed the street, stepped inside the door, and booked my ticket to Denver.

The day after I announced that I would be leaving the school and Korea in a matter of days, a large group of girls approached me in the garden recess area, led by Sue, who handed me a small box wrapped beautifully in the way I'd seen cakes decorated in shop windows—in hot pink and brilliant blue, topped with silk and satin bows. I bowed to each of them. Sue began to wail; the high-pitched heaving sound shocked me, because each time the girls laughed or giggled, they usually hid behind their hands. Now each girl was sobbing.

"Don't go, teacher, don't go," Sue cried.

"You have been wonderful students," I said. I tried to wish them happiness and luck without crying, too—not because I wanted to stay, but because I desperately wanted to leave.

Inside the box were long love letters written in broken English, pictures of fairies and queens with "I love you, teacher" written beneath them, a sketched likeness of my face next to a tabloid photograph of Brad Pitt, and an Édith Piaf tape. When my former students wrote to me, which they did for years, I waited weeks to open the letters. I could hardly stand to read their sweet words or look at thc intricatc drawings they made for me.

Mr. Adams called and spoke to Mrs. Park in Korean about what was happening. Afterward, she stayed in her room for the rest of the night, and I sat, guilt-ridden, in my bedroom. When I did see her next, she was distant and quiet. Perhaps by leaving I was shaming her or communicating to her that she was not important to me. What had Mr. Adams told her? I would never know.

I tried to explain myself to Mrs. Park, but language failed me. How could I express the complexity of my gratitude? How could I thank her for such kindness? I sat in my room, looking at the personal, intimate gifts from my students. I felt the deep ache of failure.

I knew I'd never enjoy doing tae kwon do again, but I had learned something during my predawn sweat sessions. Those desperate moments I spent alone in the empty gymnasium made me feel closer to my students than any lesson I ever taught in the classroom. As I moved and punched and shouted, waiting for the sun to rise and my fear to dissipate, I could feel the pressure the girls put on themselves to succeed. I thought of the bright, motivated, and lovely students in my classes, trying so hard to make the grade no matter what it took, trying to be extraordinary, to be the best student and the best girl, as if being perfect were the only way of being acceptable, the only way to live. It was clear to me that my students were already as perfect as they'd ever need to be. And maybe, I thought, so was I. Maybe.

On my last night in Seoul, I took my laundry off the clothesline that stretched across the narrow sun porch behind the kitchen. The neighborhood lay before me: a tangled nest of wires, clotheslines, red roofs, and rows of small back porches and patios. There wasn't a free space in sight: people living in boxes stacked on boxes stacked on the ground and then raised up as high as the sky. I pressed my face against the glass and looked down into this modern electrical net. If I fell, I might never reach the ground. Rice bubbled in the cooker behind me. The dusk light was a warm, hazy gold. A few small ants marched around the east-facing windows. A bird flew toward me and then away again, its black wings beating a clear path in the fading light.

The next morning when the taxi picked me up at the apartment, Mrs. Park took my hands and spread my palms over her warm cheeks. Her eyes were closed. Finally, she released me and shut the door. As the taxi pulled away, I looked in the rearview mirror and watched Mrs. Park's home become smaller and smaller until I could no longer find it among the other high-rise buildings.

Chapter Thirteen

SHAPE-SHIFTER

After I returned to Colorado, a friend sent me some of the letters I had written to her while I was in Korea. There was no mention of Itaewon, struggles at school, nightmares, trouble at my host family's house, or the terrifying panic attacks. Instead, there were detailed descriptions of streets, sunsets, students, and food. "I thought you were doing great there," she said.

I never let on that I wasn't having the time of my life. I could not bear to let anyone know that I was struggling. Who was I if not the overachiever who barreled through adversity with a laugh and a can-do spirit? Who was I if I could not *withstand*? Travel had failed me. How could I admit this, when months before I was so sure it would not just make me feel better, but make me whole?

After receiving the letters from my friend, I opened the box of journals I'd shipped back from Korea and read my private recollections of that time in the colorful notebooks I had purchased every week at the Kyobo bookstore in Seoul. While I was writing positive, upbeat letters, the journals tell a different story. I wrote: "I have an ill-proportioned, overweight body. What is the root of this horrible lack of self-esteem? Why does it pull on me so much? Why do I repulse people or feel like I do? Still, I must work harder. I must work harder to be better."

I did not know who—or even what—I was. I had yoked my identity to the physical appearance of my body, yet it was always changing. In that sense, it seemed to have little integrity—it was disassembled and, in a sense, violated—each night. My body felt like an unsafe place: a place I inhabited but felt disconnected from at the same time. No wonder I was afraid of the dark; I was terrified to be alone with myself.

When I returned from Korea, I felt more confused and desperate—more disembodied—than ever before. Would it ever be possible, I wondered as I closed the last journal and placed it in the box with the others, to rescue a whole from the parts, as I had so brazenly claimed to do in my senior thesis the year before?

Over the next months, I visited doctors and counselors, searching for answers and healing. Using a device that strapped around my chest, a cardiologist tracked each pulse and beat of my heart for one week, looking for signs of trouble. There was nothing wrong with my heart. The first counselor I went to prescribed heavy drugs; the next one suggested yogic retreats that involved relaxing chants and self-guided meditation. I flatly refused to do either, because the chanting made me sad and meditation made me anxious and uncomfortable. "I'm not doing that hippie shit," I told Mom.

One therapist gave me tapes of falling rain and suggested that I imagine painting the word "RELAX" on the inside of my forehead as I listened. The tapes made me giggle. None of it helped. Dad dropped me off at a different office each week. As I stepped out of the Volkswagen, he called, "Good luck!" as if this might be the person who could heal me. I stormed into the house after each appointment and announced something like "Another quack. Another insane shrink trying to tell me what to do."

Although I stopped fluctuating between feeling numb and frantic and the panic attacks eventually subsided, I felt unraveled and raw. I spent my days sleeping and reading nineteenth-century novels, taking long walks, and sitting on the porch with Fred, the family dog, after dinner. No medication or chants would supply an immediate understanding of what had happened to me. It was going to take time.

My experiences in Korea had shocked me out of a way of

thinking that had guided my life for as long as I could remember. I had been fully invested in the lie that I was able-bodied. I had practiced and perfected this fiction, living within it and according to its dictates as if it were a moral framework instead of a complex system of self-deception: I did not want to be abnormal or *less than* because of my grievous, irrevocable physical flaw, so I had to be abnormally fantastic in order to compensate. The paradox: Being extraordinary was the only way to be ordinary. This worked to my advantage in many ways. Motivated by the fear that I would be worthless if I wasn't hugely successful, I worked hard to achieve my goals. But the fear that fueled my work ethic had devastating effects on my self-image. I had convinced myself that if I admitted my limitations, if I faced the truth about my body, if I *failed* in any real or imagined way, it would ruin my life. Who could love a person so deformed and scarred? A person with a body part that was not God-given, but manufactured, artificial? How could I have pride in an embodied existence that was such an aberration? I thought overcoming my disability was the only way for me to be loved, yet I was already deeply loved by many people; I just couldn't manage to love or accept myself. The problem was mine.

I realized that if I did not break free of my faulty logic, I might spin forever in a destructive trap of my own making, and then I would never be whole. In South Korea, stripped of language and the trappings of familiar culture, I was reduced to my body, a disabled body, a malformed, disfigured body: a difficult and complicated reality to claim.

For twenty-two years, I had been living as a willing stranger in the country of my own body; the geography and landscapes of its terrain felt foreign, although I'd lived within its borders all my life. I wanted to know and accept it, but I didn't want to ask for help. I knew a change was needed, but I was so afraid that if I finally accepted my body, if I dug deeply into my feelings of shame surrounding my disability, then I would be completely ejected from the normal world. It seemed so much easier to keep "passing"—even though doing so had already cost me so much.

In an effort to impose some structure on myself, get out of the house, and also make some money, I took the job I'd had for years during the summer: selling lingerie at a store in the mall. I spoke in my "bra and panties voice" for eight hours each day; listened to women complain about how much they hated their bodies as I measured them for new undergarments; hung tiny little bras carefully on tiny little hangers; and convinced people to buy matching robes for their silk chemises. At night, I collapsed in front of the television. I didn't even have the energy to impersonate the perky sorority girls I worked with, something that had particularly entertained Dad during previous summers.

I was back home and should have felt safe, but I felt like shit. My parents tiptoed around me, giving me space, letting me sleep until the middle of the afternoon on my days off, not saying anything when I snorted angry responses at them from behind whatever book I happened to be reading.

One Saturday, I was invited to a party by a college friend who was in Denver working on her master's degree. I took hours applying glittery makeup, curling my hair, and squeezing into a pair of tight jeans and a lacy black top.

"It's good you're getting out!" Mom said, neglecting to comment on my outfit.

As I crossed the lawn to get in my friend's car and go to the party, I felt giddy. I was determined to shake this foul mood by putting all of my fears, doubts, and confusion about where I was going in my life and where I had come from into becoming as drunk and flirtatious as possible. It had partially worked in Dublin, hadn't it? Wasn't that the best year of my life? I wanted to feel like a woman; this meant having the question "Am I desirable?" answered in the affirmative. I stayed up until six in the morning, making out with a guy whose name I never bothered to learn.

When I arrived home, Mom and Dad were waiting up for me in the living room, exhausted and furious. "Where the hell have you been?" Mom asked.

"Having fun for once, what's wrong with that?" I yelled.

"You could have at least called us!" she shouted.

"I'll do what I want," I said. "I'm an adult."

"Could have fooled me," Dad said.

As a result of forging short-lived romantic flings slapped together by alcohol and adrenaline, I often found myself in precarious situations I wasn't prepared for and with people I didn't want to be with. I was addicted to the promise of intimacy. A man's desire for me instantly colored my perception of him: Suddenly he seemed perfect, and more than lust, more than anything else, I felt gratitude. Each new man held out the false hope that he might change my life, make it better, make it mine. Impulsively and without much thought to the consequences, I leapt at every opportunity for what might be reinvention, happiness, change—something.

I made promises to be responsible when I went out, and each weekend I broke that promise. "I don't do anything stupid. I'm careful," I told Mom, although standing in the front room on yet another Saturday morning with my tights balled up in one hand, I felt ridiculous, having morphed into the cliché of a rebellious high school teenager even though I was twenty-two.

After several weeks of this behavior, Mom became frantic. I was too old to be grounded, and parental lectures were having no effect. "Where are you?" she'd ask, crying while I struggled up the stairs to sleep off my hangover. "We are losing you!"

Because I couldn't always remember what happened during my drunken encounters, I got an AIDS test. Worried and frantic as I waited for the results, I followed Mom around the house, asking her if she thought I looked sick.

"What do you have to be concerned about?" Mom asked. She was in the laundry room. "You said you were safe." I poured some detergent on a pile of towels, slammed the lid shut, and adjusted the dial. "Weren't you?" She pulled the dial, and water poured into the tub.

"Tell me," she said, and as the washing machine swished and whirred, I did. I told her plenty of things she would rather not have known. We stayed through the wash and dry cycle of one complete load, and when we left the room, Mom closed the door.

"My dirty laundry," I joked.

"Not funny," she replied.

When the test came back negative, Mom really let me have it. "You will get your shit together, young lady," she said. "I'm not going through this again. I am *not*!"

After this incident, my relationship with my mother deepened and improved, in part because she had changed. As a school nurse with several districts under her partial administrative jurisdiction, she helped implement a revolutionary inclusion program that helped integrate special education kids into the regular classroom; no more hidden, corner rooms for them. Her newfound professional confidence changed her toward me, and I felt I could tell her more. She seemed less traditional somehow and much more open and free. Powerful in a new way.

At Thanksgiving, we drove to a Lutheran retreat center in the mountains. Through the car window, I watched evergreens pass in a green, spiky blur. I rolled down the window and inhaled the clean, thin, snow-tinged air of my childhood, and then I felt it. Something broke inside me. Some horrifying pressure was released. "Fuck it, fuck you! Fuck *everything*!" I yelled out the window at the stoic trees and the old snow piled between them. I banged my hands against the car windows and thrashed around in the backseat. I screamed and cried and cursed and pounded my fists against my thighs.

"What is it? What's the matter?" Dad asked, slowing down so much that the car behind us on the winding road began to tailgate impatiently.

Mom looked at me as if she didn't know me at all. I felt for a brief instant that I really had been lost and lost forever. I felt that ground of being I had been so desperate to find slip from beneath me. Soon I was sobbing, and so was Mom.

"Shit," Dad said, and pulled onto the road's shoulder. He looked straight ahead for a few moments, and then he started to cry, too. "Okay, you two," he said. For several minutes, the car shook with our crying and the trucks racing by on the steep mountain road.

That night, I tried to write letters by the fire in our cabin but found I had little to say. After Mom and Dad had gone to bed, I crept out the front door. The night was freezing and clear; the stars looked as if they were pinning down the land. For the first time in a long time, I felt gripped by the faith I'd had as a child and just as quickly released again. I felt solid, supported, taken inside my body in a way I hadn't felt in years or maybe ever before. Lumps of snow falling from the tree branches broke the quiet with a muted thump as they hit the ground. I listened to the trees creaking and shifting; I felt the cold ground beneath my boots.

In the morning, Dad was in the kitchen making the only meal he can—pancakes.

"I'm going to divinity school," I said. However fleeting the previous night's connection had been, I'd felt embodied in a way I hadn't for a long time, and I hadn't been thinking about it at all; it had been effortless. I felt faith in what would happen next, and I decided to act on it.

"Excellent plan!" Dad exclaimed. "I'm surprised, honestly, but good for you!"

"Why so surprised? Don't you think I can do it?" I sneered. I felt the fears rushing back. Maybe it was madness to pursue theology any further. Maybe I would just continue to tell nice-sounding lies. Maybe what I'd felt had been nothing more than a hoax, just another trick of the mind.

"Oh, lighten up," he said, and slid a pancake onto my plate. "Just thought you'd given up on the whole study-of-God path."

"You make seminary sound like vacation Bible school," I said.

"I would know," he replied. "Good luck with Greek."

"Listen, Happy Hank, don't be such a grump," Mom said, shaking my arm and then handing me a cup of coffee. "I can totally see you as a theologian. I think grad school is a great idea."

After the holidays, I moved to Boston with the intention of attending Harvard Divinity School. I worked with the same lingerie company and lived with friends I'd met in Dublin. Mom and Dad seemed worried but relieved to see me go.

"I'll be fine," I told them, and I briefly believed this. "I'll be too busy with grad school applications to get into trouble." But there was one more international trip I had to take.

Chapter Fourteen

SURVIVING THE BODY

In the lawn in front of the Palais des Nations in Geneva stands a giant, three-legged chair. One leg has been violently torn away, and the bits of remaining wood hang like icicles from the messy, uneven break. The symbolic wound is irreversible, the chair's original shape irretrievable. The chair is both a memorial to land mine victims and a reminder of the millions of mines that remain in the ground worldwide, waiting to kill and maim if countries fail to take the appropriate steps to remove them safely.

The first time I saw that three-legged chair, I turned my head away as the bus passed, fearful of somehow being implicated and feeling guilty that I wasn't brave enough to be. Although the trauma of losing a leg to a land mine was difficult and deeply unsettling to imagine, it was the physical image of incompleteness that resonated with me. I resisted being associated with such a symbol of brokenness.

Before entering Harvard Divinity School in autumn 1998, I served as the youth intern at the Lutheran World Federation in Geneva, Switzerland, a nine-month position. I helped design programs and resources that would empower, inspire, and assist Lutheran youth and women according to the specific needs of different geographic regions around the globe. I researched the histories of ordained women worldwide; I wrote and edited newsletter articles and tracked international correspondence; I traveled to Namibia to help administrate a theological training week for youth; I worked with colleagues from all over the world.

In my application, which I had sent away for three years earlier when I returned from Dublin, I had specifically mentioned my disability, citing my interest in theological issues of embodiment. When people asked questions about my leg, I recited an updated version of the poster child speech on autopilot, even though it had long felt inadequate and now made me feel cheap and dishonest—even weary—when I told it.

Once, after a weekly meeting, a colleague approached me. As we walked to the coffee machine, she told me that there is a word in almost every African language for disabled people that means stepped on by an elephant, a wildebeest, a bear, a god.

"I am interested in your story," she said, pouring a cup of coffee and handing it to me. "And wouldn't it be interesting to know how other women like you from different parts of the world think about God? How they live?"

I nodded, the coffee cup warm between my hands. Walking back to my office, I shuddered. I sat at my desk, holding the coffee until it went cold. I finally got back to work, but for the rest of the day I felt the shadow of those beasts looming over me—waiting to stomp and crush. I remembered hearing disabled women speaking—as if from some lost and hidden place—from the pages of a dusty, forgotten book in the corner of the St. Olaf library. I remembered those stories full of resistance and rage, truth and triumph; I remembered the insights from *The Disabled God* and how the book had literally changed my life by shifting my thinking. Looking out at the flower-filled courtyard of my workplace, I decided it was vitally important that I hear and learn from living, breathing women about how they lived; how they felt about their bodies, about God, about their place in the world. Here, in my colleague's words, was a call to action, and Geneva, a hub of the international community, was the perfect place in which to take up that call. I asked for and was granted money and space to hold a meeting for one disabled woman from each of the six regions of the Lutheran World Federation.

The women arrived during the first week of full-blown spring in Geneva. The air was fragrant with the scent of lilacs and air rinsed clean after a light rain. Bees buzzed wildly in front of the double doors of the hotel, where inside, six disabled women were gathered, introducing themselves in awkward and nervous English.

The goal of our gathering—apart from forging connections with one another—was the preparation of a document that would assist the Lutheran World Federation in making its programs more inclusive and receptive to the specific needs of disabled women throughout the world. Nancy Eiesland, the theologian I so admired, had accepted the invitation to be the special guest of the conference. She would lead us in reflection and meditation and assist with the theological language of the final document.

The first night, after everyone had gotten settled in their hotel rooms, the six of us sat around a table in the hotel conference room as Nancy led us in an exercise designed to acquaint us with one another before the week began. She passed out large sheets of butcher paper and markers and asked us to draw a timeline of our lives. Illustrating our experiences, she explained, was a way of embodying our stories; it was a physical and visual way of telling a tale that we were frequently asked to recite for others.

My first impulse was to depict myself as the beaming poster child, to paint myself as a kind of celebrity. Although I was eager to hear the women's stories, I felt that old, instinctive pull to separate myself from the group by secretly asserting or quietly insisting that I was the most normal and therefore the least disabled. I had noticed the looks from the other hotel guests and the concierge as our group gathered for dinner or slowly crossed the lobby to our conference room. As usual, I was worried to look crippled, to look different. I still wanted to be the star of any group, which meant being singled out as normal, beautiful, and bright. But as I looked around at the women at the table, I decided to take a chance. Now was the time for truth. My skin was covered in goose bumps as I began to draw. When everyone had finished, one by one we lifted the illustrated sheets of paper and explained to the others how our disabilities had affected our lives.

Ana from Argentina was first. She'd had polio as a child and now used crutches or a walker. Her approach to disability was distinctly theological: "Jesus came for the outcasts," she said. "Jesus came for the crippled and the lame." Ana was an ordained pastor serving a lively and supportive congregation; she was married and had several children. She drew herself in the wheelchair she'd used as a child. She drew her family. Her dark ropes of hair moved as she shook her head, telling her story.

Martha from Ethiopia had been disabled at birth, her foot twisted in what many believed to be an act of God. Outcast by society, she survived by the love of family, yet her life still retained in it moments of profound exile. As a child, trusted spiritual leaders informed her that her deformity was God's mark of shame, yet she resisted this classification, guided by a stronger inner conviction. "I know that I am a child of God," she said. "I have always known this." When I met her, she ran across the lobby and gave me a tight hug. "This is the best day of my life," she said. She had taken a horse, two buses, and three planes to get to Geneva. She drew an enormous church in the center of the page. "God is everything," she said. "There is no room for anything else."

Yumiko from Japan walked with a cane and a stiff leg as the result of severe arthritis that no attempted medicine or therapy had been able to resolve. A homemaker, she was integrated into her local community and had three grandchildren. She was overwhelmingly positive and good-humored, always making our group laugh and helping us laugh at ourselves. She drew herself at the center of her family.

Lizbet from Norway had longed to be ordained as a Lutheran minister, but because of her short stature, this dream was denied her. "They said nobody would listen to me because I'm too short," she explained. She drew herself tall in the picture, wearing flowing purple robes. "When I dream," she said, "I am as tall and powerful as I am in my mind." She drew a crowd of people in a circle, with herself at the center, preaching.

Then it was my turn. I had agonized over what images might accurately depict crucial moments in my life story as a disabled woman. Without mentioning the poster child title or rattling off my accomplishments, I didn't know what to render, what to illustrate. I thought of listing the dates of my surgeries and recording memories of each; I realized I had no idea when my surgeries took place. Instead, I drew my body as it had changed with each subsequent operation: First the foot was taken, then the hip surgery, the knee fusion, the way prosthetic limbs had changed with each passing year of growth and technological advancement. My hands shook as I lifted my piece of paper. It was the first time I had talked about my disability without mentioning the poster child experience. At the end of the page, I drew myself standing legless in front of a mirror. "I think my life is about running," I said, and this felt like the final piece of an accumulated awareness—an epiphany—that had been building and falling, building and falling, for many years, perhaps since the day I became the poster child. I had not made myself look or sound extraordinary. I said, "I have always hated my body," and realized that this was an accurate statement. It was so true, it nearly took my breath away. The women nodded and listened. In their eyes was understanding, empathy, and a unique kind of sisterhood—unspoken but felt—that I had never experienced before. I had never felt so terrified and free. My words did not reach back to slap me; they did not dissipate but stayed buoyed in the room with the expansive lightness of the truth.

As a child on camping trips, I would sprinkle birdseed in my hand and wait for a bird to alight. When it did, its body was always more substantial than I expected, yet remarkably light as well, the weight delicate and tender, as if I were holding a lightbulb filled with heavy hair. For a few moments as the bird's feet stepped lightly in the creases of my open palm, picking at the seed with its tiny beak, I watched its calm, hot eyes and felt the energy of its fluttering heart weighing down the hollow of my hand. After it flew away, my hand felt both lighter—free of the little body—and more grounded, as if I had been touched and rooted to something beyond me. This is the feeling I had now—in my chest, in my heart—as the day drew to a close.

That night, unable to sleep, I left my hotel room at midnight and took a taxi to my flat on Avenue de Soret. After the day's events, I craved the comforts of my own space: my pictures, my books, my clothes, my piles of letters. Lying in bed, I heard people chatting at the late night café below, sometimes a drunken laugh. Before dawn, I would smell the familiar odor of espresso and fresh croissants and hear the quick chatter of the morning customers. Although my fear of the dark had made it difficult for me to sleep since I had arrived in Geneva seven months before, that night I slept calmly and well. I didn't close and lock the windows or leave the lights and radio on all night as I usually did. I left the windows open to the night breeze and didn't worry about anyone sneaking in to murder me or attack me; I didn't worry about being seen. My mind raced, full of the women's stories. Why had I been so terrified of the dark all these years? Perhaps I lived in fear that someone was going to force me to speak the truth. Nobody could take my story now; I had already told it. I remembered the words of Psalm 139: *For you created my inmost being; you knit me together in my mother's womb. I praise you because I am fearfully and wonderfully made . . . my frame was not hidden from you when I was made in the secret place, when I was woven together in the depths of the earth.* I thought of patterns and the efforts of their resistance. I imagined stepping into the shadow of a beast's—any beast's—heavy foot and coming out crushed through the ground of an experience with the proof of a vision—unique and my own—alight in my palm, a savage spinning. I put my hands on my chest and felt the perfect organ of my heart beating immaculate inside the body squashed. As the psalm promises, I felt known by a higher power—*you have searched me and you know me*—and known to myself.

I didn't feel peace so much as equilibrium and a desire to stop hiding the truth about my disability from others and from myself; in contrast with the way I had been living, this was a state of calm powerful enough to put me to sleep.

The week progressed with Bible study, more stories, meals, outings, and the formation of practical ideas that would help existing Lutheran World Federation structures become more accessible to disabled women worldwide. The suggestions we finalized and typed up in a conference room continue to guide efforts of greater inclusivity in LWF program planning worldwide.

On the last day of the gathering, our group met in the LWF office building. The reactions in the building varied: Some people stared; others smiled and brought cookies and coffee to the meeting room; others stood in the doorways of their offices and watched us process by; many of my colleagues engaged the women in conversations, asking them questions. Regardless of people's individual reactions, the physical presence of the women created a palpable shift in the office environment. There was a detectable change in the air, an opening and a new energy. For weeks after the women returned to their homes, I received e-mails from my colleagues telling me how their ideas about disability had changed radically. All we'd done was tell the truth about our bodies without shame, without apology, and without fear.

The next time I was on the bus as it passed the three-legged chair at the Palais des Nations, I did not look down or away. I faced its broken, uneven frame and did not feel ashamed. I saw the faces of the women; I heard their voices and their stories. The broken chair told its own story and provided its own call to action. So did we. The women had their stories, and I had mine, and what we shared was a responsibility to tell them.

"Hey, look what I found." Dad placed a huge cardboard box at my feet. "Look inside."

"What is it?" I asked.

"Just open it."

After I returned from Geneva, my parents' upcoming move from Denver to Cheyenne had triggered weeks of clearing closets and emptying storage spaces. I was sitting on the floor of the garage, sorting through a stack of Dad's old seminary books, putting aside the Greek lexicon and the Martin Luther biography to take with me to Harvard.

The overstuffed box Dad set before me was bulging at the seams. I opened the flaps. Inside was a mess of artificial limbs heaped on top of one another, with ankles and calves and knees stacked end over end. Metal knees bent stiffly over calves and thighs; the soles of two SACH feet were pressed together; the mess of twisted waist straps resembled coiled snakes. My metal brace hovered over the pile like a tiny seesaw.

"Should we get them out?" Dad asked.

"Why not?" I replied.

"Here's the supplement," Mom said. She handed me four garbage bags; two were full of stump socks I'd used with the wooden legs, their edges frayed and torn; two held old silicone liners that were decorated with strange sweat patterns from long-ago workouts and the occasional sprinkle of bloodstains from wounds now healed, the source of injury forgotten. "I didn't throw any of them out," Mom said. "You never know."

I piled up the liners and the carefully laundered and folded socks. They made three tall, neat piles next to the row of limbs.

"Look at that," Dad said.

"It's amazing to see them all right there, lined up like that," Mom said.

The metal frame of the tiny brace was tarnished, its straps filthy; the white orthopedic shoe was dirty and worn. The whole apparatus looked as if it belonged in a small-town museum that was infrequently visited; a place of moldy-smelling rooms filled with dusty mannequins wearing old fashions, stained embroidered cloths draped over fabric-worn rockers, laceless shoes piled in a corner near rickety baby carriages.

"How the hell did I walk in that awful contraption?" I asked.

"You did all right," Mom said.

The bright orange foot of the first wooden leg was covered in uneven splotches of dirt that looked like a child's muddy fingerprints—probably mine. The bottom of the socket was dusty and scarred from scraping against sidewalks and floors. There was a visible line of uneven stitches where the strap had been repaired with an additional piece of canvas. The metal hinges lined the outside of the socket from top to bottom; the calf was slender, and between it and the foot was a two-inch wood brick. "You grew a lot that year," Mom said.

The next leg was slightly bigger. The socket was wider at the top from weight gain, and the foot was dark with dirt and nearly ruined. A peg had been added on the inside where the socket met the shank to lessen the severity of the clumping sound when the leg swung through, which produced its own muted thumping noise. The peg looked hammered down. "I think we called that one the clunker," Mom said.

"I thought the clunker was a different one," Dad said.

"No, it was that one," Mom replied. "I'm sure of it."

The third leg had at least five inches added at the ankle. The foot had never been screwed on exactly right and looked as if it were sliding away from the leg, as if the additional piece were made of slick mud that had never dried. Mom explained that I had switched feet in the middle of the leg's life. This was the prosthesis I'd been wearing when Brian called me peg leg. I remembered, too, that Andy and I—in a reference to the *Star Wars* movies we loved—had called it "the leg bites back" after we were convinced that a mosquito had died trying to pierce the wood-flesh of the leg.

The next leg was Schmidt's last. The waist strap was more like a harness; the man's-size Seattle foot bore permanent stripes from a pair of black sandals I'd worn to Disney World; the Florida heat had melted the crisscross pattern into the foot, making the rubber toes look diseased. The front of the socket looked bumpy, like bad papier-mâché. "I remember he kept making the socket tighter and looser," I said.

"That was not a good day," Dad said. "I remember feeling really pissed off at Schmidt."

The next leg was the tallest and slimmest yet, the socket curved to match my expanding hips; the ankle was thin and sculpted. This was Larry's first leg. The leather patch at the back of the thigh was added to keep me from sliding out of my desk chair at school.

I switched back from the Seattle to the SACH foot for the next leg so I could wear different shoes—Mom and I called them "girly shoes"—that were made for slender feet. This leg was the first that took on a true womanly shape. I had grown at least three inches, and the thigh was markedly curvier than the others. I had gotten a new foot at some point, and the seam between the foot and the ankle was plastered over in a different shade of paint.

The next leg was the one I had worn when I resolved to be as thin as possible. It had taken me through hours of grueling aerobics in high school and college. The frayed waist strap was practically destroyed from arduous, sweaty workouts; there were messy holes I had burrowed in the strap as I quickly lost weight. This was the leg I had tossed off the top of my loft during the first year of college, the one Liz and I had nicknamed "Creaky Malone" for the cracking sounds in the knee joint when the Minnesota winter temperatures dropped below zero. This was the leg I had been so happy to discard when I got my first hydraulic prosthesis.

Out of place, at the end of the row, was the leg with the failed suction socket; the one that made the farting noises, the one in which I had placed so much hope. What was intended to be the suction mechanism looked like a doll's painted eye covered with a patch of skin. I had painted the foot's toenails; since I couldn't wear it, I clearly hadn't been worried about getting tired of the color.

"I can't believe I actually wore these," I said. "They're so ugly!"

"Well," Mom said, picking up the legs one by one and setting a blanket under the feet so they wouldn't rest directly against the concrete and get even more dirty. "That's why you're such a spoiled little shit. I took one look at those and felt sorry for you."

"Thanks, I think," I said.

"Oh, I'm joking," she said, standing up. She bumped my hip with hers. "Sort of."

"Should we leave them up?" Dad asked. I nodded.

After my parents left the garage, I looked at the legs again, one by one. Individually, they looked strange to the point of being comical, but gathered together like this, they were not so ugly but instead had an idiosyncratic, brutal, and unassuming beauty that also told a larger story.

Since I received my first wooden leg in 1978, the prosthetic industry has changed dramatically, with advances in technology and design that were unimaginable even a decade ago. Now there are sleek, well-designed Web sites that advertise the precise benefits of specific feet, knees, and other prosthetic components. I am suddenly a valued customer, treated politely by prosthetic companies that actively compete for my business. This is a far cry from the days when a young female amputee had to wear a man's prosthetic foot if she wanted the latest design.

Articles about souped-up prosthetics appear in national newspapers. There are new technological developments all the time, new legs and knees, some of them phenomenally expensive and outside the realm of possibility for many amputees, with or without insurance. The microprocessor knee (about $35,000), or "C-leg," features a computerized device that learns the parameters of your gait; if you sway to the side, the knee automatically corrects your movement and keeps you from falling. As my prosthetist, Nick, has heard from his clients who wear it, "It's as if you don't have to think about walking at all." This development is so astounding to me, it is almost unbelievable. There continue to be different types of Flex-Feet developed for varying activity levels; there are feet equipped with shock absorption and rotation capabilities. Elite disabled athletes are continually confounding our notions of what a body can do. A leg at the high end of technology—complete with external silicone spray that closely resembles human skin (and is particularly marketed to women)—costs about $50,000, double the price of my current leg.

Liner technology has advanced as well. While my first leg featured a cloth sock and a simple wooden socket with a waist strap as a method of suspension, I now wear a full contact leg, featuring a hybrid suction socket that makes the most of the residual limb's end-bearing capabilities. Owing to the shape of my stump, which has always been an issue in a good prosthetic fit, I wear a custom-made silicone liner, which is more expensive than injected silicone. On the wall in the back room at the prosthetist's office where liner molds are kept for easy reference, my long, thin mold juts out alongside other rounder, shorter molds. "Your shape is unique," Nick explained. "It narrows so dramatically from hip to tip." Once the liners begin to fray from the sweat of exercise and the pressure and friction of movement, they are less durable and functional, apart from smelling absolutely horrible. Nick tells me that in light of current developments, I may soon be able to wear a new injected silicone socket, reducing the cost of my leg and improving its overall capabilities.

Now, when I visit Web sites of major prosthetic manufacturers, it's as if amputees can change their bodies—and their identities—as easily as snapping on a new running foot, a new knee, a newly designed cosmetic cover, or a state-of-the-art ankle. In Internet chat rooms and on national and international Listservs, amputees discuss their needs and desires, they talk freely and excitedly about what they want to do. You want to run, sprint, leap, pole-vault, windsurf, or swim? You want to run a marathon or compete in a triathlon? Want to golf or just walk comfortably? Somebody makes a part or a combination of parts that will enable an amputee to do so. Many of these parts have sleek and enticing names: The Cheetah foot is custom-made for track sprinting; the Elite foot claims to be the best bet for vertical shock capabilities; the Rheo Knee promises to let amputees "walk your way" and analyzes gait, automatically adjusting resistance. I recently ordered a waist belt called the Gunslinger Waist Power Belt. Like a girdle, it holds the leg at the top and enables me to run longer distances with greater comfort. The body can literally become a wonder of technology and engineering. If you have enough money, the right insurance plan, or the appropriate athletic sponsors, the possibilities seem endless.

But here, in my parents' garage and assembled before me now, was the physical history of *my* body—individual, imperfect, and unique. The hydraulic prosthesis I was wearing had taken me all over Europe and Asia. This leg had been with me during my college graduation and my first sexual experience; it had witnessed my moment of truth telling in Geneva. These legs had borne my body through train trips, plane rides, and countless other encounters. Unlike my washable skin or the inevitable fading of some memories, they still bore the marks of these journeys. Here were the moments of my life laid out before me—embodied—in wood and canvas and plastic and metal. Touchstones for a history.

I visited the legs every day, sometimes twice a day. I liked looking at them set out before me against the garage wall. Each time I looked at them, I remembered a story or a memory.

How did that get there? I wondered, noticing a new scrape or mark I hadn't seen before. *When did that change?* I thought, looking at a chunk that was missing from one of the heels. When I asked my parents, our stories often differed. "Was that when I crashed my bike in the high school parking lot?" I'd ask, bringing them to the garage and pointing out a deep groove, like a rut, near the hinges of the second leg.

"No, you fell off the swing set," Dad said. "I remember."

"No, she fell out of the tree in the backyard," Mom said. "That's what happened."

"Well, which was it?" I asked. They shrugged.

What was the real story? Nobody seemed to know. It was strange that after a lifetime of scrutinizing the body, when faced with its history, there were still things about it that I did not know; there were facts that failed to add up.

"You need to box up those legs tonight," Mom said. The move to our new home was imminent. "The truck is coming tomorrow."

"Ready?" Dad asked, a roll of packing tape in his hand. Mom walked in with a new moving box that she'd carefully labeled in black marker "Emily's Legs."

"I padded the inside with a quilt," she said.

But I wasn't quite ready to put them away. "I'll do it in the morning," I said.

"Well, do it before eight," Mom said, and left the box at the end of the row.

Only one person knew my body better than I did. I called Dr. Elliot the next day. He quickly returned my call, and without any of my medical records before him, he specifically recalled certain details of my body and my particular PFFD case. I was surprised and moved by this instant recall. I may have been willfully oblivious, but there had been someone who had always known what was going on with me, who knew me, I would discover, literally inside out. My life and my body had been in his hands many times.

I asked Dr. Elliot questions about my different operations. I asked him to clarify when they were performed and to explain what each procedure was supposed to do.

"And is it true," I asked finally, with all the other facts carefully noted down, "that we don't know how or why PFFD occurs?"

"We don't know why, but we do know that it is a defect in the DNA when the body is formed."

I had had no idea that my disability was literally written into my DNA. Stories carved into wood through scars and scuffs were one thing, but a disability from the inside out? I had never considered this possibility. Although the defect was not inherited and therefore impossible to pass to my future children (there is no specifically identifiable DNA strand for PFFD), it did indicate a spontaneous mutation.

This discovery left me speechless and angry. A defect in the DNA, a twist in the genetic ladder, a chance mutation in the delicate braiding of informational strands, felt so permanent, so preordained, so *unfair.* I realized how desperately I wanted to continue passing off my disability as a random accident, as a fluke, as just, "you know, one of those things," as I used to say in my pert poster child speeches, which I had recycled in countless ways throughout my life. My disability was indeed random and accidental, but it was also *a mutation.* The word felt sticky in my mouth.

Later that night, I looked over my notes again. Because I had written them so quickly as Dr. Elliot had talked and especially at the end of our conversation, in a kind of stunned fury, there was an exchange I had originally glossed over.

"If you can create the part that's missing," Dr. Elliot had said, "why wouldn't you make someone whole with a prosthesis? It's just like anything else we might use to survive in the world."

Survive in the world. This had and has been my daily business throughout my life. The knowledge that I could not outrun or out-achieve my own design came as a complicated relief. After all those years of overachievement, after all that work trying to physically transform my body or solve its problems intellectually, as if this would finally make it mine, it had belonged to me all along; there was no overcoming my DNA. I could not argue with the realities of creation.

"Know what I mean?" Dr. Elliot had asked.

"I think I do," I had replied. The body was not a problem or a puzzle that could be solved by the mind, in the arms of a man, in flattery and attention from strangers, in the pleasure of academic accolades, in locations far from home, at divinity school, or anywhere else. The answers were literally staring at me in the face, lined up against one wall of the garage. But did the answers give me the peace I had hoped for?

I returned to the garage for the last time. As I looked at the legs, I remembered the women gathered in Geneva who had strengthened me with the stories and ordinary facts of their existence, each of them extraordinary in some way and yet profoundly normal as well. It would be a lie to say that I found peace in my body. I did not and have not; perhaps I never will. But I did discover a sense of ownership, and I did find a voice.

There was one more thing to do before boxing up my legs. I took off the prosthesis that had walked me through the streets of Dublin and kept me standing up in Korea. I slipped it through the mouth of my shorts and hopped over to set it at the end of the row. The body wasn't meant to be solved or resolved—it was meant to speak and tell its own story, and here I was, standing on one leg before the pieces of mine. I did not feel happiness or even relief. I felt sadness mixed with a quiet resignation. I may never fully understand or even accept the body I live in and with, but it does tell a story, and that story can be told.

Finally, the only claim I can make with any certainty about my body is this: It is mine.

ACKNOWLEDGMENTS

I am deeply grateful to the Corporation of Yaddo, the Fine Arts Work Center, the James A. Michener Center for Writers at the University of Texas at Austin, the Jentel Arts Foundation, the Mary Roberts Rinehart Foundation at George Mason University, and the Philip Roth Residency at the Stadler Center for Poetry at Bucknell University for the financial support that provided invaluable time and space at different times during the writing of this book.

My heartfelt thanks to the following individuals: to Annik LaFarge, editor and friend, whose enthusiasm, sharp wit, intelligence, and sincere belief in this work surpassed my expectations and encouraged me each step of the way; to my agent, Esther Newberg, for her support, insight, hard work, unflinching honesty, and quick response to panicked e-mails; to Christine Earl and Kari Stuart at ICM for keeping everything in order. A writer could ask for no greater team.

I am also indebted to the editors of *The Sun* magazine, for publishing the essay "Surviving the Body" that grew into *Poster Child*; the *Atlantic Monthly,* for recognition of this work; my classmates at the University of Texas at Austin and my students in the Provincetown Adult Education memoir course who read the manuscript at different stages and provided helpful direction; Charles Beneke and Viet Nguyen for careful reading; Sarah Reinertsen and Jillian Weise for knowing this story; Susan Briante, Julie Gateas, Paige Kaltsas, Philip Pardi, Jeff Severs, Chris Simpson, Devon Shaw, and Betsy Wheeler for the gift of friendship and sharp editorial insight;

Madalyn Aslan, Caeli Bourbeau, Monika Bustamante, Kate Hill Cantrill, Kate Weldon LeBlanc, Emily Miles, Lisa Railsback, Carrie Scanga, Mira Urosev, Ryann Watson, and Jennifer Weber for humor, love, and unflagging belief in me; Paulette Bates Alden, David Bradley, Paula Closson Buck, Chris Camuto, Katie Ford, Maria Flook, Marie Howe, Denis Johnson, Shara McCallum, Naomi Shihab Nye, Patricia Powell, Robert Rosenberg, Brad Watson, and Joy Williams for encouragement and much-appreciated support; Nancy Eiesland for showing me a different way; Barbara Pitkin and Edmund Santurri for thirteen years of mentorship; Marla Akin, Emil Kresl, and Cristina Zambrano for making things happen.

A special thanks to Barbara Belejack, Laura Furman, Steve Harrigan, and James Magnuson for their extraordinary vision and tireless support of my work.

To Glen and Ann Rebka for your gracious and boundless enthusiasm for all of my endeavors, my thanks.

To my family—Andy, Jen, Iain, James, Lois, Abe, and B. F. Rapp, the Eigsti family, and the Gorman family; for your faithful presence in my life, thank you.

Finally, to Mary and Roger Rapp for the rare gift of unconditional love, my deepest gratitude.

A NOTE ON THE AUTHOR

Emily Rapp was born in Nebraska and grew up in Wyoming and Colorado. Born with a congenital defect, she has worn a prosthetic limb ever since her left foot was amputated at age four. A former Fulbright scholarship recipient, she was educated at Harvard University, St. Olaf College, and the University of Texas at Austin, where she was a James A. Michener Fellow. She has received awards and recognition for her work from the *Atlantic Monthly, StoryQuarterly,* the Mary Roberts Rinehart Foundation, the Jentel Arts Foundation, the Corporation of Yaddo, and the Fine Arts Work Center in Provincetown, where she was a winter writing fellow. She was recently the Philip Roth Writer-in-Residence at Bucknell University. She lives in Los Angeles, where she is a core faculty member in the MFA program at Antioch University-Los Angeles.